Nadine Gordimer:
A Bibliography of Primary & Secondary Sources
1937-1992

Bibliographical Research in African Literatures

General Editor:
Bernth Lindfors
Professor of English, University of Texas at Austin

No. 1: Ngugi wa Thiong'o: A Bibliography of Primary and
Secondary Sources, 1957-1987
CAROL SICHERMAN

No. 2: A New Bibliography of the Lusophone Literatures of
Africa/*Nova Bibliografia das Literaturas Africanas de
Expressão Portuguesa*
GERALD MOSER & MANUEL FERREIRA

No. 3: Black African Literature in English, 1987-1991
BERNTH LINDFORS

No. 4: Nadine Gordimer: A Bibliography of Primary and
Secondary Sources, 1937-1992
DOROTHY DRIVER, ANN DRY,
CRAIG MACKENZIE & JOHN READ

Nadine Gordimer
A Bibliography of Primary and Secondary Sources, 1937-1992

Compiled by

Dorothy Driver, Ann Dry, Craig MacKenzie and John Read

With an introduction by
Dorothy Driver

HANS ZELL PUBLISHERS

London • Melbourne • Munich • New Jersey • 1994

British Library Cataloguing in Publication Data

Nadine Gordimer : Bibliography of Primary and Secondary Sources, 1937 -1992
    (Bibliographical Research in African Literatures: No. 4)
    I. Driver, Dorothy II. Series
    016.823

    ISBN 1-873836-26-0

Library of Congress Cataloging-in-Publication Data

Nadine Gordimer : a bibliography of primary and secondary sources, 1937-1992 / compiled by
    Dorothy Driver ... [et al.] : with an introduction by Dorothy Driver.
    357p. 210cm. – (Bibliographical research in African literatures : no. 4)
    Includes index.
    ISBN 1-873836-26-0
    1. Gordimer, Nadine – Bibliography. 2. South Africa in literature – Bibliography.
    I. Driver, Dorothy II. Series
    Z8355.9.N3 1994
    [PR9369.3.G6]
    016.823 - - dc20   93-37446
                                                       CIP

Published by Hans Zell Publishers, an imprint of Bowker-Saur Ltd,
60 Grosvenor Street, London W1X 9DA, United Kingdom.
Tel: +44 (0) 71 493 5841 Fax: +44 (0) 71 580 4089

Bowker-Saur Ltd, a division of REED REFERENCE PUBLISHING.

Published in association with The National English Literary Museum, Private Bag 1019,
Grahamstown 6140, Republic of South Africa

Cover design by Robin Caira
Printed on acid-free paper.
Printed and bound in Great Britain
by Antony Rowe Ltd., Chippenham, Wiltshire.

Cover illustration: Photograph of Nadine Gordimer by Gisele Wulfsohn/Southlight
p. xvi: Sketch of Nadine Gordimer by Nils Burwitz (original in the collection of the National English Literary Museum).

CONTENTS

ABBREVIATIONS

In addition to standard abbreviations for periodical titles, and those recommended by MLA, the following abbreviations are used in this bibliography:

* An asterisk indicates that an item has not been personally verified by the compilers and is not in NELM's holdings.

ent.	entitled
A.P.B.	Afrikaanse Pers Boekhandel
Africa	Africa World Press
Africana	Africana Publishing Company
Acacia	Acacia Books
Académiai	Académiai Kiadó
Allen	Allen and Unwin
Anchor	Anchor Press
Arbeiderspers	De Arbeiderspers
Arnold	Edward Arnold (Publishers) Ltd.
Art	Art Editora Ltd.
BBC	BBC Books
Bakker	Bert Bakker
	Gerrit Bakker
Ball	Jonathan Ball
Barker	Arthur Barker Ltd.
Bateleur	Bateleur Press
Blackwell	Basil Blackwell
Bloomsbury	Bloomsbury Publishing Ltd.
Bøker	Nye Bøker
Bonniers	Albert Bonniers Verlag
Burgess	Owen Burgess Publishers
CNA	Central News Agency Limited
Cape	Jonathan Cape Ltd.
Chatto	Chatto & Windus
Claasen	Claasen Verlag
Collins	Rex Collins
Contact	Uitgeverij Contact
Currey	James Currey
Dangaroo	Dangaroo Press
Dekker	An Dekker
Dell	Dell Publishing Co., Inc.
Dent	J. M. Dent & Sons Ltd.

Dial	The Dial Press
Dobson	Dennis Dobson Ltd.
Donker	Ad. Donker
Doubleday	Doubleday and Co., Inc.
Espasa	Espasa-Calpe
Estate	Fourth Estate Ltd.
Eule	Verlag Die Blaue Eule
Evans	Evans Brothers Limited
Faber	Faber and Faber
Fischer	S. Fischer Verlag
Fontana	Fontana Press
France	France-Loisirs
Gale	Gale Research Co.
Garland	Garland Publishing, Inc.
Gollancz	Victor Gollancz
Guidelines	Guidelines (Pty) Ltd.
Gyldendal Norsk	Gyldendal Norsk Forlag
Hall	G. K. Hall & Son
Harcourt	Harcourt Brace Jovanovich, Inc.
Harper	Harper and Row Publishers, Inc.
Harrap	George C. Harrap and Co., Ltd.
Hodder	Hodder and Stoughton
Holt	Holt, Rinehart and Winston, Inc.
Houghton	Houghton Mifflin Co.
Huebeck	Max Huebeck Verlag
Junction	Junction Avenue Press
Juta	Juta & Co., Ltd.
Kayor	Kayor Publishers
Kiepenheur	Kiepenheur & Witsch
Knopf	Alfred A. Knopf
Liberty	The Liberty Book Club
Lippincott	J. B. L. Lippincott & Co.
London Magazine	London Magazine Editions
Longman	Longman Southern Africa (Pty) Ltd.
Lorton	Lorton Publications
Louisiana State UP	Louisiana State University Press
Macmillan	Macmillan Publishing Co., Inc.
Magvetö	Magvetö Könyvkiadó
McGraw	McGraw-Hill, Inc.
Micah	Micah Publications
Michel	Albin Michel
Miller	Maskew Miller

Miller Longman	Maskew Miller Longman
Minerva	Heinemann Minerva
Mondadori	Arnoldo Mondadori Editore
Muntinga	Maarten Muntinga
Murray	John Murray
Narr	Gunter Narr Verlag
NELM	National English Literary Museum
Nelson	Thomas Nelson and Sons Ltd.
OUP	Oxford University Press
Ohio UP	Ohio University Press
Otava	Kustannusosakeyhtio Otava
Outrigger	Outrigger Publishers
Oved	Am Oved
P.E.N	The South African P.E.N Centre
Paladin	Paladin Grafton Books
Pandora	Pandora Press
Perskor	Perskor Publishers
Philip	David Philip
Potchefstroom U for CHE	Potchefstroom University for Christian Higher Education
Prentice	Prentice-Hall, Inc.
Profile	Profile Books
Purnell	Purnell & Sons (S.A.) Pty., Ltd.
Quixote	Dom Quixote
Ravan	Ravan Press
Reader's Digest	Reader's Digest Association, South Africa
Reijger	Reijger Publishers
Renoster	Renoster Books
Rinehart	Rinehart and Winston
Rizzoli	Rizzoli Editore
Routledge	Routledge & Kegan Paul
Salem	Salem Press
Schöningh	Ferdinand Schöningh
Seaver	Seaver Books
Seix Barral	Editorial Seix Barral, S.A.
Shuter	Shuter & Shooter
Silver Leaf	Silver Leaf Books
Simon	Simon and Schuster, Inc.
Slovensky	Slovensky Spisovatel
Southern	Southern Book Publishers
St. James	St. James Press
St. Martin's	St. Martin's Press, Inc.

Struik	C. Struik (Pty) Ltd.
Sylvester	Sylvester & Orphanos
Synora	Nea Synora
Tartaruga	La Tartaruga
Third	The Third Press
Three Continents	Three Continents Press
Timmins	Howard B. Timmins
UCT	University of Cape Town
UNISA	University of South Africa
U of Utah P	University of Utah Press
Ungar	Frederick Ungar Publishing Co.
Viking	Viking Press
Virago	Virago Press
Volk	Verlag Volk und Welt
Weidenfeld	Weidenfeld and Nicolson
Wilson	H. W. Wilson Co.
Wolfe	Wolfe Publishing Ltd.
Yayinlari	Simavi Yayinlari
Yoseloff	Thomas Yoseloff
Zed	Zed Books Ltd.

PREFACE

Research towards this bibliography was begun more than five years ago by Dorothy Driver who documented many of the critical articles on Gordimer and procured for the Museum a facsimile of the Gordimer newspaper clipping archive of Jonathan Cape which is included in the section on reviews of individual works. As the years went by she became aware that her numerous commitments did not leave her enough uninterrupted time to complete the project. She therefore approached Craig MacKenzie, then a curator at NELM, to share the work with her. He started documenting most of the sections covered in this work, and began the scanning of the critical articles for the index. However by January 1992 it became clear to both of them that they did not have the time to see the project through to conclusion. It was then that I was approached to finish the task. With the help of Ann Dry, also a curator at NELM, who undertook to document the section on reviews of individual works and the chronology, the task has been completed and I would want to express my appreciation of all the work that these people have done over the years which is reflected throughout the pages of this book. During the last year and a half they have been generous in their advice and encouragement, but in the final analysis any defects in style and arrangement of the whole work must be my own!

I have, in the main, followed the bibliographic style of the Modern Language Association of America (MLA) except in those cases where certain punctuation marks would have proved confusing or even possibly misleading. For example, I have been consistent in the use of colons before all page numbers for ease of reading, even when periods would have been more correct. Listing of the publication of individual short stories is documented under three sections: short story collections by the author, short stories in journals and newspapers, and short story anthologies. This, together with the use of the relevant index, makes for tidy presentation and easy retrieval of the material. But all other publication instances of a particular entry follow one another in block formation in one entry. Each critical work, article, thesis and interview has been scanned and, where applicable, the various works and stories discussed are placed in square brackets after each entry, as well as being indexed for ease of retrieval.

Bibliographic information has been given as succinctly as possible in each entry, necessitating the use of abbreviations. In accordance with MLA, I have abbreviated all familiar publishers' names and a key to the full name appears on the preceding pages. Full publication details of a work are given only in the first instance of its appearance; subsequent citations within that particular section comprise only title and page numbers. Volume and part numbers of periodicals have been furnished in parenthesis in preference to the month of publication, unless the latter is customary.

Entries have been checked for accuracy by personal inspection of the items concerned. Where this has not been possible, the item in the bibliography has been indicated by means of an asterisk. I would welcome confirmation by readers who have access to these items, as well as further documentation in this area. In the process of compiling this bibliography the Museum has built up a substantial collection of works by and about Nadine Gordimer, and will furnish material in its holdings upon request, subject to the provisions of the relevant copyright legislation, and for a reasonable research fee.

My special gratitude goes to Nadine Gordimer who allowed me to look at her private collection of journal and newspaper clippings, as well as her collection of translations of her work. In this regard I am also indebted to Linda Shaughnessy of A. P. Watt Ltd., Nadine Gordimer's literary agent, for the time and trouble she took in providing a detailed listing of such translations, and to Craig MacKenzie who listed the translations in Gordimer's private collection. The relevant section in the bibliography is, in large measure, due to their willing co-operation. Reference has already been made to Jonathan Cape Publishers from whom we acquired photocopies of their newspaper review archive on Gordimer's work. Dawid Malan, Senior Reference Librarian (English) at UNISA also gave unstintingly of his time when I was researching material in the library, and also in sending me relevant material throughout the year. The staff of the various departments of the Johannesburg Public Library and the William Cullen Library, University of the Witwatersrand, also gave valued assistance during my visit last year.

Finally, I wish to thank my colleagues at the Museum: Basil Mills for the photographs, Anne Warring for her help in choosing them, Ellenore Bowles for her work in tracking down entries through inter-library loan, Julie Strauss for her assistance in setting up the programme on Inmagic for the index and Ann Dry for her invaluable help with the compilation of the indices. A special word of gratitude must go to my wife, Catherine Woeber, also a curator at the Museum, who assisted me in my research trip to the libraries on the Witwatersrand. Without her constant support, encouragement and patience, this work would never have seen the light of day.

It is the hope of all of us who have had a hand in the compilation of this work that it will prove a valuable foundation on which scholars and researchers can build. More than that, the Museum hopes that it will prove a fitting tribute to South Africa's first Nobel Prize winner for literature, and one of the most important writers of our time.

John Read
Grahamstown, 1993

BIBLIOGRAPHIC SOURCES

In addition to the documentation which is held at the Museum, the following bibliographic sources were consulted.

Annual Bibliography of English Language and Literature. 1937-1992. London: Modern Humanities Research Association (formerly Cambridge UP).

British Humanities Index. 1937-1992. London: Library Association Publishing Ltd.

Humanities Index. 1937-1992. New York: The H. W. Wilson Company.

Short Story Index. 1937-1992. New York: The H. W. Wilson Company.

Book Review Digest. 1939-1992. New York: The H. W. Wilson Company.

Book Review Index. 1939-1992. Detroit, MI: Gale Research Company.

MLA International Bibliography of Books and Articles on the Modern Languages and Literatures. 1939-1980. New York: Modern Language Association of America.

Index to South African Periodicals (ISAP). 1937-1992.

Readers' Guide to Periodical Literature. 1939-1992. New York: The H. W. Wilson Company.

Dissertation Abstracts International. 1939-1992. Ann Arbor, MI: University Microfilms International.

Index to Theses with Abstracts Accepted for Higher Degrees by the Universities of Great Britain and Ireland and the Council for National Academic Awards. 1939-1992. London: ASLIB.

Union Catalogue of Theses and Dissertations of South African Universities. 1939-1992. Potchefstroom: Potchefstroom University for CHE.

The latest editions of Periodicals in South African Libraries (PISAL) and Ulrichs's *International Periodicals Directory* were checked for library holdings and journal origins. *Benn's Media Directory Incorporating Benn's Press Directory 1987* and *Willing's Press Guide 1986* were checked for newspaper origins.

I also searched the periodical holdings of the University of South Africa, and the William Cullen Library, University of the Witwatersrand. The newspaper holdings and the Africana collection of the Strange Library at the Johannesburg Public Library were also consulted. As mentioned in the preface, Miss Gordimer's literary agent, A. P. Watt Ltd., provided me with a complete listing of translations of her works and Jonathan Cape Ltd., the Museum with a facsimile of their Gordimer newspaper review clippings archive. The Museum is indebted to both these organisations for their invaluable contribution to this project.

Finally Nadine Gordimer kindly allowed us to check translations of her books and publications of short stories in periodicals in her own private collection.

The sum of various
alienations is the
state of our arts
in
relevant music
words
commitment
from within

the cataract
of imprecision
that is thrown
over our vision
dynamism of disintegration
we can think of a post
apartheid art
the following to end on the cautionary deprecate

6

INTRODUCTION

When Nadine Gordimer was awarded the Nobel Prize for Literature in 1991, her body of work included ten novels and over two hundred short stories, as well as a large amount of literary and sociopolitical criticism, and collaborations in various television films and two photographic studies of South African life. She has also been extremely generous with interviews and talks, through which she has become known as an authoritative informant on South African cultural and political life. The bibliography being offered here stands, first of all, as a homage to a woman who, seventy years old this year, has done a great deal to shape a South African literary tradition, besides helping, through her own work and her dedication to the work of others, to place South African writing in an international context.

Readers and critics may continue to look forward to new work from Gordimer, for her career as writer and commentator is by no means over. This bibliography includes all her work thus far, whatever its generic category, including translations, and all known criticism of her writing, along with a considerable amount of occasional comment. As a listing that has had to proclaim an arbitrary deadline, it is necessarily unfinished: indeed, the ultimate aspiration of a bibliography must be for its own incompletion, since its nature is to encourage new texts to be spawned from the old. As it stands, the bibliography not only provides a history of Gordimer's own career from its start in 1937 but also attests to the range of interest her work has elicited. Even as a young writer, she received a good deal of critical attention in South Africa and abroad; this critical attention grew as she established herself, as her works were increasingly translated, and as her literary and political views were more and more widely solicited. Among the relatively few books of criticism solely devoted to her writing, two have been particularly influential: Stephen Clingman's *The Novels of Nadine Gordimer: History from the Inside* (1986), and, to a lesser extent, Judie Newman's *Nadine Gordimer* (1988), which is considerably briefer. Scholars are fortunate also to have access to the best of Gordimer's essays in *The Essential Gesture: Writing, Politics and Places* (1988), edited by Stephen Clingman, to the bulk of her interviews in *Conversations with Nadine Gordimer* (1990), edited by Nancy Topping Bazin and Marilyn Dallman Seymour, and to a selection of critical essays on her in *Critical Essays on Nadine Gordimer* (1990), edited by Rowland Smith.

In part because Gordimer's writing has been nationally and internationally acclaimed at a time when South Africa has had limited cultural intercourse with the rest of the world, criticism of her work has not always managed to engage in dialogue with itself: that is, critics do not necessarily feel the need to attend to what has been said by others or to choose a path not already trampled. American criticism, for example, which has been so ready to take up Gordimer as a spokesperson on the South African situation, has often found it possible to ignore what a generation of well-informed South African readers have had to say, and South African critics have tended to limit her work by seeing it as a response simply to South Africa, without placing it in the context offered by contemporary literary theory. Moreover, addressing a writer with a reputation based on her novels, critics all too often feel able to speak of these novels, or even one or two of them, without feeling a need to see them in the literary context created by her short stories. This separation of short and long fiction tends to serve rather than enrich or adjust critics' views of Gordimer's "realism". Though the primary aim of this bibliography is to encourage further research simply by listing a set of relevant titles, it is also intended to bring to the notice of critics working in any one area of interest what has been written elsewhere, and to impress on scholars the generic range of Gordimer's writing. Such refinement is all the more important in light of the recent interest in the world's "new literatures".

What are the major tendencies of critical work on Gordimer? No doubt because of the political demands of the time, to say nothing of the "spectacular" nature of apartheid (to take over Njabulo Ndebele's now well-known epithet), criticism has tended to engage with the historical and political dimensions of her writing. Stephen Clingman's work on Gordimer is the best of this kind, taking sociological criticism to its limit by seeing Gordimer's writing as "history from the inside", history as experienced by individuals who are themselves products of history in all its complexity and contradictions. Clingman took his lead from specific solicitations from the writer herself, most notably a statement made in 1982: "I have to offer you myself as my most closely observed specimen." For Clingman, Gordimer writes not just of the events and movements of South African history, but also of what it has been like to live *through* them, along with the transformation of consciousness that this implies.

In this regard, it is quite appropriate that Clingman sees Gordimer's writing in terms of "development". Gordimer herself often talks about the changes in her fiction as a reflection of social and historical change and the writer's own changing apprehension, as in the oft-cited preface to her first *Selected Stories*. All the other critics thus far who have produced books entirely or largely about Gordimer follow her career chronologically. Robert Haugh, who wrote the first book on Gordimer, has been the only one to see her development in negative terms, arguing that she had increasing difficulty in integrating her primary interest in the personal with a set of political themes. In contrast, Michael Wade, one of Gordimer's earliest serious critics, looks at her increasing turn to "Africa" not just as a change of topic in her writing but, more importantly, as a move towards a new perspective. He has continued this line of argument in recently published work. John Cooke, who (unusually among her commentators) focuses on individual psychology, addressing the importance of Gordimer's childhood and adolescence to her writing, argues that the novels may be seen in terms of an increasing liberation from the mother's confining world. Thus to Cooke, too, Gordimer's development is positive, moving from a private to a public frame of reference.

Judie Newman builds on work done by Clingman and Cooke but takes a poststructuralist approach. Where Clingman sees South African history as the conditioning force behind Gordimer's fiction, and where Cooke sees the nature of Gordimer's relation with her mother as the crucial determinant, Newman argues that Gordimer's intersection of racial, colonial and sexual themes, with an increasingly sophisticated focus on gender, takes her work into a reassessment of narrative realism. Thus Newman extends the debate initiated by Clingman regarding the relation between Gordimer's realism and white South African constructions of reality: she argues that Gordimer's deconstruction of realism as a way of knowing South African reality opens up a new route to cultural and political decolonization.

Her reading resonates interestingly with that offered earlier by Abdul JanMahomed in *Manichean Aesthetics* (1983), whose interest is specifically in the deconstruction of some of the binary oppositions that underpin the colonial enterprise (he does not concern himself with gender), and leads, further, into work recently published by David Ward in *Chronicles of Darkness* (1989) and, as suggested earlier, Michael Wade in *White on Black in South Africa* (1993).

Although the recent criticism by Wade and Ward does not extend into book-length studies solely on Gordimer's work, it calls for comment here. The two critics complement each other in useful ways. Seeing in Gordimer's fiction a steady movement away from chronicle to prophecy, Ward pays detailed attention to her narrative strategy. In the process, especially in relation to the short stories, he addresses with intelligence and tact what has hitherto been pejoratively regarded as detachment or coldness in Gordimer's art. For Ward, Gordimer's detachment is a fault neither of the writing nor of the writer herself, but an aspect of her ability to produce her narrator as "other", alienated not just from the presented world but also from pre-existing ways of seeing reality. Thus Gordimer's art produces the recognition not simply that there is always another way of seeing or experiencing the world, but, more importantly, that seeing and experiencing the world is necessarily "other" to itself: flawed, contradictory, not after all in command.

Although Wade's work was unfortunately not quite finished at the time of his death, he very usefully places the "otherness" of the white South African observer in its political, historical and economic context, seeing Gordimer's writing as an address to those mythic structures or ideologies that have been used to maintain white South Africans' visions of themselves: he asserts that her project is to try to adjust those mythic structures quite as much as it is to record and judge them. For both critics, a distance is set up between observer and observed at every point: the observer is placed at one remove, and so are the strategies used to place the observed. What one might add here is that such detachment belongs to a writer who is always watching her language, who is always aware that *she* is being written even as she taps the typewriter keys. Thus paradoxically, given what has been said about "development", the critic needs also to be on the lookout for signs of repressiveness in the very texture of the writing.

One limitation, perhaps unavoidable, of many of the critical essays on Gordimer thus far flows from the fact that they see themselves as introductory, aiming to present the writing to a public unfamiliar with other accounts of her writing, or else aiming to introduce an aspect of Gordimer's writing not hitherto addressed. Researchers have rarely seen their way clear to producing highly specialized and specifically focused academic research. However (and, in this regard, the present bibliography is surely coming at just the right time), a critical ground both solid and fertile seems on the point of being established. One senses this not merely because the most recent critics cannot but take account of the work of Clingman, at least, which has by now been published in Britain, the United States, and South Africa, but also because some too easily established opinions about Gordimer are in the process of being overturned. The most glaring of these has been the view that Gordimer's writing represents an opposing trend in South African fiction to that of J. M. Coetzee. This, I believe, points to a second limitation of much critical thinking on Gordimer thus far. Although there is of course a difference between Gordimer and Coetzee, criticism has tended to place them in such radical opposition to one another that the opposition keeps mindlessly reproducing itself rather than being offered up for interrogation. Perhaps, given the excellent work done by Clingman, and the later contributions of Newman and Ward, as well as hints in Wade's recent work, critics might feel emboldened to turn more decisively to close textual analysis of Gordimer's writing in such a way as to see beyond this opposition. Gordimer's work is concerned with the interplay between two commitments: one to the craft of writing, and the other to the duties of the white South African writer. Encouraged by recent developments in the South African political situation, critics may now start to read the relations between art and politics in her writing not simply at the level of content but also at the level of form.

Earlier, I noted that Clingman's work had been responsive to Gordimer's own invitations about how she should be read. Gordimer also claimed, "nothing I say [is] as true as my fiction." Despite Clingman's desire to respond, he did not give this assertion its full weight. In Gordimer's fiction, contrary to what she has sometimes said on public platforms or in occasional writings, any "authority" accorded to the narrative point of view is continually questioned. Thus her fiction is "true" first of all in the sense that "truth" *is* fiction, constructed under social and political conditions which are themselves historically and culturally specific, and secondly in the sense that writing is "truth" by default, for it expands, questions and subverts the concepts on which "truth" is grounded. If we wish to attend to the relations set up in her writing between art and politics, or the private and the political, we must examine the ways the writing itself produces and negotiates these relations. At times the negotiation is conducted with difficulty in her work, and the writing sometimes buckles under the orthodoxies it has elsewhere questioned. In this regard Gordimer's work is especially interesting, for its invaluable self-consciousness renders white South Africa visible to itself.

At the start of this introduction I suggested that Gordimer had helped shape a South African literary tradition. She has also shaped the direction of South African cultural and political life, both through her own writing and through the increasingly sophisticated critical responses her work has given rise to. It has seemed worth spending some time on two of the most recent critics not only because other commentators, notably Rowland Smith, have already summarised earlier critical trends, and not only because these two illustrate so clearly the benefits gained by building on other readings, but also because they are themselves the products of her writing. Indeed, it is Gordimer's writing that has empowered her best critics to recognise in her work the portrayal of a specific white South African neurosis and to speak of the particular urgencies, and difficulties, of experiencing the world from the point of view of the "other", taking into account differences of gender and class as well as race. As Clingman wrote of Gordimer's essays, in a remark we may extend to her fiction, "Whatever future culture develops in South Africa, it could do far worse than to be based on the kind of rigorous, questioning independence of mind that we see in her essays." Gordimer's writing tells us, over and again, that we must keep asking questions about the past and the present, as well as about the kind of future which the past and present produce.

Dorothy Driver
University of Cape Town, 1993

CHRONOLOGY

1923.   Nadine Gordimer born on 20 November in Springs, near Johannesburg. Her father, Isidore Gordimer, a Lithuanian emigrant at thirteen, was a watchmaker and jeweller by trade. Her mother, Nan Myers Gordimer, emigrated to South Africa from England with her parents when she was six. Gordimer was educated at the Convent of Our Lady of Mercy in Springs until the age of eleven after which she received private tuition until she was fifteen or sixteen.

1937.   First published story, "The Quest for Seen Gold", appeared in the Children's Section of the *Sunday Express*, 13 June.

1939.   First adult fiction, "Come Again Tomorrow", published in *The Forum* (Johannesburg).

1945.   Attended the University of the Witwatersrand, but left after one year.

1949.   Married Dr Gerald Gavron. Publication of *Face to Face: Short Stories*.

1950.   Daughter, Oriane, born on 6 June.

1952.   Publication of *The Soft Voice of the Serpent and Other Stories*. Divorced from Dr Gavron.

1953.   Publication of *The Lying Days*.

1954.   Married Reinhold Cassirer, an art dealer originally from Heidelberg, Germany.

1955.   Son, Hugo, born on 28 March.

1956.   Publication of *Six Feet of the Country.*

1958.   Publication of *A World of Strangers*, banned till 1970.

1960.   Publication of *Friday's Footprint and Other Stories.*

1961.   Awarded the W. H. Smith Literary Award for *Friday's Footprint* (1960) and the Ford Foundation Fellowship to the United States as Visiting Lecturer at the Institute of Contemporary Arts, Washington, D.C.

1963.   Publication of *Occasion for Loving.*

1965.   Publication of *Not for Publication and Other Stories.*

1966.   Publication of *The Late Bourgeois World*, banned till 1976.

1967.   Edited *South African Writing Today* with Lionel Abrahams.

1969.   Granted Thomas Pringle Award for creative writing in English in South African magazines (South Africa). Visiting Lecturer, Harvard University (Cambridge, Massachusetts) and Northwestern University (Illinois).

1970.   Publication of *A Guest of Honour.* Visiting Lecturer at the University of Michigan (Ann Arbor).

1971.   Publication of *Livingstone's Companions.* Appointed Adjunct Professor of Writing, Columbia University (New York).

1972.   Awarded James Tait Black Memorial Prize (England) for *A Guest of Honour.*

1973.   Publication of *The Black Interpreters: Notes on African Writing* and *On the Mines* (with David Goldblatt).

1974.   Publication of *The Conservationist.* Awarded CNA Prize (South Africa) for *A Guest of Honour* and joint winner of the Booker Prize (England) for *The Conservationist.*

1975.   Publication of *Selected Stories.* Awarded CNA Prize for *The Conservationist* and Grand Aigle d'Or Prize (France). Visiting Gildersleeve Professor at Barnard College (New York).

1976.   Publication of *Some Monday for Sure.*

1978.   Publication of *No Place Like: Selected Stories.*

1979.   Publication of *Burger's Daughter*, banned 11 July and reinstated in August. Appointed Honorary Member of the American Academy and Institute of Arts and Letters.

1980. Awarded CNA Prize for *Burger's Daughter*. Publication of *A Soldier's Embrace, Town and Country Lovers*, and *What Happened to Burger's Daughter or How South African Censorship Works*. Appointed Honorary Member of the American Academy of Arts and Sciences.

1981. Publication of *July's People* and broadcasting of "A Terrible Chemistry" - Writers and Places Television Series, England. Scripted screenplays for four of the seven television dramas collectively entitled "The Gordimer Stories" 1981-1982 ("Country Lovers", "A Chip of Glass Ruby", "Praise", and "Oral History"). Awarded Scottish Arts Council Neil M. Gunn Fellowship, the Common Wealth Award for Distinguished Service in Literature (USA) and the CNA Prize for *July's People*. Honorary Doctorate of Literature conferred by the University of Leuven, Belgium.

1982. Granted Modern Language Association Award (USA).

1983. Co-scripted and co-produced "Choosing for Justice: Allan Boesak" with Hugo Cassirer.

1984. Publication of *Something Out There*. Awarded Honorary Doctorate of Literature by the University of the Witwatersrand.

1985. Awarded the Premio Malaparte (Italy) for her contribution to literature. Honorary Doctorates of Literature conferred by Smith College (Northampton, Massachusetts) and Mount Holyoke College (South Hadley, Massachusetts). Awarded Honorary Doctorate of Humane Letters, City College of New York.

1986. Publication of *Lifetimes: Under Apartheid*. Awarded Nelly Sachs Prize (West Germany), Officier de l'Ordre des Arts et des Lettres (France), and Brockport Writers Forum International Award (State University of New York, Brockport). Honorary Doctorates of Literature conferred by Harvard University (Cambridge, Massachusetts), Yale University (New Haven, Connecticut) and University of Cape Town (South Africa). Assisted in organizing the Anti-Censorship Action Group (ACAG).

1986-87. Elected Vice President of P.E.N.

1987.   Publication of *A Sport of Nature*. Awarded Honorary Doctorates of Literature by Columbia University (New York), the New School for Social Research (New York City) and York University (England). Elected Patron and Regional Representative, Congress of South African Writers (COSAW).

1988.   Publication of *The Essential Gesture: Writing, Politics and Places*.

1989.   Scripted and narrated a documentary in BBC series "Frontiers: Gold and the Gun" concerning the South Africa-Mozambique frontier. Broadcast 6 June 1990 on BBC1 Television.

1990.   Publication of *My Son's Story*.

1991.   Elected Publicity Secretary of COSAW. Awarded the CNA Prize for *My Son's Story*. Publication of *Jump and Other Stories* and *Crimes of Conscience*. Awarded the Nobel Prize for Literature, October. Granted the highest French Art and Literature decoration, the Commandeur dans l'Ordre des Arts et Lettres, November.

1992.   Elected COSAW Vice President. Participated in the Mayibuye Community Arts Academy held in Port Elizabeth from 15-20 December concerning the role of the arts in the transformation of South Africa. Honorary Doctorates of Literature conferred by the University of Durban-Westville and from Cambridge University (England). Participated in the Grahamstown Festival Winter School Lectures, 5 July. Publication of *Why Haven't You Written? Selected Stories—1950-1972*.

1993.   Elected member of a board of trustees charged with the responsibility of overseeing a proposed Foundation for Arts and Culture concerned with the process of transformation and cultural reconstruction in South Africa, under the wing of the ANC's Department of Arts and Culture.

WORKS OF NADINE GORDIMER

A. FICTION: NOVELS AND SHORT STORY COLLECTIONS

1949.   1. *Face to Face*. Johannesburg: Silver Leaf.

> **Contents:**
> "The Soft Voice of the Serpent."   9-15.
> "Ah, Woe Is Me."   16-25.
> "The Umbilical Cord."   26-35.
> "The Battlefield at No. 29."   36-48.
> "In the Beginning."   49-62.
> "A Commonplace Story."   63-71.
> "The Amateurs."   72-81.
> "A Present for a Good Girl."   82-93.
> "The Train from Rhodesia."   94-100.
> "La Vie Bohème."   101-114.
> "Is There Nowhere Else Where We Can Meet?"   115-
>   119.
> "The Kindest Thing to Do."   120-127.
> "The Last of the Old-Fashioned Girls."   128-132.
> "No Luck To-Night."   133-143.
> "The Talisman."   144-155.
> "Monday Is Better than Sunday."   156-164.

1952.   2. *The Soft Voice of the Serpent and Other Stories*. New York: Simon. * Toronto: Musson. Repr. London: Gollancz, 1953. *New York: NAL, 1956. New York: Viking, 1962. Harmondsworth: Penguin, 1962. *Toronto: Macmillan, 1962.

Contents:
"The Soft Voice of the Serpent."   1-7.
"The Catch."   8-25.
"The Kindest Thing to Do."   26-33.
"The Hour and the Years."   34-47.
"The Train from Rhodesia."   48-55.
"A Watcher of the Dead."   56-67.
"Treasures of the Sea."   68-75.
"The Prisoner."   76-91.
"Is There Nowhere Else Where We Can Meet?"   92-96.
"The Amateurs."   97-106.
"A Present for a Good Girl."   107-118.
"La Vie Bohème."   119-132.
"Ah, Woe Is Me."   133-143.
"Another Part of the Sky."   144-155.
"The Umbilical Cord."   156-165.
"The Talisman."   166-177.
"The End of the Tunnel."   178-193.
"The Defeated."   194-212.
"A Commonplace Story."   213-221.
"Monday Is Better than Sunday."   222-230.
"In the Beginning."   231-244.

1953.   3. *The Lying Days*. *New York: Simon. London: Gollancz. *Toronto: Musson. Repr. *New York: NAL, 1955. London: Cape, 1978. London: Virago, 1983.

1956.   4. *Six Feet of the Country: Fifteen Short Stories*. New York: Simon. Also pub. as *Six Feet of the Country: Short Stories*. London: Gollancz [this edition omits the story "The White Goddess and the Mealie Question" and rearranges the sequence].

Contents:
"Six Feet of the Country."   1-15.
"Face from Atlantis."   17-39.
"A Bit of Young Life."   41-55.

"Enemies." 57-68.
"Which New Era Would That Be?" 69-85.
"Out of Season." 87-97.
"My First Two Women." 99-114.
"The White Goddess and the Mealie Question."
   115-128.
"Clowns in Clover." 129-138.
"A Wand'ring Minstrel, I." 139-150.
"Happy Event." 151-167.
"Charmed Lives." 169-183.
"Horn of Plenty." 185-204.
"The Cicatrice." 205-213.
"The Smell of Death and Flowers." 215-241.

1958. 5. *A World of Strangers*. *New York: Simon. London: Gollancz. Repr. Harmondsworth: Penguin, 1961, 1981. London: Cape, 1976.

1960. 6. *Friday's Footprint*. London: Gollancz. *Toronto: Macmillan. Also pub. as *Friday's Footprint and Other Stories*. New York: Viking [this edition omits "Something for the Time Being"].

Contents:
"Friday's Footprint." 11-33.
"The Last Kiss." 34-43.
"The Night the Favourite Came Home." 44-57.
"Little Willie." 58-67.
"A Style of Her Own." 68-81.
"The Bridegroom." 82-91.
"Check Yes or No." 92-103.
"The Gentle Art." 104-120.
"The Path of the Moon's Dark Fortnight." 121-138.
"Our Bovary." 139-152.
"A Thing of the Past." 153-166.
"Harry's Presence." 167-178.
"An Image of Success." 179-224.
"Something for the Time Being." 225-236.

1963. 7. *Occasion for Loving*. *New York: Viking. London: Gollancz. Repr. London: Cape, 1978. London: Virago, 1983.

1965. 8. *Not for Publication and Other Stories*. New York: Viking. Also pub. as *Not for Publication*. London: Gollancz [this edition omits "Something for the Time Being"].

Contents:
"Not for Publication."   3-19.
"Son-in-Law."   21-31.
"A Company of Laughing Faces."   33-50.
"Through Time and Distance."   51-61.
"The Worst Thing of All."   63-85.
"The Pet."   87-92.
"One Whole Year, and Even More."   93-116.
"A Chip of Glass Ruby."   117-127.
"The African Magician."   129-145.
"Tenants of the Last Tree-House."   147-165.
"Good Climate, Friendly Inhabitants."   167-180.
"Vital Statistics."   181-198.
"Something for the Time Being."   199-210.
"Message in a Bottle."   211-216.
"Native Country."   217-229.
"Some Monday for Sure."   231-248.

1966. 9. *The Late Bourgeois World*. New York: Viking. London: Gollancz. Repr. London: Cape, 1976. Harmondsworth: Penguin, 1982.

1970. 10. *A Guest of Honour*. New York: Viking. Repr. London: Cape, 1971. Harmondsworth: Penguin, 1973, 1983.

1971. 11. *Livingstone's Companions*. New York: Viking. Repr. London: Cape, 1972. Harmondsworth: Penguin, 1975.

Contents:
"Livingstone's Companions."   3-37.
"A Third Presence."   39-50.
"The Credibility Gap."   51-60.
"Abroad."   61-82.
"An Intruder."   83-92.
"Inkalamu's Place."   93-105.
"The Life of the Imagination."   107-122.
"A Meeting in Space."   123-137.
"Open House."   139-151.
"Rain-Queen."   153-163.
"The Bride of Christ."   165-181.

"No Place Like." 183-191.
"Otherwise Birds Fly In." 193-206.
"A Satisfactory Settlement." 207-218.
"Why Haven't You Written?" 219-231.
"Africa Emergent." 233-248.

1974. 12. *The Conservationist.* London: Cape. Repr. New York: Viking, 1975. *New York: McGraw, 1977. Harmondsworth: Penguin, 1978, 1983.

1975. 13. *Selected Stories.* London: Cape. Repr. New York: Viking, 1976. Also repr. as *No Place Like: Selected Stories.* Harmondsworth: Penguin, 1978, 1983. [Author's selection from earlier collections.]

Contents:
"Is There Nowhere Else Where We Can Meet?" 15-18.
"The Soft Voice of the Serpent." 19-23.
"Ah, Woe Is Me." 24-30.
"The Catch." 31-42.
"The Train from Rhodesia." 43-47.
"A Bit of Young Life." 48-58.
"Six Feet of the Country." 59-69.
"Which New Era Would That Be?" 70-82.
"Enemies." 83-91.
"Happy Event." 92-104.
"The Smell of Death and Flowers." 105-124.
"Friday's Footprint." 125-143.
"The Night the Favourite Came Home." 144-155.
"The Bridegroom." 156-163.
"The Last Kiss." 164-171.
"The Gentle Art." 172-184.
"Something for the Time Being." 185-194.
"A Company of Laughing Faces." 195-210.
"Not for Publication." 211-224.
"A Chip of Glass Ruby." 225-233.
"Good Climate, Friendly Inhabitants." 234-245.
"The African Magician." 246-259.
"Some Monday for Sure." 260-274.
"Abroad." 275-292.
"Livingstone's Companions." 293-320.
"An Intruder." 321-328.
"Open House." 329-338.

"Rain-Queen."   339-347.
"No Place Like."   348-355.
"The Life of the Imagination."   356-368.
"Africa Emergent."   369-381.

1976.   14. *Some Monday for Sure*. African Writers Series No. 177.
London: Heinemann [shorter version of *Selected Stories*].
Repr. 1980, *1991.

Contents:
"Is There Nowhere Else Where We Can Meet?"   2-5.
"Ah, Woe Is Me."   6-13.
"Six Feet of the Country."   14-25.
"Which New Era Would That Be?"   26-39.
"The Smell of Death and Flowers."   40-60.
"The Bridegroom."   61-69.
"The African Magician."   70-84.
"Not for Publication."   85-99.
"Something for the Time Being."   100-110.
"A Chip of Glass Ruby."   111-120.
"Some Monday for Sure."   121-137.
"Open House."   138-148.
"Africa Emergent."   149-162.

1979.   15. *Burger's Daughter*.   New York: Viking.   London: Cape.
Repr. Harmondsworth: Penguin, 1980.

1980.   16. *A Soldier's Embrace: Stories*. New York: Viking. London:
Cape. Repr. Harmondsworth: Penguin, 1982.

Contents:
"A Soldier's Embrace."   7-22.
"A Lion on the Freeway."   23-27.
"Siblings."   29-44.
"Time Did."   45-53.
"A Hunting Accident."   55-66.
"For Dear Life."   67-72.
"Town and Country Lovers *One*."   73-84.
"*Two*."   85-93.
"A Mad One."   95-104.
"You Name It."   105-112.
"The Termitary."   113-120.
"The Need for Something Sweet."   121-132.
"Oral History."   133-144.

1980.   17. *Town and Country Lovers*. Los Angeles, CA: Sylvester. [These two stories also pub. as "City Lovers" and "Country Lovers."]

1981.   18. *July's People*. Johannesburg: Ravan/Taurus. New York: Viking. London: Cape. Repr. Harmondsworth: Penguin, 1982.

1982.   19. *Six Feet of the Country*. Harmondsworth: Penguin. Repr. New York: Viking Penguin, 1986. [Pub. as a result of a television series of 6 one-hour films by Profile Productions, South Africa and Telepool, Germany, 1981. The series, supplemented with a half-hour interview with Nadine Gordimer, omitted in the book, was televised in Britain, West Germany, Italy, Switzerland, Holland, Scandinavia and U.S.A., but not released in South Africa due to its politically controversial nature. Eventually the films were screened in Johannesburg in March, 1983, except for "A Chip of Glass Ruby" which remained banned. The whole series was shown at the 1984 Boston ASA meetings. The series is distributed by Teleculture, Inc., 420 Lexington Ave., New York, NY 10017.]

Contents:
"Six Feet of the Country." 7-20.
"Good Climate, Friendly Inhabitants." 21-35.
"A Chip of Glass Ruby." 36-47.
"City Lovers." 48-60.
"Country Lovers." 61-70.
"Not for Publication." 71-89.
"Oral History." 90-101.

1984.   20. *Something Out There*. *New York: Viking. London: Cape. Johannesburg: Ravan/Taurus. Repr. Harmondsworth: Penguin, 1985.

Contents [pagination of Cape edition]:
"A City of the Dead, A City of the Living." 9-26.
"At the Rendezvous of Victory." 27-38.
"Letter from His Father." 39-56.
"Crimes of Conscience." 57-63.
"Sins of the Third Age." 65-77.
"Blinder." 79-88.
"Rags and Bones." 89-96.

"Terminal." 97-101.
"A Correspondence Course." 103-115.
"Something Out There." 117-203.

1987.   21. *A Sport of Nature*. New York: Knopf. London: Cape. Cape Town: Philip. Repr. *New York: Penguin, 1988. Harmondsworth: Penguin, 1988.

1990.   22. *My Son's Story*. New York: Knopf. London: Bloomsbury. Cape Town: Philip; Johannesburg: Taurus. Repr. London: Penguin, 1991.

1991.   23. *Crimes of Conscience*. Oxford: Heinemann.

> **Contents:**
> "'A City of the Dead, A City of the Living.'" 1-17.
> "Country Lovers." 18-25.
> "A Soldier's Embrace." 26-41.
> "A Hunting Accident." 42-53.
> "Blinder." 54-62.
> "A Correspondence Course." 63-74.
> "The Termitary." 75-81.
> "Crimes of Conscience." 82-87.
> "Oral History." 88-98.
> "At the Rendezvous of Victory." 99-109.
> "The Ultimate Safari." 110-121.

24. *Jump and Other Stories*. Cape Town: Philip. London: Bloomsbury.

> **Contents:**
> "Jump." 3-20.
> "Once upon a Time." 23-30.
> "The Ultimate Safari." 33-46.
> "A Find." 49-54.
> "My Father Leaves Home." 57-66.
> "Some Are Born to Sweet Delight." 69-88.
> "Comrades." 91-96.
> "Teraloyna." 99-107.
> "The Moment before the Gun Went Off." 111-117.
> "Home." 121-140.
> "A Journey." 143-158.
> "Spoils." 161-179.
> "Safe Houses." 183-209.

"What Were You Dreaming?" 213-225.
"Keeping Fit." 229-243.
"Amnesty." 247-257.

1992.   25. *Why Haven't You Written? Selected Stories 1950—1972.*
London: Penguin.

Contents:
"The Kindest Thing to Do." 3-8.
"The Defeated." 9-23.
"A Watcher of the Dead." 24-32.
"Treasures of the Sea." 33-38.
"The Prisoner." 39-50.
"The Amateurs." 51-58.
"A Present for a Good Girl." 59-67.
"La Vie Bohème." 68-77.
"Another Part of the Sky." 78-86.
"The Umbilical Cord." 87-94.
"The Talisman." 95-103.
"The End of the Tunnel." 104-115.
"Monday Is Better than Sunday." 116-122.
"In the Beginning." 123-133.
"A Third Presence." 137-146.
"The Credibility Gap." 147-155.
"Inkalamu's Place." 156-166.
"The Bride of Christ." 167-181.
"A Meeting in Space." 182-195.
"Otherwise Birds Fly In." 196-208.
"A Satisfactory Settlement." 209-219.
"Why Haven't You Written?" 220-231.

B. SHORT STORIES IN JOURNALS AND NEWSPAPERS

1937.   26. "The Quest for Seen Gold." *Children's Sunday Express*
(part of *Sunday Express*) 13 June: 38.

1938.   27. "Beady Eye's Christmas Gift." *Children's Sunday Express*
(supp. to *Sunday Express*) 4 Dec.: 1.

28. "The First Rainbow." *Children's Sunday Express* (supp. to
Sunday Express) 5 June: 1.

1938.   29. "The Valley Legend." *Children's Sunday Express* (supp. to *Sunday Express*) 18 Sept.: 1.

1939.   30. "Come Again Tomorrow: 'An Immeasurable Blessing Had Been Born of the Disgrace.'" *The Forum* 18 Nov.: 14.

1943.   31. "Bombs over Joh'burg." *P.S.* Apr.: 3-4.

32. "No Place Like Home." *P.S.* Dec.: 7-8.

1944.   33. "The Day." *P.S.* Apr.: 18-19, 32.

34. "No Luck Tonight." *South African Opinion* (1.6): 18-20, 31.

35. "The Shoes." *South African Opinion* (1.3): 21-22.

1945.   36. "The Kindest Thing to Do." *South African Opinion* (2.9): 7-9.

37. "The Menace of the Years." *South African Opinion* (2.4): 18-20.

38. "The Peace of Respectability." *South African Opinion* (1.12): 10-11, 31. [Rev. as "The Hour and the Years."]

1946.   39. "Music Teacher." *Vandag* (1.7): 46-50.

1947.   40. "Ah, Woe Is Me." *Common Sense* (8.12): 537-541.

41. "Is There Nowhere Else Where We Can Meet?" *Common Sense* (8.9): 387-389.

42. "The Train from Rhodesia." *Trek* (11.21): 18-19. Repr. in *Insig* Nov., 1991: B1-B2.

1948.   43. "The Amateurs." *Common Sense* (9.12): 540-544.

44. "The Two of Us." *Trek* (12.1): 22-23. [Also pub. as "The Soft Voice of the Serpent."]

45. "The Umbilical Cord." *Trek* (12.11): 14-15, 22.

46. "A Watcher of the Dead." *Jewish Affairs* (3.4): 31-35. Rev. in *The New Yorker* 9 June, 1951: 74, 76-81.

1949.   47. "Poet and Peasant." *Hasholom* (28.1): 26-29, 31, 47.

48. "A Present for a Good Girl." *Criteria* (1): 55-63. Repr. in *Harper's Magazine* Apr., 1952: 45-50.

49. "Sweet Dreams Selection." *Common Sense* (10.11): 501-505.

1950. 50. "The Hour and the Years." *The Yale Review* (40.2): 261-272. [Orig. version pub. as "The Peace of Respectability."]

51. "Treasures of the Sea." *Trek* (14.6): 8-11.

1951. 52. "The Catch." *Virginia Quarterly Review* (27.3): 386-400.

53. "A Sunday Outing." *Trek* (15.10): 8-9.

1952. 54. "A Bit of Young Life." *The New Yorker* 29 Nov.: 37-42.

55. "The Soft Voice of the Serpent." *Harper's Magazine* May: 87-90. [Orig. pub. as "The Two of Us."]

56. "A Story from the Top Shelf." *Jewish Affairs* (7.4): 41-44.

1953. 57. "Clowns in Clover." *The New Yorker* 10 Oct.: 111-117.

58. "Happy Event." *The Forum* (2.8): 34-40. Repr. as "A Matter of Adjustment." *Charm: The Magazine for Women Who Work* Mar., 1954: 96-97, 151-159.

59. "Six Feet of the Country." *The Forum* (1.11): 25-29. Rev. in *The New Yorker* 23 May: 32-38. [Ending changed for *The New Yorker*. This rev. edition used in future publications.]

1954. 60. "Out of Season." *The New Yorker* 20 Mar.: 31-34.

61. "The Scar." *Harper's Magazine* Mar.: 35-39. [Also pub. as "The Cicatrice."]

62. "The Smell of Death and Flowers." *The New Yorker* 15 May: 34-42.

63. "A Wand'ring Minstrel." *Harper's Magazine* Aug.: 60-65. [Also pub. as "A Wand'ring Minstrel, I."]

1955. 64. "Which New Era Would That Be?" *The New Yorker* 9 July: 25-30.

1956. 65. "Charmed Lives." *Harper's Bazaar* Feb.: 110, 178, 180, 183, 193.

66. "Face from Atlantis." *The Paris Review* (13): 101-121.

67. "The Pretender." *The New Yorker* 24 Mar.: 33-38. [Also pub. as "My First Two Women."]

68. "A Sense of Survival." *The New Yorker* 19 May: 31-36. [Rev. as "Enemies."]

1957. 69. "Check Yes or No." *Mademoiselle* June: 82-83, 122-126.

1957.   70. "The Last Kiss." *The London Magazine* (4.2): 14-21.

71. "Little Willie." *The New Yorker* 30 Mar.: 28-31.

72. "Our Bovary." *The New Yorker* 28 Sept.: 41-46.

1958.   73. "Christmas in Johannesburg." *The New Yorker* 4 Jan.: 22-28. [Rev. and pub. as chapter 12 of *A World of Strangers*.]

74. "The Lady's Past." *Cosmopolitan* Dec.: 88-93. [Also pub. as "A Style of Her Own."]

75. "The Path of the Moon." *Mademoiselle* Oct.: 68, 122-130. [Also pub. as "The Path of the Moon's Dark Fortnight."]

1959.   76. "The Bridegroom." *The New Yorker* 23 May: 36-39.

77. "The Gentle Art." *Mademoiselle* Nov.: 106-107, 135-138, 140-143.

78. "An Image of Success." *Cosmopolitan* Aug.: 72-83.

79. "A Thing of the Past." *Encounter* (13.3): 3-10.

80. "A View of the River." *The New Yorker* 11 Apr.: 40-50. [Rev. and pub. as "Friday's Footprint."]

1960.   81. "A Chip of Glass Ruby." *Contrast* (1.1): 13-22. Repr. in *The Atlantic* Feb., 1961: 66-70.

82. "A Company of Laughing Faces." *Mademoiselle* July: 57-63.

83. "Neighbours and Friends." *Cosmopolitan* Aug.: 76-83.

84. "Something for the Time Being." *The New Yorker* 9 Jan.: 26-31.

85. "Something Unexpected." *Cosmopolitan* June: 89-93.

1961.   86. "The African Magician." *The New Yorker* 15 July: 27-34.

1962.   87. "Message in a Bottle." *The Kenyon Review* (24.2): 227-232.

88. "The Pet." *The New Yorker* 24 Mar.: 34-36.

89. "Tenants of the Last Tree House." *The New Yorker* 15 Dec.: 39-46.

1962.	90. "Through Time and Distance." *The Atlantic* Jan.: 46-50. Repr. in *Contrast* (2.1): 16-25. *Sunday Times Colour Magazine* (supp. to *Sunday Times*) 22 Dec., 1963: 25-26, 28, 30.

1964.	91. "One Whole Year, and Even More." *The Kenyon Review* (26.1): 93-115. Repr. in *The Classic* (1.4) 1965: 23-42.

 	92. "Stranger in Town." *Harper's Magazine* Nov.: 108-110, 112+. [Also pub. as "Good Climate, Friendly Inhabitants."]

1965.	93. "Inkalamu's Place." *Inkululeko* (1.3): 53-56. Repr. in *Contrast 18* (5.2) 1968.: 13-23.

 	94. "Not for Publication." *Contrast 12* (3.4): 14-29. Slightly alt. as "Praise" in *The Atlantic* Apr.: 99-105.

 	95. "The Proof of Love." *Ladies' Home Journal* Feb.: 80, 90, 93-94, 96. [Also pub. as "Native Country."]

 	96. "Some Monday for Sure." *Transition* (4.18): 9-15.

 	97. "Son-in-Law." *The Reporter* 11 Mar.: 37-40.

 	98. "A Third Presence." *Cosmopolitan* July: 95-96, 98-99. Repr. in *London Magazine* (6.6) 1966: 75-84.

 	99. "Vital Statistics." *The Kenyon Review* (27.1): 27-48.

 	100. "The Worst Thing of All." *The London Magazine* (4.11): 3-21.

1966.	101. "Say Something African." *The New Yorker* 20 Aug.: 34-40. [Also pub. as "A Meeting in Space."]

 	102. *"The Visit." *Jewish Chronicle* 9 Sept.: 39.

1967.	103. "The Bride of Christ." *Nova*: 88-91, 93. Repr. in *The Atlantic* Aug.: 58-64.

 	104. "A Meeting in Space." *The Cornhill Magazine* (Summer): 122-135. [Also pub. as "Say Something African."]

 	105. "Out of the Walls." *The New Yorker* 11 Feb.: 34-37. Repr. in *Daily Telegraph Magazine* (supp. to *Daily Telegraph*) 22 Sept.: 41, 45-46. [Also pub. as "An Intruder."]

1968.	106. "Abroad." *The Southern Review* (4.3): 725-744. Repr. in *Contrast 24* (6.4) 1970: 9-28.

1968.   107. "The Life of the Imagination." *The New Yorker* 9 Nov.: 61-67.

108. "A Satisfactory Settlement." *The Atlantic* Jan.: 54-58.

1969.   109. "Livingstone's Companions." *The Kenyon Review* (31.2): 181-214.

110. "Open House." *Encounter* (32.2): 8-14.

111. "Otherwise Birds Fly In." *The Cornhill Magazine* (Summer): 296-308.

112. "Rain Queen." *Cosmopolitan* Mar.: 142-147. Repr. as "The Rain Queen." *Nova* Feb., 1970: 60, 62-63.

1971.   113. "Africa Emergent." *London Magazine* (11.3): 19-32.

114. "No Place Like." *The Southern Review* (7.3): 906-914.

115. "Why Haven't You Written?" *The New Yorker* 27 Feb.: 37-42.

1972.   116. "An Intruder." *Cosmopolitan* July: 128-130. [Also pub. as "Out of the Walls."]

1974.   117. "You Name It." *London Magazine* (14.2): 5-11.

1975.   118. "The Children." *Okike* (9): 42-49. [Also pub. as "Country Lovers."]

119. "City Lovers." *The New Yorker* 13 Oct.: 40-46. Repr. as "Town Lovers." *Harpers & Queen* Mar., 1976: 117-119. [Rev. as "Town and Country Lovers *One*."]

120. "A Lion on the Freeway." *Harper's Magazine* Mar.: 77-78. Also pub. in *The New Review* (1.10): 30-31.

121. "Siblings." *Encounter* (45.1): 3-10.

1975/6. 122. "The Termitary." *London Magazine* (15.5): 5-11.

1976.   123. "Country Lovers." *London Magazine* (16.3): 39-46. [Also pub. as "The Children" and rev. as "Town and Country Lovers *Two*."]

124. "A Soldier's Embrace." *Harper's Magazine* Jan.: 44, 46, 51-53, 56, 57. Repr. in *Contrast 39* (10.3): 8-22. *Harpers & Queen* Aug.: 66-68, 94, 116.

1977.   125. "For Dear Life." *New Statesman* 14 Jan.: 64-65.

1977. 126. "A Hunting Accident." *Encounter* (48.3): 3-8.

127. "The Need for Something Sweet." *The New Review* (3.34/35): 47-50.

128. *"Oral History." *Playboy* May. Repr. in *Harpers & Queen* July: 78-79, 140.

129. "Time Did." *London Magazine* (17.5): 11-17.

1979. 130. "Rags and Bones." *Harper's Magazine* Oct.: 88-90, 92.

1980. 131. "A Mad One." *Harpers & Queen* Apr.: 156, 158.

1981. 132. "Bushcraft: A Chapter from the Novel *July's Children* [sic] by Nadine Gordimer." *Staffrider* (4.1): 37-38. Repr. as "An Unaccustomed Killer at the Watering Hole." *The Times* 7 Aug.: 9. [Slightly different from version used in novel.]

133. "A Correspondence Course." *The New Yorker* 16 Feb.: 42-48. Repr. in *Literary Review/Quarto* Oct., 1982: 44-47. *The Literary Half-Yearly* (23.1) 1982: 3-14.

134. "Crimes of Conscience." *Index on Censorship* (10.6): 44-45. Repr. in *Frontline* (3.2) 1982: 16-17. *New Statesman* 22 Oct., 1982: 27-28.

1982. 135. "A City of the Dead, A City of the Living." *The New Yorker* 5 Apr.: 44-52. Repr. as "City of the Dead, City of the Living." *Granta 6: A Literature of Politics* 1983: 277-293.

136. "Sins of the Third Age." *Cosmopolitan* Aug.: 136-141, 146.

1983. 137. "At the Rendezvous of Victory." *Mother Jones* Feb./Mar.: 35-40.

138. "Blinder." *The Boston Globe Magazine* (supp. to *The Boston Globe*) 24 July: 13, 16-19, 22.

139. "Letter from His Father." *London Review of Books* 20 Oct.-2 Nov.: 20-23. Repr. in *The Threepenny Review* (18) 1984: 3-6.

140. "Terminal." *The Fiction Magazine* (2.1): 14-15. *Repr. in *The Argus* Mar.

141. "Tourism." *London Magazine* (23.3): 5-11.

1984. 142. "Something Out There." *Salmagundi* (62): 118-192.

1985.   143. "What Were You Dreaming?" *Granta 15*: 153-164. Repr. in *Kunapipi* (7.2&3): 99-106.

1986.   144. "Children with a House to Themselves." *The Paris Review* (100): 172-186. [Early version of a section from *A Sport of Nature*.]

1987.   145. *"Balancing Rocks." *Michigan Quarterly Review* (26): 34-47.

146. "Spoils." *Granta 22*: 195-208.

147. "Teraloyna." *The Boston Globe Magazine* (supp. to *The Boston Globe*) 31 May: 20-22, 24, 26, 28, 30. *Repr. in *COSAW Journal* (1) 1988: 28-32.

1988.   148. "Home." *The New Yorker* 25 Apr.: 34-42. Repr. in *Cosmopolitan* Dec., 1991: 224, 226, 228, 230, 232, 234, 236.

149. "The Moment before the Gun Went Off." *Harper's Magazine* Aug.: 63-65.

1988/9. 150. "Once upon a Time: A Fairy Tale of Suburban Life." *The Weekly Mail* 23 Dec.-12 Jan.: 31. Exp. as "Once upon a Time." *Salmagundi* (81) 1989: 67-73.

1989.   151. "Across the Veld." *The Paris Review* (113): 99-111. [Early version of a section from *My Son's Story*.]

152. "A Journey." *Weekend* (supp. to *The Irish Times*) 8 July: 1-2.

153. "Jump." *Harper's Magazine* Oct.: 55-61.

154. "The Ultimate Safari." *Granta 28: Ten Year Birthday Special*: 58-69.

1990.   155. "Amnesty." *The New Yorker* 27 Aug.: 39-42.

156. "A Find." *New Statesman & Society* 10 Aug.: 24-26. Repr. in *Salmagundi* (88-89) 1990/91: 72-77.

157. "My Father Leaves Home." *The New Yorker* 7 May: 40-43.

1991.   158. "Nobel Nadine's New Short Stories: 'Comrades.'" *The Weekly Mail* 11-17 Oct.: 30.

C. SHORT STORIES IN ANTHOLOGIES

[1948.]   159.   *The South African Saturday Book: A Treasury of Writing and Pictures of South Africa, Old and New, Homely and Extraordinary.* Comp. Eric Rosenthal and arr. by Richard F. Robinow. London: Hutchinson.

"The Defeated." 169-182.

1950.   160.   *Towards the Sun: A Miscellany of Southern Africa.* Comp. Roy MacNab. London: Collins.

"The Catch." 87-99.

[1952.]   161.   *'Silver Leaves': A South African Collection of Good Reading.* Johannesburg: Silver Leaf.

"A Present for a Good Girl." 20-28.

1954.   162.   *South African P.E.N Year Book 1954.* Johannesburg: CNA.

"Out of Season." 50-57.

1956.   163.   *Footprints: An Anthology of Modern South African English Prose.* Ed. C. Murray Booysen. Johannesburg: A.P.B.

"The Soft Voice of the Serpent." 142-147.

1957.   164.   *South African P.E.N Year Book 1956-1957.* Cape Town: Timmins.

"The Path of the Moon's Dark Fortnight." 67-82.

165.   **Stories.* Ed. Frank G. Jennings and Charles J. Calitri. New York: Harcourt.

"My First Two Women."

[1958.]   166.   *Anthology of Short Stories by South African Authors.* Ed. A. D. Dodd. Cape Town: Juta.

"Ah, Woe Is Me." 186-194.

1960.   167.   *40 Best Stories from Mademoiselle, 1935-1960.* Ed. Cyrilly Abels and Margarita G. Smith. London: Gollancz. Also pub. *New York: Harper.

"The Path of the Moon." 217-233.

1960.   168. *Following the Sun: 17 Tales from Australia, India, South Africa*. Berlin: Seven Seas.

"The Smell of Death and Flowers."   134-160.

169. *P.E.N 1960: New South African Writing and a Survey of Fifty Years of Creative Achievement*. Johannesburg: P.E.N.

"The Bridegroom."   44-47.

170. *South African Stories*. Ed. David Wright. London: Faber.

"Which New Era Would That Be?" 65-78.

171. *Stories from* The New Yorker *1950-1960*.   New York: Simon.

"Six Feet of the Country."   687-697.

1963.   172. *Encounters: An Anthology from the First Ten Years of* Encounter *Magazine*. Ed. Stephen Spender, Irving Kristol and Melvin J. Lasky. London: Weidenfeld.

"A Thing of the Past."   418-428.

173. *Modern Jewish Stories*.   Ed. Gerda Charles.   London: Faber. *Repr. Englewood Cliffs, NJ: Prentice, 1965.

"Face from Atlantis."   49-67.

174. *Short Stories from Southern Africa*.   Ed. A. G. Hooper. Cape Town: OUP.

"Another Part of the Sky."   28-36.
"The Bridegroom."   37-45.
"Enemies."   46-55.

175. **Short Stories of Our Time*.   Ed. Douglas R. Barnes. London: Harrap. Repr. Walton-on-Thames, Surrey: Nelson, 1984.

"A Present for a Good Girl."   94-105. [Nelson ed.]

176. *Tales of South Africa: An Anthology of South African Short Stories*. Comp. C. Murray Booysen. Cape Town: Timmins.

"Enemies."   125-137.

177. **Yisröel: The First Jewish Omnibus*.   Rev. ed.   Ed. Joseph Leftwich. New York: Yoseloff.

"The Path of the Moon's Dark Fortnight."

[1964.] 178. *16 Stories by South African Writers*. Ed. Clive Millar. Cape Town: Miller.

"A Watcher of the Dead." 18-27.
"The Gentle Art." 73-89.

1964. 179. *New South African Writing, No 1*. Ed. Tony Fleischer. Cape Town: Purnell.

"The African Magician." 1-16.

180. **The Rinehart Book of Short Stories*. Alternate ed. Ed. C. L. Cline. New York: Holt.

"Another Part of the Sky."

181. *Short Story International*. Ed. Samuel Tankel. New York: Short Story International.

"One Whole Year, and Even More." 62-85.

1965. 182. *English Short Stories of Today*. Third Series. Ed. T. S. Dorsch. London: OUP. Repr. as *Charmed Lives: Classic English Short Stories*. Oxford: OUP, 1988.

"Charmed Lives." 144-156.

1966. 183. **Gallery of Modern Fiction: Stories from* The Kenyon Review. Ed. Robie Macauley. Assoc. Ed. George Lanning and David Madden. New York: Salem.

"Message in a Bottle."

184. *Modern African Narrative: An Anthology*. Comp. Paul Edwards. London: Nelson.

"Six Feet of the Country." 75-90.

1967. 185. *More Tales of South Africa: An Anthology of South African Short Stories*. Comp. C. Murray Booysen. Cape Town: Timmins.

"Little Willie." 169-180.

186. *South African Writing Today*. Ed. Nadine Gordimer and Lionel Abrahams. Harmondsworth: Penguin.

"Some Monday for Sure." 119-135.

[1968.] 187. *More Short Stories by South African Writers*. Comp. A. D. Dodd. Cape Town: Juta.

"The Train from Rhodesia." 126-131.

1968. 188. *Best Theatre Stories*. Ed. Guy Slater. London: Faber.

"The Worst Thing of All." 100-124.

1969. 189. **Short Stories International*. Ed. E. W. Johnson. Boston: Houghton.

"The Defeated."

190. *Stories South African*. Ed. A. Lennox-Short and R. E. Lighton. Johannesburg: A.P.B.

"Treasures of the Sea." 80-87.

1970. 191. *Penguin Modern Stories 4*. Ed. Judith Burnley. Harmondsworth: Penguin.

"A Satisfactory Settlement." 38-49.
"Abroad." 50-71.

192. *Seismograph: Best South African Writing from* Contrast. Comp. Jack Cope. Cape Town: Reijger.

"A Chip of Glass Ruby." 28-36.

193. **Stories in Black and White*. Ed. Eva H. Kissin. Philadelphia: Lippincott.

"Which New Era Would That Be?"

1971. 194. *Herman Charles Bosman as I Knew Him*. By Bernard Sachs. *S.A. Opinion—Trek Anthology*. Ed. Bernard Sachs. Johannesburg: Dial.

"No Luck To-Night." 119-128.
"The Menace of the Years." 226-232.

1972. 195. *London Magazine Stories 7*. Comp. Alan Ross. London: London Magazine.

"Africa Emergent." 45-58.

196. *Short Stories from Seven Countries*. Ed. Alan Lennox-Short. Cape Town: Juta.

"A Wand'ring Minstrel, I." 1-11.

1973. 197. *Writers' Territory.* Ed. Stephen Gray. Cape Town: Long-man.

"Message in a Bottle." 149-153.

[1974.] 198. *Selected Stories from Southern Africa: An Anthology of South African Short Stories.* Comp. C. Murray Booysen. Cape Town: Timmins.

"Little Willie." 167-178.

1974. 199. *Great Short Stories of the World.* Vol. 1. Cape Town: Reader's Digest.

"Six Feet of the Country." 241-253.

200. *London Magazine Stories 9.* Comp. Alan Ross. London: London Magazine.

"You Name It." 106-112.

201. *On the Edge of the World: Southern African Stories of the Seventies.* Ed. Stephen Gray. Johannesburg: Donker.

"You Name It." 63-70.

202. *South of Capricorn: Stories from Southern Africa.* Comp. Leon Hugo and Betty Hugo. Pretoria: Academica.

"Ah, Woe Is Me." 97-104.

1975. 203. *Cut-Glass Bottles: A Selection of Stories for South African Schools.* Ed. G. E. de Villiers. Johannesburg: Macmillan.

"Enemies." 151-168.

204. **Modern Stories in English.* Ed. W. H. New and H. J. Rosengarten. New York: Crowell. *2nd ed. Longman, 1986.

"No Place Like."

1976. 205. *Quarry '76: New South African Writing.* Ed. Lionel Abrahams and Walter Saunders. Johannesburg: Donker.

"A Lion on the Freeway." 185-188.

206. *Winter's Tales 22.* Ed. James Wright. London: Macmillan; New York: St. Martin's.

"Town and Country Lovers." 35-59.

1978.   207. *A Century of South African Short Stories.* Ed. Jean Marquard. Johannesburg: Donker.

> "The Train from Rhodesia." 171-175.
> "The Bridegroom." 176-183.

208. *Literary Gems: Selected Short Stories.* Ed. B. Scheffler. Johannesburg: Perskor.

> "Little Willie." 147-155.
> "Harry's Presence." 156-167.

209. *Motherlove: Stories by Women about Motherhood.* Ed. Stephanie Spinner. New York: Dell.

> "A Chip of Glass Ruby." 98-110.

210. **Women and Fiction 2: Short Stories by and about Women.* Ed. Susan Cahill. New York: NAL.

> "The Train from Rhodesia."

1979.   211. *Best for Winter: A Selection from Twenty-Five Years of Winter's Tales.* Ed. A. D. Maclean. London: Macmillan; New York: St. Martin's.

> "Town and Country Lovers." 388-401.

[1980.]   212. **Short Story International 32.* Great Neck, NY: International Cultural Exchange.

> "Oral History."

1980.   213. *Modern South African Stories: Revised and Expanded Edition of On the Edge of the World.* Ed. Stephen Gray. Johannesburg: Donker.

> "You Name It." 99-104.

214. *Winter's Tales 26.* Ed. A. D. Maclean. London: Macmillan.

> "Rags and Bones." 117-123.

1981.   215. *Between the Thunder and the Sun: An Anthology of Short Stories.* Ed. John Gardner. Cape Town: OUP.

> "The Train from Rhodesia." 143-148.

1982.   216. *Echad 2: South African Jewish Voices.* Ed. Robert and Roberta Kalechofsky. Marblehead, MA: Micah.

> "A Hunting Accident." 71-81.

1982.   217. *Modern Short Stories 2, 1940-1980.* Ed. Giles Gordon. London: Dent.

"Happy Event." 205-220.

218. *Under the Southern Cross: Short Stories from South Africa.* Ed. David Adey. Johannesburg: Donker.

"A Company of Laughing Faces." 166-181.

219. *A Web of Feelings: A Spectrum of South African Short Stories.* Ed. Paul A. Scanlon. Pietermaritzburg: Shuter.

"The Children." 36-43.
"The Catch." 108-120.

1983.   220. *Ex-Africa Stories for Secondary Schools.* Ed. Frances M. M. Olver and Sylvia van Straaten. Johannesburg: Hodder.

"The Soft Voice of the Serpent." 83-86.

221. **An International Treasury of Mystery and Suspence.* Ed. Marie R. Reno. New York: Doubleday.

"Africa Emergent."

222. *Stories from Central & Southern Africa.* African Writers Series, No. 254. Ed. Paul A. Scanlon. London: Heinemann.

"A Soldier's Embrace." 78-91.

223. **The Story and Its Writer.* Ed. Ann Charters. St. Martin's.

"A Chip of Glass Ruby."

224. *Unwinding Threads: Writing by Women in Africa.* African Writers Series, No. 256. Ed. Charlotte H. Bruner. London: Heinemann.

"Inkalamu's Place." 119-128.

1984.   225. *To Kill a Man's Pride and Other Stories from Southern Africa.* Ed. Norman Hodge. Johannesburg: Ravan.

"Six Feet of the Country." 150-165.

1985.   226. *African Short Stories.* Ed. Chinua Achebe and C. L. Innes. London: Heinemann.

"The Bridegroom." 115-123.

1985.   227. *Fiction 100*. Ed. Pickering. Macmillan.

"The Train from Rhodesia."

228. *Fictions*. Ed. Trimmer and Jennings. Harcourt.

"The Train from Rhodesia."

229. *The Penguin Book of Southern African Stories*. Ed. Stephen Gray. Harmondsworth: Penguin.

"At the Rendezvous of Victory." 297-305.

230. *Short Stories International 53*. Ed. Samuel Tankel. International Cultural Exchange.

"Town Lovers."

231. *The Signet Classic Book of British Short Stories*. Ed. Karl. NAL.

"The Defeated."

1986.   232. *The Art of the Tale: An International Anthology of Short Stories 1945-1985*. Ed. Halpern. Viking.

"The Life of the Imagination."

233. *Classic Short Fiction*. Ed. Bohner. Prentice.

"The Train from Rhodesia."

234. *A Double Colonization: Colonial and Post-Colonial Women's Writing*. Ed. Kirsten Holst Petersen and Anna Rutherford. Mundelstrup, Denmark: Dangaroo.

"What Were You Dreaming?" 99-106.

235. *A Land Apart: A South African Reader*. Ed. André Brink and J. M. Coetzee. London: Faber.

"A Lion on the Freeway." 19-22.

236. *London Magazine 1961-85*. Ed. Alan Ross. London: Chatto. Repr. as *London Magazine 1961-1985*. London: Paladin, 1989.

"Country Lovers." 203-209.

237. *Reef of Time: Johannesburg in Writing*. Ed. Digby Ricci. Johannesburg: Donker.

"A Satisfactory Settlement." 245-253.

1986. 238. *The World of the Short Story*. Ed. Fadiman. Houghton.

"Letter from His Father."

1987. 239. *Dark Arrows: Great Stories of Revenge*. Ed. Manguel. Potter.

"Letter from His Father."

240. *Enjoying Stories*. Ed. Atwan and Wiener. Longman.

"The Termitary."

241. *The Secret Self 2: Short Stories by Women*. Ed. Hermione Lee. London: Dent.

"A City of the Dead, A City of the Living."

242. *The Short Story: 30 Masterpieces*. Ed. Lawn. St. Martin's.

"Six Feet of the Country."

243. *Sometimes When It Rains: Writings by South African Women*. Ed. Ann Oosthuizen. London: Pandora.

"What Were You Dreaming?" 19-28.

244. *The Story and Its Writer*. 2nd ed. Ed. Ann Charters. St. Martin's. *Repr. 1990.

"Town and Country Lovers."

245. *A Third Book of Modern Prose*. Comp. Margaret Flower. 2nd impression. Johannesburg: Southern. 1st impression. *Johannesburg: Macmillan.

"Treasures of the Sea." 135-142.

246. *To Read Fiction*. Ed. Hall. Rinehart.

"The Train from Rhodesia."

1988. 247. *Full Measure: Modern Short Stories on Ageing*. Ed. Sennett. Graywolf.

"Enemies."

248. *The Heath Introduction to Fiction*. 3rd. ed. Ed. Cherry Clayton. Heath.

"A Correspondence Course."

1988. 249. *Ourselves in Southern Africa: An Anthology of Southern African Writing*. Ed. Robin Malan. London: Macmillan.

"The Bridegroom." 37-44.

250. **Selected Stories from* The Southern Review: *1965-1985*. Ed. Simpson, Stanford, Olney and Gulledge. Louisiana State UP.

"Abroad."

251. *Somehow Tenderness Survives: Stories of Southern Africa*. Ed. Hazel Rochman. New York: Harper.

"Country Lovers." 49-59.
"A Chip of Glass Ruby." 105-118.

252. **The Story: Readers and Writers of Fiction*. Ed. Bergman. Macmillan.

"The Train from Rhodesia."

1989. 253. **Among Sisters*. Ed. Susan Cahill. NAL.

"La Vie Bohème."

254. *Cross-Currents: An Anthology of Short Stories*. Ed. Ian Ferguson, Melissa King, Pamela Ryan, Karen Scherzinger and Michael Williams. Pretoria: Acacia.

"Six Feet of the Country." 243-253.

255. **The Houghton Mifflin Anthology of Short Fiction*. Ed. Hampl. Houghton.

"Africa Emergent."
"Sins of the Third Age."

256. *Prize Writing: An Original Collection of Writings by Past Winners to Celebrate 21 Years of the Booker Prize*. Ed. Martyn Goff. London: Hodder.

"Benoni - Son of Sorrow." 67-75.
[Slightly altered sections from *My Son's Story* published in 1990.]

257. **Sudden Fiction International*. Ed. Shapard and Thomas. Norton.

"Terminal."

1990. 258. *Colours of a New Day: Writing for South Africa*. Ed. Sarah Lefanu and Stephen Hayward. Johannesburg: Ravan.

"Teraloyna." 324-330.

259. *Flight: A Selection of Stories*. Ed. Rudolph Anderson and Victoria Shepherd. Cape Town: Hodder.

"The Soft Voice of the Serpent." 93-96.

260. *The Minerva Book of Short Stories 1*. Ed. Giles Gordon and David Hughes. London: Minerva. First pub. as *Best Short Stories*. London: Heinemann, 1988.

"Spoils." 74-88.

261. *Raising the Blinds: A Century of South African Women's Stories*. Ed. Annemarié van Niekerk. Johannesburg: Donker.

"Good Climate, Friendly Inhabitants." 80-90.

1991. 262. *The Best of South African Short Stories: Over Seventy Illustrated Stories of Our Land and Its People*. Ed. Anne Turner. Cape Town: Reader's Digest.

"Enemies." 208-221.
"The Train from Rhodesia." 222-224.

263. *Best Short Stories*. Ed. Giles Gordon and David Hughes. Heinemann.

"A Find."

264. *Short and Tall: A Collection of Short Stories*. Comp. A. G. Ullyatt, N. P. le Roux and W. J. Greyling. Pretoria: Academica.

"Enemies." 128-136.

265. *Wordsmiths: An Approach to Short Story Study*. Comp. J. O. Hendry. Cape Town: Miller Longman.

"The Catch." 207-216.

D. DRAMA

1949. 266. "The First Circle." *Six One-Act Plays by South African Authors*. Pretoria: J. L. van Schaik: 43-70.

E. TRANSLATIONS OF WORKS

The Soft Voice of the Serpent and Other Stories

1965. 267. *De zachte stem van de slang en andere verhalen.* Trans. Katja Vranken. Compass Books ed. Amsterdam: Contact. Repr. in Moderne Klassieken ed. Amsterdam: Dekker, 1989.

The Lying Days

1955. 268. *Lögnens dagar.* Trans. Margareta Åstrand. Stockholm: Bonniers.

1956. 269. *Entzauberung: Roman.* Trans. Wolfgang von Einsiedel. Frankfurt: Fischer. Repr. Frankfurt: Goverts, 1978. *Frankfurt: Fischer Taschenbuch, 1980.

Six Feet of the Country (1956)

1958. 270. *En plats i jorden: Noveller.* Trans. Saga and Claës Gripenberg. Stockholm: Bonniers.

1959. 271. *Sechs Fuß Erde: Erzählungen.* Trans. Wolfgang v. Einsiedel. Frankfurt: Fischer. Repr. as *Sechs Fuß Erde.* Trans. Peter Kleinhempel. Berlin: Volk, 1980. Also pub. as *Clowns in Glück: Erzählungen.* Trans. Wolfgang von Einsiedel. Frankfurt: Fischer, 1982 [i.e. under title *Clowns in Clover* with the story "Six Feet of the Country" not included].

A World of Strangers

1959. 272. *En verden av fremmede.* Trans. Ragnar Kvam. Oslo: Gyldendal Norsk.

273. *Främlingars värld.* Trans. Saga and Claës Gripenberg. Stockholm: Bonniers.

1959. 274. *I fremmed land. Trans. Helga Vang Lauridsen. Copenhagen: Fremad. Repr. Copenhagen: Gyldendal.

1961. 275. Un mundo di straniere. Trans. Marco Guarnaschelli. Milan: Feltrinelli. Repr. Milan: Feltrinelli (Universale Economica ed.), 1980.

1962. 276. Fremdling unter Fremden: Roman. Trans. Wolfgang von Einsiedel. Frankfurt: Fischer Repr. Frankfurt: Fischer Taschenbuch, 1982.

1964. 277. Mundo de extraños. Trans. M.ª Luisa Borrás. Barcelona: Seix Barral.

278. Swiat Obcych Ludzi. Trans. Maria Boduszynska-Borowikowa. Warsaw: Panstwowy Instytut Wydawniczy.

1979. 279. *Un monde d'étrangers. Trans. Lucienne Lotringer. Paris: Michel. Repr. *Paris: Livre de Poche, 1989.

1986. 280. *Un Mundo de Estranhos. Lisbon: Difel.

1991. 281. *Vieraat toisilleen. Helsinki: Otava.

Occasion for Loving

1965. 282. Rakkaus kielletty. Trans. Suomentanut Kyllikki Hämäläinen. Helsinki: Otava. *Repr. 1991.

283. Tillfälle att älska. Trans. Saga and Claës Gripenberg. Stockholm: Bonniers.

1983. 284. Anlaß zu lieben: Roman. Trans. Margaret Carroux. Frankfurt: Fischer. Repr. *Frankfurt: Deutscher Bücherbund, 1989. Orig. pub. *Cologne: Kiepenheur.

1984. 285. Occasione d'amore. Trans. Pier Francesco Paolini. Milan: Feltrinelli.

1987. 286. *Ocasion de amor. Barcelona: Versal.

Not for Publication and Other Stories

1991. 287. Niet voor publicatie en andere verhalen. Trans. Heleen ten Holt. Amsterdam: Bakker.

The Late Bourgeois World

1967. 288. *En bortgången värld.* Trans. Marianne Gerland-Ekeroth. Stockholm: Bonniers. *Repr. 1975.

1968. 289. *De bourgeoiswereld van weleer.* Trans. N. Funke- Bordewijk. Amsterdam: Contact. Repr. as *De bourgeoiswereld van vroeger.* Amsterdam: Muntinga (Rainbow Pocketboeken), 1987.

1976. 290. *Den senborgerlige verden.* Copenhagen: Fremad. Repr. *Copenhagen: Gyldendal.

1979. 291. *Kesie Polgarvillag.* Budapest: Magvetö.

1982. 292. *Den senborgerlige verden.* Trans. Inger-Sophie Manthey. Oslo: Gyldendal Norsk.

1985. 293. *O Falecido Mundo Burguês.* Trans. Carlos Sussekind. São Paolo: Art.

1987. 294. *El ultimo mundo burgues.* Barcelona: Versal.

1989. 295. *Il mondo tardo borghese.* Milan: Feltrinelli.

296. *The Late Bourgeois World.* Athens: Medusa.

1991. 297. *Heimur feigrar stettar.* Reykjavic: Mal og Menning.

1993. 298. *Feu le monde bourgeois.* Trans. Pierre Boyer. Paris: Plon.

The Late Bourgeois World and Not for Publication

1969. 299. *Na pewno w którys poniedziayek: Opowiadania.* Trans. Agnieszka Glinczanka. Warsaw: Panstwowy Instytut Wydawniczy.

A Guest of Honour

1974 300. *Un huésped de honor.* Trans. Enrique Riambau. Barcelona: Nueva Galéria Literaria: Editorial Noguer. Repr. *Barcelona: Tusquets.

1977. 301. *Hedersgästen: Roman.* Trans. Magnus Kison Lindberg. Stockholm: Bonniers.

1979.	302.	*Gosc Honorowy.* Trans. Zofia Kierszys. Warsaw: Ksiazka i Wiedza.
1981.	303.	**Aeresgaest.* Copenhagen: Gyldendal.
	304.	**A Guest of Honour.* Tel Aviv: Oved.
1985.	305.	*Un ospite d'onore.* Trans. Mariagiulia Prati. Milan: Feltrinelli.
1986.	306.	*Der Ehrengast: Roman.* Trans. Klaus Hoffer. Frankfurt: Fischer/Goverts.
1988.	307.	**Een eregast.* Trans. Heleen ten Holt. Amsterdam: Bakker.

Livingstone's Companions

| 1976. | 308. | *Livingstone bajtársai.* Trans. Mária Borbás. Budapest: Magvetö. |

The Conservationist

1975.	309.	*Bevararen.* Trans. Magnus Kison Lindberg. Stockholm: Bonniers.
1976.	310.	**Bevareren.* Oslo: Gyldendal Norsk.
1977.	311.	*Az örzö.* Trans. Judit Gyepes. Budapest: Magvetö.
	312.	*Der Besitzer: Roman.* Trans. Victoria Wocker. Düsseldorf: Claassen. Repr. **Frankfurt: Fischer, 1989.
1978.	313.	**Ejerne.* Trans. Birgitte Brix. Copenhagen: Fremad. Repr. Copenhagen: Gyldendal, 1988.
1979.	314.	*Posestnik.* Trans. Boris M. Verbic. Ljubljana: Pomurska Zalozba.
1982.	315.	*O Amante da Natureza.* Trans. Wilma Feitas Ronald de Carvalho. Rio de Janeiro: Codecri.
	316.	*Zachowac swój Swiat.* Trans. Jadwiga Milnikiel. Warsaw: Ksiazka i Wiedza.
1983.	317.	**El conservador.* Madrid: Tusquets.

1987.   318. *De milieubeheerder.* Trans. Tineke Funhof. Amsterdam:
              Arbeiderspers. First pub. as *Een dode zwarte man.*
              Amsterdam: Contact.

         319. *Il conservatore.* Trans. Sandro Ossala. Milan: Tartaruga.

1988.   320. *The Conservationist.* Tel Aviv: Schocken.

         321. *Le conservateur: Roman.* Trans. Antoinette Roubichou-
              Stretz. Paris: Michel. Repr. Paris: Le Grand Livre du Mois,
              1991.

         322. *Status Quo.* Trans. Magda Záryová. Bratislava: Pravda.

1992.   323. *The Conservationist.* Athens: Nepheli.

         324. *O Conservador.* Trans. Ana Luisa Faria. Lisbon: Edições
              ASA.

Selected Stories

1984.   325. *Zapach Kwiatòw Ismierci.* Trans. Agnieszka Glinczanka,
              Blanka Kuczborska and Piotr Niklewicz. Warsaw: Ksiazka
              i Wiedza.

Some Monday for Sure

1980.   326. *Numa Segunda - Feira de Certesa.* Vozes de Africa, 16.
              Trans. Adelaide Mendes de Carvalho. Lisbon: Edições 70.

1981.   327. *Kurzgeschichten.* Frankfurt: Volk.

Burger's Daughter

1979.   328. *Burger's datter.* Copenhagen: Gyldendal.

         329. *Burgers datter.* Trans. Ingebjørg Nesheim. Oslo: Gylden-
              dal Norsk. Repr *1981. *Oslo: Den Norske Bokklubben,
              1980.

         330. *La figlia di Burger: Romanzo.* Trans. Ettore Capriolo. Milan:
              Mondadori. Repr. *Milan: Club degli Editori, 1980.

1980. 331. *Burgerin tytär.* Trans. Seppo Loponen. Helsinki: Söderström. Repr. Helsinki: Söderström, 1991.

332. *Burgers dotter.* Trans. Annika Preis. Stockholm: Bonniers.

1981. 333. *Burgers Tochter: Roman.* Trans. Margaret Carroux. Frankfurt: Fischer. Repr. Frankfurt: Fischer Taschenbuch, 1982.

1982. 334. *Burger's dochter.* Trans. Dorinde van Oort. Amsterdam: Arbeiderspers.

335. *Fille de Burger.* Trans. Guy Durand. Paris: Michel. Repr. *Paris: Livre de Poche.

1984. 336. *Burger's Daughter.* Tel Aviv: Oved.

1985. 337. *A Filha de Burger.* Rio de Janeiro: Rocco.

1986. 338. *H KOPH TOY MNEPTZEP.* Athens: Odysseas.

339. *La hija de Burger.* Barcelona: Tusquets.

1988. 340. *Burger jeva hci.* Maribor: Zalozba Obzerja.

1992. 341. *A Filha de Burger.* Trans. J. Teixeira de Aguilar. Lisbon: Edições ASA.

A Soldier's Embrace

1983. 342. *Il bacio di un soldato.* Trans. Marisa Caramella. Milan: Tartaruga.

1993. 343. *A Soldier's Embrace.* Barcelona: Espasa.

July's People

1982. 344. *Hans hvide mennesker.* Copenhagen: Gyldendal.

345. *Julys Folk.* Oslo: Gyldendal Norsk. Repr. *Oslo: Den Norske Bokklubben, 1986.

346. *Julys folk.* Trans. Else Lundgren. Stockholm: Bonniers.

347. *Julys Leute: Roman.* Trans. Margaret Carroux. Frankfurt: Fischer/Goverts. *Repr. in omnibus with four stories from *Jump.* Frankfurt: Coron, 1992.

1982. 348. *Pavelijaja herra*. Helsinki: Söderström.

1983. 349. *Ceux de July*. Trans. Annie Saumont. Paris: Michel. Repr. *Paris: Livre de Poche.

350. *July's mensen*. Trans. Dorinde van Oort. Amsterdam: Bakker. *Orig. pub. Amsterdam: Arbeiderspers.

351. *July's People*. Jerusalem: Keter.

352. *La gente de July*. Trans. Barbara McShane and Javier Alfaya. Barcelona: Ediciones Grijalbo, S. A. Repr. *Barcelona: Circulo de Lectores, 1988.

1984. 353. *July nepe*. Budapest: Magvetö.

354. *Luglio*. Trans. Hilia Brinis. Milan: Rizzoli Editore. Repr. *Milan: Feltrinelli, 1991.

1987. 355. *A Gente de July*. Lisbon: Circulo dei Leitores. Repr. *Lisbon: Teorema.

1988. 356. *O Pessoal de July*. Rio de Janeiro: Rocco.

1991. 357. *July's People*. Athens: Synora.

1992. 358. *July a jeho l'udia*. Trans. Elena Diamantova. Bratislava: Slovensky.

Six Feet of the Country (1982)

1982. 359. *Gutes Klima, nette Nachbarn: Erzählungen*. Trans. Wolfgang von Einsiedel, Peter Kleinhempel and Walter Hartmann. Frankfurt: Fischer. [Under title *Good Climate, Friendly Inhabitants* with stories in different order from the English ed.]

Something Out There

1985. 360. *Eine Stadt der Toten, eine Stadt der Lebenden: Erzählungen*. Trans. Inken Bohn. Frankfurt: Fischer/ Goverts.

361. *Etwas da Draussen: Erzählungen*. Trans. Inken Bohn. Frankfurt: Fischer. [Novella published on its own without accompanying short stories.]

1985. 362. *Quelque chose la-bas.* Trans. Jean Guiloineau. Paris: Michel.

1986. 363. *Der er noget derude.* Copenhagen: Gyldendal.

364. *Qualcosa la fuori.* Trans. Marisa Caramella. Milan: Feltrinelli.

1987. 365. *Hal algoa ahi fuera.* Barcelona: Alianza.

1990. 366. *Something Out There and Three Other Stories.* Moscow: Khudozhestvennaya.

A Sport of Nature

1987. 367. *Ein Spiel der Natur: Roman.* Trans. Eva Schönfeld. Frankfurt: Fischer/Goverts.

368. *Luonnonoikku.* Trans. Seppo Loponen. Helsinki: Söderström. Repr. Helsinki: Söderström. Also pub. *Helsinki: New Books, 1990.

369. *Una forza della natura.* Milan: Feltrinelli.

1988. 370. *Een speling der natuur.* Trans. Heleen ten Holt. Amsterdam: Bakker.

371. *Et naturens lune.* Copenhagen: Gyldendal.

372. *Et villskudd.* Trans. Johan Hambro. Oslo: Gyldendal Norsk.

373. *Hillela.* Trans. Else Lundgren. Stockholm: Bonniers. *Repr. 1990.

374. *Un capricho de la naturaleza.* Madrid: Versal.

1989. 375. *Um Capricho da Natureza.* Trans. Miguel Serras Pereira. Lisbon: Quixote. Also pub. *Lisbon: Circulo dei Leitores.

1990. 376. *Uma Mulher sem Ignal.* Rio de Janeiro: Rocco.

377. *Un caprice de la nature.* Trans. Gabrielle Merchez. Paris: Michel. Repr. *Paris: Livre de Poche, 1992. Also pub. *Paris: France, 1991.

1991. 378. *A Sport of Nature.* Tel Aviv: Kinneret.

The Essential Gesture

1989. 379. *Breven från Johannesburg.* Trans. Else Lundgren. Stockholm: Bonniers.

380. **Le geste essentiel.* Trans. Jean-Pierre Richard. Paris: Bourgois.

1990. 381. *Vivere nell' interregno.* Trans. Franca Cavagnoli. Milan: Feltrinelli.

1992. 382. **O Gesto Essencial.* Rio de Janeiro: Rocco.

My Son's Story

1991. 383. **A Historia do Meu Filho.* Lisbon: Presenca.

384. *Die Geschichte meines Sohnes: Roman.* Trans. Stephanie Schaffer-de Vries. Frankfurt: Fischer.

385. *Het verhaal van mijn zoon.* Trans. Heleen ten Holt. Amsterdam: Bakker.

386. **La història del meu fill.* Barcelona: Edicions de l'Eixample, S. A. Repr. Barcelona: Cercle di Lectors, 1992. Trans. Roser Berdugue and Mònica Martín.

387. **La historia di mi hijo.* Barcelona: Ediciones B. Repr. *Barcelona: Circulo dei Leitores.

388. **La historia di mi hijo.* Bogotá: Editorial Norma.

389. *Min sønns historie.* Trans. Karin Bang. Oslo: Gyldendal Norsk. Repr. *Oslo: Bøker.

390. *Min søns historie.* Trans. Finn Holten Hansen. Copenhagen: Gyldendal.

391. *Oglumun öyküsü.* Trans. Seckin Selvi. Istanbul: Yayinlari.

392. **Poikani tarina.* Trans. Kristiina Drews. Helsinki: Söderström. Repr. Helsinki: Söderström.

393. **Saga sonar mins.* Reykjavic: Mal og Menning.

394. *Storia di mi figlio.* Trans. Franca Cavagnoli. Milan: Feltrinelli. Repr. *Milan: Club degli Editori.

1992. 395. *A História do Meu Filho*. Trans. Geraldo Galvão Ferraz. São Paolo: Siciliano.

396. **L'histoire de mon fils*. Trans. Pierre Boyer. Paris: Bourgois.

397. **Min sons historia*. Stockholm: Bonniers.

398. **My Son's Story*. Athens: Kastaniotis.

Jump and Other Stories

1992. 399. **Die endgültige Safari*. Frankfurt: Fischer. *Four stories repr. in omnibus with *July's People*. Frankfurt: Coron.

400. *El salt i altres històries*. Trans. Dolors Udina. Barcelona: Edicions de l'Eixample, S. A.

401. **El salto*. Barcelona: Ediciones B.

402. *Hopp og andre noveller*. Trans. Ragnhild Eikli. Oslo: Gyldendal Norsk.

403. *Il salto*. Trans. Franca Cavagnoli. Milan: Feltrinelli.

404. *Il salto y otros cuentos*. Trans. Javier Escobar Isaza. Bogotá: Editorial Norma.

405. **Jump and Other Stories*. Stockholm: Bonniers.

1993. 406. **Le safari de votre vie*. Paris: Plon.

Selections of Stories [chosen by publishers].

1983. 407. **Moscow: Innostrannaya Literatura. [8 stories.]

1984. 408. **16 Noveller*. Oslo: Gyldendal. [16 stories.]

409. **Et billede pa success*. Copenhagen: Gyldendal. [16 stories.]

410. **Tåget från Rhodesia*. Trans. Else Lundgren. Stockholm: Bonniers. [16 stories.]

1986. 411. **Tokyo: Shobunsha. [7 stories.]

412. **Perjantain jalan jalki*. Helsinki: Söderström. [16 stories.]

1989.   413. **Oatkova slepj.* Prague: Mlada Fronta. [16 stories.]

F. EXTRACTS

The Lying Days

1953.   414. "Believe the Heart." *Mademoiselle* Oct.: 90-91, 141-151.

415. "The World Repeated Upside Down." *New World Writing: Fourth Mentor Selection.* New York: NAL: 253-257.

1965.   416. "Helen." *Onward from Table Mountain: An Anthology of South African Prose.* Ed. W. Waldman. London: Arnold; Cape Town: Juta: 89-99.

1982.   417. Extract from *The Lying Days. Upbeat* (2.6): 9.

The Late Bourgeois World

1966.   418. "The Late Bourgeois World." *Encounter* (26.6): 19-26. [Chapter 1 of *The Late Bourgeois World.*]

A Guest of Honour

1970.   419. "Dinner on a Golden Plate." *London Magazine* (10.9): 5-12.

1992.   420. "It's Unlucky Not to Take a Chance." *A Book of Hope.* Cape Town: Philip: 82.

The Conservationist

1973.   421. "The Conservationist." *Playboy* Mar.: 91-92, 94, 102, 165.

1974.   422. "The Dogs." *Contrast 34* (9.2): 37-48. Also pub. in *The New Review* (1.5): 63-67.

423. "Golden Reclining Nudes of the Desert." *Encounter* (43.1): 3-6.

424. "Plenty." *Southern Review* (7.1): 29-35.

Burger's Daughter

1979. 425. "Lunch in the Park." *Telegraph Sunday Magazine* (supp. to *Sunday Telegraph*) 3 June: 105, 108, 110, 114.

426. "The Meeting: *Work in progress*." *Staffrider* (2.2): 34.

1986. 427. "from *Burger's Daughter*." *A Land Apart: A South African Reader*. Ed. André Brink and J. M. Coetzee. London: Faber: 89-93.

1987. 428. "Excerpt from *Burger's Daughter*." *For Nelson Mandela*. Ed. Jacques Derrida and Mustapha Tlili. New York: Seaver/Holt: 5-9.

July's People

1981. 429. "July's People." *Mother Jones* July: 44-57.

Something Out There

1986. 430. "Extract from *Something Out There*." *Reef of Time: Johannesburg in Writing*. Ed. Digby Ricci. Johannesburg: Donker: 294-295.

A Sport of Nature

1987. 431. "A Sport of Nature." *Cosmopolitan* Apr.: 172, 174, 176-177, 180, 183.

432. "Two Excerpts from *A Sport of Nature*." *TriQuarterly 69*. Special issue ent. *From South Africa: New Writing, Photographs and Art* (Spring): 307-322.

My Son's Story

1990. 433. "The Body Speaks and All Is Silenced." *Review/Books* [supp. to *The Weekly Mail*] 26 Oct.-1 Nov.: 10.

434. "from *My Son's Story*." *New Contrast 71* (18.3): 6-14.

1990.   435.   "My Son's Story." *Femina* Nov.: 158-159, 200-201, 203.

1991.   436.   **Sunday Times* 6 Oct.: 6.

G. NON-FICTION

1943.   437.   ***"Close-Up: Katie Kagan." *P.S.* Dec.: 18-19.

1953.   438.   ***"Some Important Fall Authors Speak for Themselves: Nadine Gordimer in Johannesburg." *New York Herald Tribune Book Review* 11 Oct.: 20.

1954.   439.   "A South African Childhood: Allusions in a Landscape." *The New Yorker* 16 Oct.: 121-143.

440.   "Writing Belongs to Us All." *The Forum* (3.6): 9-10.

1955.   441.   "Hassan in America." *The Forum* (3.11): 13-19.

442.   "Johannesburg." *Holiday* (18.2): 46, 49-50, 57-59.

1957.   443.   "South African Riviera." *Holiday* (22.6): 166, 168, 171.

1958.   444.   "Chief Luthuli: Bulletin Biography, no. 1." *Treason Trial Bulletin* (2): 4-6. [Issued by Treason Trial Defence Fund, Johannesburg.]

1959.   445.   "Apartheid." *Holiday* (25.4): 94-95, 133-134.

446.   "Chief Luthuli." *The Atlantic* Apr.: 34-39. Repr. in *The Essential Gesture: Writing, Politics and Places.* Ed. Stephen Clingman. Johannesburg: Taurus; Cape Town: Philip, 1988: 31-41.

447.   "Egypt Revisited." *The National and English Review* Jan.: 47-53. Repr. in *The Essential Gesture*: 125-131. [Orig. typescript under title "A View of the Nile", Dec. 1958.]

448.   "Where Do Whites Fit In?" *The Twentieth Century* Apr.: 326-331. Repr. in *The Essential Gesture*: 25-30.

1960.   449.   ***"The English Novel in South Africa." *The Novel and the Nation: Being a Series of Lectures Delivered at the Winter School of the National Union of South African Students at the Witwatersrand University, July 1959.* Ed. Hugh Lewin. Cape Town: NUSAS, U of Cape Town: 16-21. Orig. extr. in two parts as "The Novel & the Nation: Creative in Uncreative Circumstances." *Contact* 8 Aug., 1959: 11; and

"The Novel & the Nation II." *Contact* 5 Sept., 1959: 15.
Complete lecture rev. as "The Novel and the Nation in
South Africa." *Times Literary Supplement* 11 Aug., 1961:
520-523. Also in *Radcliffe Quarterly* (47.2) 1963: 21-44.
Also in *African Writers on African Writing*. Ed. G. D. Killam.
London: Heinemann, 1973: 33-52. Extr. in *Modern Black
Writers*. Ed. Michael Popkin. New York: Ungar, 1978: 4.
[Further rev. paper presented as The Anne Radcliffe Lecture
1961 whilst Gordimer was a visiting professor under the
international exchange programme of the Institute of
Contemporary Arts, Washington.]

1961. 450. "The Congo River." *Holiday* (29.5): 74-79, 88, 92, 97-103.
Repr. in *The Essential Gesture*: 133-155. [Orig. two
typescripts ent. "Towards the Heart of Darkness" and "Africa
1960: The Great Period", 1960.]

451. "The Man Who Burned His Pass: Chief Luthuli." *Heroes of
Our Time*. London: Gollancz: 84-93.

1963. 452. "'Censored, Banned, Gagged': Letter from Johannesburg."
Encounter (20.6): 59-63. Repr. as "Censored, Banned,
Gagged" in *The Essential Gesture*: 49-56.

453. "Great Problems in the Street." *I Will Still Be Moved:
Reports from South Africa*. Ed. Marion Friedmann.
London: Barker, for Amnesty International: 117-22. Repr.
in *The Essential Gesture*: 43-47.

454. "Leaving School—II." *London Magazine* (3.2): 58-65.
Repr. as "Invincible Summer." *Harper's Bazaar* Aug., 1964:
86-87, 155, 162-163. "The Bolter and the Invincible
Summer." *Antæus* (45/46) 1982: 104-113. "A Bolter and
the Invincible Summer." *The Essential Gesture*: 15-22.
Also in *Sunday Times* 4 Sept., 1988: G8-G9.

455. "Party of One." *Holiday* (34.1): 12, 14-17.

1964. 456. "Notes of an Expropriator." *Times Literary Supplement* 4
June: 482.

457. "Poet in the Dove-Cote: Writers on Their Task." *Contrast
10* (3.2): 89-90. [Response to N. P. van Wyk Louw's article
in *Sestiger* (3).]

1964. 458. "Why Must the Door Be Shut in His Face?" Letter. *Rand Daily Mail* 24 Sept.: 8. [Protesting the refusal of SA Government to grant Nat Nakasa a passport.]

1965. 459. "Plays and Piracy: A Discussion." *Contrast 12* (3.4): 53-55.

1966. 460. "The Fischer Case." *London Magazine* (5.12): 21-30.

461. "One Man Living through It." *The Classic* (2.1): 11-16. [On Nat Nakasa.] Repr. as "One Man Living through It: New Kind of Man." *Atlas: The Magazine of the World Press* (12.1): 10-13. Repr. as "One Man Living through It" in *The Essential Gesture*: 67-72. Also pub. as introduction to *The World of Nat Nakasa: Selected Writings of the Late Nat Nakasa*. Ed. Essop Patel. Johannesburg: Ravan/Bateleur, 1975: xx-xxvi.

462. "The Voices We May Not Hear." *Rand Daily Mail* 13 Aug.: 8. Repr. as "How Not to Know the African." *Contrast 15* (4.3) 1967: 44-49.

463. "Why Did Bram Fischer Choose Jail?" *New York Times Magazine* 14 Aug.: 30-31, 80-81, 84. Repr. in *The Essential Gesture*: 57-65. [*Orig. typescript ent. "Profile: Abram Fischer."]

464. "Zambia." *Holiday* (39.6): 38, 40, 42-43, 45-46, 86, 88-89.

1967. 465. "*The Classic*: Nadine Gordimer Replies." Letter. *South Africa: Information and Analysis* (52): 1-2.

466. *South African Writing Today*. Ed. with Lionel Abrahams. Harmondsworth: Penguin.

1968. 467. "The International Symposium on the Short Story: South Africa." *The Kenyon Review* (30.4): 457-463. Extr. as "The Flash of Fireflies." *Short Story Theories*. Ed. Charles E. May. Ohio: Ohio UP: 178-181.

468. "South Africa: Towards a Desk Drawer Literature." *The Classic* (2.4): 64-74. *Extr. as "Politics: A Dirtier Word than Sex!" *Solidarity* (3.11): 69-71. Also extr. in "Politics: A Dirtier Word than Sex!" by Lewis Nkosi. *South Africa: Information and Analysis* (65): 1-4. [Orig. talk given to students of the University of the Witwatersrand.]

469. *"Topics: The Word, Too, Falls Victim of Apartheid." *New York Times* 31 Aug.: 22, sec. 1.

1968. 470. "The Witwatersrand: A Time & Tailings." *Optima* (18.1): 22-23, 25-26. With David Goldblatt. Repr. as introductory essay to *On the Mines*, by David Goldblatt and Nadine Gordimer. Cape Town: Struik, 1973: n.p. *Extr. as "On the Mines." *Management* Dec., 1973: 52-55.

1969. 471. "The Interpreters: New Africa through African Writers' Eyes." *Africa Contemporary Record: Annual Survey and Documents 1968-1969*. Ed. Colin Legum and John Drysdale. London: Africa Research: 883-891. Rev. as "Themes and Attitudes in Modern African Writing." *Michigan Quarterly Review* (9.4) 1970: 221-229. Rev. as "The Interpreters: Some Themes and Directions in Modern African Fiction." *African Literature: The Lectures Given on This Theme at the University of Cape Town's Public Summer School, February 1972*. Cape Town: Board of Extra Mural Studies, U of Cape Town, 1972. These lectures pub. as chapters entitled "Themes" and "Politics of Fate" in *The Black Interpreters: Notes on African Writing*. Johannesburg: Spro-Cas/Ravan, 1973: 19-45. [Orig. paper *"The Interpreters: Theme as Communication in the African Novel" presented at National Arts Winter School, U of the Witwatersrand, Johannesburg, 1968.]

472. "A Sestiger for the 70s." Open letter to André Brink. *The Star* 17 Jan.: 18.

[1970.] 473. Foreword. *The Discarded People: An Account of African Resettlement*. By Cosmas Desmond, O.F.M. Braamfontein: Christian Institute of S.A.: 5-10. Repr. Harmondsworth: Penguin, 1971: xiii-xvii.

1970. 474. "Censorship and the Primary Homeland." *Reality* (1.6): 12-15. Adapt. as "Apartheid and 'the Primary Homeland.'" *Index on Censorship* (1.3/4) 1972: 25-29.

475. "The Interpreters: Some Themes and Directions in African Literature." *The Kenyon Review 128* (32.1): 9-26. Repr. as "Origins and Directions" in *African Literature: The Lectures Given on This Theme at the University of Cape Town's Public Summer School, February 1972*. Slightly rev. and pub. as "Origins and Directions" in *The Black Interpreters*: 5-17.

1970. 476. Preface. *Familiarity Is the Kingdom of the Lost.* By Dugmore Boetie. New York: Dutton; Greenwich, CT: Fawcett: 3-4.

477. "Some Notes on African Writing." *South African Outlook* Oct.: 172-174. Repr. in *The Black Interpreters*: 7-9, 28-29, 33-34, 35, 44. Also in *African Literature: The Lectures Given on This Theme at the University of Cape Town's Public Summer School, February 1972.*

478. "Themes and Attitudes in Modern African Writing." *Michigan Quarterly Review* (9.4): 221-230. Extr. in *Modern Black Writers*: 278-279, 327-328.

1971. 479. Foreword. *Sounds of a Cowhide Drum: Poems.* By Oswald Joseph Mtshali. Johannesburg: Renoster: v-viii. Repr. New York: Third, 1972: xi-xv. London: OUP, 1972: ix-xiii. Johannesburg: Donker, 1982: 9-14.

480. "The Life of Accra, the Flowers of Abidjan: A West African Diary." *The Atlantic* Nov.: 85-89. Repr. as "Merci Dieu, It Changes" in *The Essential Gesture*: 177-184.

481. *"Pack Up, Black Man." *New York Times* 15 Jan.: 43, sec. 1.

482. *Speak Out: The Necessity for Protest.* Sixth E.G. Malherbe Academic Freedom Lecture, delivered at U of Natal, Durban, 11 Aug. Durban: Academic Freedom Committee, Students' Representative Council, U of Natal. Repr. in *The Essential Gesture*: 73-85. Extr. as "White Proctorship and Black Disinvolvement." *Reality* (3.5): 14-16.

1972. 483. *African Literature: The Lectures Given on This Theme at the University of Cape Town's Public Summer School, February 1972.* Cape Town: Board of Extra Mural Studies, U of Cape Town.

> **Contents:**
> "Origins and Directions." Lecture 1.
> **The Interpreters: Some Themes and Directions in Modern African Fiction.**
> "Themes." Lecture 2.
> "Some Political Novels in Africa." Lecture 3.

Repr. as "Modern African Fiction in English" in *The Black Interpreters*: 5-45. Extr. as "Recurring Themes: Heroes Who Affirm a Literature of Commitment." *The Star* 29 Sept.: 6.

1972. 484. "Far-Off Land of the White Man." Letter. *The Star* 22 Mar.: 19.

485. *"In a World They Never Made: Five Black South African Poets Write about Life in the White-Makes-Right Land of Apartheid." *Playboy* May: 166-169. [Refers to Joyce Nomafa Sikakane, Stanley Motjuwadi, Oswald Mbuyiseni Mtshali, Sydney [Sipho] Sepamla, Mongane Wally Serote.]

486. *"Unchaining Poets." *New York Times* 9 Dec.: 35, sec. 1.

1973. 487. *"98 Kinds of Censorship." *American Pen* (5.4): 16-21. Repr. as "98 Kinds of Censorship in South Africa" in *Hekima* (1) 1980: 115-119.

488. *The Black Interpreters: Notes on African Writing*. Johannesburg: Spro-Cas/Ravan Press.

Contents:
Section One: Modern African Fiction in English.
"Origins and Directions." 5-17.
"Themes." 19-32.
"Politics as Fate." 33-45.
Section Two: New Black Poetry in South Africa.
"New Black Poetry in South Africa." 51-70.

489. "New Black Poetry in South Africa." *The Black Interpreters*: 51-70. Repr. as "Writers in South Africa: The New Black Poets." *Dalhousie Review* (53.4) 1973/74: 645-664. Repr. in *Exile and Tradition: Studies in African and Caribbean Literature*. Ed. Rowland Smith. London: Longman, 1976: 132-151.

490. "Pula." *London Magazine* (12.6): 90-103. Rev. as "Pula!" in *The Essential Gesture*: 167-175.

491. "Reports and Comment: Tanzania." *The Atlantic* May: 8, 10, 12, 14-18.

1974.   492. "Apartheid and Censorship." *The Grey Ones: Essays on Censorship.* Ed. J. S. Paton. Johannesburg: Ravan, in association with Aquarius and the Programme for Social Change: 2-6.

493. "Gordimer vs. Paton: Top SA Writers Clash." By Caroline Clarke. *Sunday Times* 22 Dec.: 2. [Includes an open letter from Gordimer to Paton in response to his attack on her reported interview in *The Times* of London.]

494. "Literature and Politics in South Africa: Public Address by Nadine Gordimer, 14 March 1974, Writers' Week, Adelaide Festival of Arts." *Southern Review: An Australian Journal of Literary Studies* (7.3): 205-227. Repr. in **Translation* (3) 1976: 19-35. Rev. as "Literature and Politics in South Africa." *Journal of Southern African Studies* (2.2) 1976: 131-150. Repr. in *Aspects of South African Literature.* Ed. Christopher Heywood. London: Heinemann: 99-120. [Orig. paper given at Writers' Week, Adelaide Festival of Arts, 14 March 1974 under title "English-Language Literature". Rev. paper given at conference on "Literature in the Conditions of Southern Africa" under title "English-Language Literature and Politics in South Africa", U of York, 4-7 Apr. 1975. Also presented at U of Cape Town Summer School Session on "S.A. Prose in English", Jan. 1976.]

1975.   495. "The Books They Ban Along with Underpants." *Rand Daily Mail* 6 Sept.: 8.

496. "Boycott: A Matter of Personal Taste or Public Principle?" *Index on Censorship* (4.2): 21-22. [Response to Question-naire.]

497. "Can a Dying Fischer Be a Living Threat?" Letter. *Rand Daily Mail* 5 Mar.: 18.

498. *"Catalogue of the Ridiculous." *The Times* 2 July: 11.

499. Introduction. *Selected Stories.* London: Cape: 9-14. Repr. in *No Place Like: Selected Stories.* Harmondsworth: Penguin, 1978: 9-15. Also pub. as "Selecting My Stories." *The Essential Gesture*: 93-98. Extr. as "What Makes Us Write?" *The Writer* Oct., 1976: 23-24.

1975. 500. "A Writer's Freedom." *New Classic* (2): 11-16. Repr. in *English in Africa* (2.2): 45-49. *Index on Censorship* (5.2) 1976: 53-55. *They Shoot Writers, Don't They?* Ed. George Theiner. London: Faber, 1984: 134-140. *The Essential Gesture*: 87-92. [Orig. paper given at a conference on "Writings from Africa: Concern and Evocation", South African Indian Teachers' Association, Durban, Dec.]

1976. 501. "Banned in South Africa." *Index on Censorship* (5.1): 42. [Extr. from a speech at a public symposium on the New Censorship Act, 4 June 1975.]

502. "The Children Who Face Bullets: Nadine Gordimer Describes the Anguish of White People Like Herself Who Oppose Apartheid Yet Are Helpless against a Regime That Shoots Children." *The Observer Review* 12 Dec.: 21.

503. "Letter from South Africa." *New York Review of Books* 9 Dec.: 3-4, 6, 8, 10. Repr. as "Letter from Johannesburg, 1976" in *The Essential Gesture*: 99-110.

504. "A Morning in the Library." *Quarry '76: New South African Writing.* Ed. Lionel Abrahams and Walter Saunders. Johannesburg: Donker: 27-35.

505. "No Protection." *Index on Censorship* (5.1): 44. [Extr. from a speech at a public symposium on the New Censorship Act, 4 June 1975.]

1977. 506. "From Apartheid to Afrocentrism." *South African Outlook* Dec.: 181-183. Rev. in *The AUETSA Papers 1979*: 46-50. Proc. of a conference of the Association of University English Teachers of Southern Africa, U of Durban-Westville, July 1979. Repr. in *English in Africa* (7.1) 1980: 45-50. [Orig. paper presented at NUSAS seminar, May.]

507. "*Mother Courage* . . . Nadine Gordimer Has the Last Word." *The Star* 29 Oct.: 5. [Response to review by Robert Greig of Barney Simon's production of *Mother Courage* by Bertolt Brecht.]

508. "People in SA Have a Second Birth." *Evening Post* 12 Sept.: 6, 11. [Extr. from an address given at U of Cape Town, Sept.]

1977. 509. "What Being a South African Means to Me." *South African Outlook* June: 87-89, 92. *Repr. as "Search for a New Consciousness; Being South African: White." *Christianity and Crisis* 12 Dec.: 293-298. Extr. in *South Africa - The Privileged and the Dispossessed.* Ed. Geoffrey Davis and Michael Senior. Paderborn, Munich: Schöningh, 1983: 117-121. [Orig. paper presented at the Africanisation Culture Week, U of Cape Town.]

1978. 510. Foreword. *Ukubamba Amadolo: Workers' Struggles in the South African Textile Industry.* By Bettie du Toit. London: Onyx Press: 1-5.

511. *"Transkei: A Vision of Two Blood-Red Suns." *Geo* Apr.: 8-42. Repr. as "A Vision of Two Blood-Red Suns" in *The Essential Gesture*: 185-199.

1979. 512. "An Appreciation of Kurt Jobst." *Kurt Jobst: Goldsmith and Silversmith: Art Metal Worker.* Comp. Dieter and Arno Jobst. Johannesburg: Bakker: 44-46.

513. "My Johannesburg." *Geo* Aug.: 116-141.

514. "Nadine Gordimer: Geagte Redaksie." Letter. *Die Transvaler* 17 July: 10.

515. "Relevance and Commitment." Paper delivered and circulated at a conference on "The State of Art in South Africa." U of Cape Town, July. Repr. in *The Essential Gesture*: 111-119. Rev. version presented at the Radcliffe Forum, Harvard University, Oct.; at the Neil Gunn Fellowship Address, Edinburgh 1981. This version pub. as "Apprentices of Freedom." *The Arts in Adversity* (supp. to *New Society*) 24-31 Dec., 1981: ii-v. Further rev. paper presented at congress in aid of Amnesty International on "The Writer and Human Rights", U of Toronto, Oct. 1981. Pub. as "Apprentices of Freedom: Relevance and Commitment in South African Arts." *The Writer and Human Rights.* Ed. Toronto Arts Group for Human Rights. Garden City, NY: Anchor/Doubleday: 18-22. Repr. as "Art & the State in South Africa: Procrustean Bedfellows I." *The Nation* 24 Dec., 1983: 657-659. *Extr. *In These Times* 27 Jan.-2 Feb., 1982: 12-13. [*Paper also presented at a conference on "Culture and Resistance", Gaborone, Botswana, July 1982.]

1980. 516. "Censorship and the Word." *The Bloody Horse* (1): 20-24. Repr. as "The Unkillable Word" in *The Essential Gesture*: 203-207. [Orig. address at CNA Literary Awards Dinner, 17 Apr.]

517. "Facts and Interpretation." Letter. *African Communist* (82): 109. [Reply to rev. of *Burger's Daughter* by Z. N. ent. "The Politics of Commitment" in *African Communist* (80): 100-102.]

518. "Letter from the 153rd State." *New York Review of Books* 6 Nov.: 12, 14, 16-17.

519. "New Forms of Strategy — No Change of Heart." *Critical Arts* (1.2): 27-33. Repr. as "The South African Censor: No Change." *Index on Censorship* (10.1) 1981: 4-9. Also as "Censorship and Unconfessed History." *The Essential Gesture*: 209-217. Extr. as "Censorship Changes — a Victory for Whom?" *Rand Daily Mail* 6 Aug.: 11. [Orig. address given at a conference on censorship, U of Cape Town, 24 Apr.]

520. "An Unkillable Rabbit-Family." *Contrast 50* (13.2): 25-26. [Part of a piece ent. "Three Notes for an Anniversary" by Nadine Gordimer, Jan Rabie and Richard Rive written on the occasion of *Contrast's* 20th anniversary.]

521. *What Happened to Burger's Daughter or How South African Censorship Works.* Essays by Nadine Gordimer and John Dugard with statements by Director of Publications et al. Johannesburg: Taurus.

1981. 522. "Nadine Gordimer's Anatomy of Protest." *Weekend Post* 14 Mar. [Extr. of address given at the Transvaal region of the Black Sash in 1971.]

523. "Women Who Took the Literary Lead." *Rand Daily Mail* 14 May.: 4. Abbr. version of "A Note on Women and Literature in South Africa", address given at launch of "Women in Publishing" organisation, Johannesburg, 8 May.

1982. 524. "20 Years of Bannings Have Not Killed S African Writing." *The Argus* 29 May: 24.

1982. 525. *"On Literary Tradition: A Symposium." *Shenandoah* (33.3): 3-46 [Gordimer: 27-46]. [Symposium sponsored by the Virginia Foundation for the Humanities and Public Policy, George Mason U, 4-5 Apr.]

526. "Start Democracy from Scratch." Letter. *Sunday Times* 21 Nov.: 31.

1983. 527. *"Between Death and Birth: Writing in South Africa Today." *The Age Monthly Review* (3.3): 9.

528. "Censorship in South Africa." *The Writer and Human Rights*: 166-172. Repr. as "Art & the State in South Africa: Procrustean Bedfellows II." *The Nation* 24 Dec.: 659-661. [Orig. paper presented at a conference in aid of Amnesty International on "The Writer and Human Rights", U of Toronto, Oct. 1981.]

529. "*Classic* Banning an Act of Suppression." Letter. *Rand Daily Mail* 26 Jan.

530. *D. C. S. Oosthuizen Memorial Lecture 1 September 1983: Nadine Gordimer.* Grahamstown, SA: Academic Freedom Committee, Rhodes U. [Address ent. "Living in the Interregnum" but totally different from the William James Lecture 1982 (pub. 1983) except for first few paragraphs.] Extr. as "Living in the Interregnum." *Rand Daily Mail* 2 Sept.: 10.

531. *David Goldblatt: So Far / Tot Dusver.* Cape Town: SA National Gallery. Text of address at opening of the exhibition "David Goldblatt: Thirty-Five Years of Photographs" at the South African National Gallery, 13 Apr. Abbr. as "David Goldblatt: So Far" in *Granta 17*, 1985: 125-127.

532. "Drawing the Line: A Discussion." With Susan Sontag, Julius Tomin and Carolyn Forché. *The Writer and Human Rights*: 235-240. [Discussion emanating from the session ent. "The Writer's Role" at a conference on "The Writer and Human Rights", U of Toronto, Oct. 1981.]

533. "The Grand Inquisitor: A Discussion." With Julius Tomin, Susan Sontag and Margaret Atwood. *The Writer and Human Rights*: 30-32. [Discussion emanating from the

session ent. "The Writer and Community: Isolation and Commitment" at a conference on "The Writer and Human Rights", U of Toronto, Oct. 1981.]

1983. 534. "Living in the Interregnum." *New York Review of Books* 20 Jan.: 21-22, 24-29. Slightly rev. version of the William James Lecture presented at the New York U Institute for the Humanities, 14 Oct., 1982. Orig. version pub. in *The Essential Gesture*: 219-237. Also pub. in *Race and Literature / Ras en Literatuur*. Ed. Charles Malan. Censal Publication No 15. Pinetown: Burgess, 1987: 209-225.

535. "Talking about Angus Wilson." *Twentieth Century Literature* (29.2): 118-120.

1984. 536. "Gordimer in Defence of Breytenbach Book." Letter. *Rand Daily Mail* 7 Sept.: 8. [Criticises *Rand Daily Mail* review of Breytenbach's *Mouroir*.]

537. "South Africa: A Letter from Nadine Gordimer." *The Sampson Letter* 25 Sept.: 11-12.

538. *"South Africa Boycott: What Should Writers Do?" *Writers' News* (3.1): 5-10 [Gordimer: 7].

1985. 539. "The Axing of a Sapling of Free Expression." *The Sunday Star* 12 May.: 17. [Article written in response to the repeated bannings of editions of *SASPU National*.]

540. "The Essential Gesture: Writers and Responsibility." *The Tanner Lectures on Human Values VI 1985*. Ed. Sterling M. McMurrin. Salt Lake City, Utah: U of Utah P; Cambridge: CUP: 1-19. Repr. as "The Essential Gesture." *The Essential Gesture*: 239-250. Also pub. in slightly altered form in *Granta 15*: 135-151. Extr. as *"The Essential Gesture: Writers and Responsibility." *The Age Monthly Review* Dec./Jan. 1984/85: 13-15. Also extr. as "The Position of the White Writer in South Africa." *Realities* (Spring): 2-3. [Orig. presented as the Tanner Lecture on Human Values, U of Michigan, 12 Oct. 1984.]

541. "Guarding 'The Gates of Paradise': A Letter from Johannesburg." *New York Times Magazine* (supp. to *New York Times*) 8 Sept.: 34-36, 38, 106-108. Extr. as "The White Lie." *Sunday Tribune* 8 Sept.: 18. Repr. as "Clothed Only

in Their White Skins, Just Like the Emperor." *The Sunday Star* 8 Sept.: 18. Orig. different version pub. as "Letter from Johannesburg, 1985" in *The Essential Gesture*: 251-258.

1985.   542. *"'Nadine Gordimer: Boesak's Answer to Pretoria." *The Village Voice* 3 Sept.: 16, 18.

543. Preface. *Call Me Woman*. By Ellen Kuzwayo. Johannesburg: Ravan: xi-xii.

1986.   544. "Address by Nadine Gordimer, South African Writer, at the Graduation Ceremony on December 12, 1986 at 2.30pm." *University of Cape Town Graduation Addresses December 1986*. Cape Town: UCT: 22-26.

545. "Censorship Control Is Creaking." *Third World Book Review* (2.1&2): 27.

546. *Lifetimes: Under Apartheid*. With David Goldblatt. London: Cape. [Text consists of extracts from Gordimer's novels and short stories.]

547. "People's Education Will Deal with Future Realities." *The Cape Times* 23 Dec.: 8. [Extracts from graduation address, Faculty of Arts and Music, U of Cape Town, Dec.]

548. "'The Writer's Imagination and the Imagination of the State: Two Views.'" With Norman Mailer. *New York Review of Books* 13 Feb.: 23-25.

1987.   549. "Bennett Award Acceptance Speech, 1986." *The Hudson Review* (40.2): 182-183.

550. "Censorship of 'The Word.'" *Africa Report* (32.4): 50-52.

551. *Leben im Interregnum: Essays zu Politik und Literatur*. Ed. and intro. Stephen Clingman. Trans. Manfred Ohl and Hans Sartorius. Frankfurt: Fischer. [Shorter version of *The Essential Gesture* which does not include the chapters that form the section "A Writer in Africa."]

552. "Natural Selection." *Washington Post Magazine* (supp. to *Washington Post*) 18 Oct.: 20-28, 30. Extr. as "Preying to the Gallery." *Sunday Times Travel* (supp. to *Sunday Times*) 17 Jan.: F1, F2.

1987. 553. "Nelson Mandela: A Tribute." *For Nelson Mandela*. Ed. Jacques Derrida and Mustapha Tlili. New York: Seaver/Holt: 3-4.

1988. 554. "Censorship and the Artist." *Staffrider* (7.2): 11-16.

555. *The Essential Gesture: Writings, Politics and Places*. Ed. and intro. Stephen Clingman. Johannesburg: Taurus; Cape Town: Philip. New York: Knopf. London: Cape. Repr. New York: Penguin, 1989.

> **Contents** [pagination of Taurus/Philip edition]:
> **Beginnings.**
> "A Bolter and the Invincible Summer." 15-22.
> **A Writer in South Africa.**
> "Where do Whites Fit In?" 25-30.
> "Chief Luthuli." 31-41.
> "Great Problems in the Street." 43-47.
> "Censored, Banned, Gagged." 49-56.
> "Why did Bram Fischer Choose Jail?" 57-65.
> "One Man Living through It." 67-72.
> "Speak Out: The Necessity for Protest." 73-85.
> "A Writer's Freedom." 87-92.
> "Selecting My Stories." 93-98.
> "Letter from Johannesburg, 1976." 99-110.
> "Relevance and Commitment." 111-119.
> **A Writer in Africa.**
> "Egypt Revisited." 125-131.
> "The Congo River." 133-155.
> "Madagascar." 157-166.
> "Pula!" 167-175.
> "Merci Dieu, It Changes." 177-184.
> "A Vision of Two Blood-Red Suns." 185-199.
> **Living in the Interregnum.**
> "The Unkillable Word." 203-207.
> "Censorship and Unconfessed History." 209-217.
> "Living in the Interregnum." 219-237.
> "The Essential Gesture." 239-250.
> "Letter from Johannesburg, 1985." 251-258.

556. "Huddleston: A Sign." *Trevor Huddleston: Essays on His Life and Work*. Ed. Deborah Duncan Honor. Oxford: OUP: 5-9.

1988. 557. *"Who Writes? Who Reads? The Rise of a People's Literature in South Africa." *Radcliffe Quarterly* (74.3): 2-4.

1989. 558. "Bedevilment of Double Translation." Letter. *The Star* 30 Oct.: 8. [Corrects a mistranslated comment ascribed to Gordimer by *The Star*.]

559. Foreword. *Olive Schreiner: A Biography*. By Ruth First and Ann Scott. London: The Women's Press: 3-8.

560. "The Gap Between the Writer and the Reader." *New York Review of Books* 28 Sept.: 59-61.

561. Letter. *The Weekly Mail* 10-16 Nov.: 12. [In response to *The Weekly Mail* article alleging the predominance of the SACP at an ANC rally. Replies to this letter in *The Weekly Mail* 17-23 Nov.: 14.]

562. "Sunday Was a Beautiful Day, Com: Nadine Gordimer Celebrates Last Weekend's Historic ANC Rally in Soweto." *The Observer* 5 Nov.: 16.

563. "Threats of Death Not Empty, Here." Letter. *Akal* Aug.: 42. Repr. as "COSAW and *The Weekly Mail*." *Index on Censorship* (18.2): 3. [Response to Charlotte Bauer's article "Disinvested: Why Salman Rushdie Was Prevented from Attacking State Censorship." *Index on Censorship* (17.10) 1988: 33.]

564. "The Value of a Conference: Introduction." *Culture in Another South Africa*. Ed. Willem Campschreur and Joost Divendal. London: Zed: 10-12.

565. "Words for Salman Rushdie." *New York Times Book Review* 12 Mar.: 28.

1990. 566. *"African Earth." *House & Garden* July: 40.

567. ". . . and a Writer's Case for." *Review/Books* (supp. to *The Weekly Mail*) 23 Feb.-1 Mar.: 7. [Written in defence of Salman Rushdie, in sequence with an article by John le Carré ent. "A Writer's Case Against Rushdie."]

568. "Censorship and Its Aftermath." *Index on Censorship* (19.7): 14-16. Extr. in *Harper's Magazine* Nov.: 27, 30. [Orig. address to English P.E.N's International Writers' Day, London, 2 June.]

1990.   569. "The Ingot and the Stick, the Ingot and the Gun: Mozambique—South Africa." *Frontiers*. London: BBC: 50-77.

570. "Let's Break Our Habit of Violence with Just Laws." *The Weekly Mail* 9-15 Nov.: 34. [Extr. of keynote address to *The Weekly Mail* Book Week.]

571. "Letter from Johannesburg." *African Commentary: A Journal of People of African Descent* June: 4-6.

572. "Living Life to the Full, Day by Unpredictable Day." *The Star* 3 Jan.: 10.

573. "Sorting the Images from the Man." *Newsweek* 26 Feb.: 47. [American ed.]

574. "Who Writes? Who Reads? The Concept of a People's Literature." *Staffrider* (9.1): 36-41. [Orig. paper presented at symposium of UNESCO Working Group, Senegal, 1989.]

575. "With Open Eyes." *Values Alive: A Tribute to Helen Suzman*. Ed. Robin Lee. Johannesburg: Ball: 115-119. Repr. in *Cosmopolitan* Sept.: 30, 32, 38.

1991.   576. *Nobel Lecture: 1991*. Stockholm: The Nobel Foundation. Repr. as "Writing and Being." *Staffrider* (10.2) 1992: 5-10. "Turning the Page: African Writers on the Threshold of the Twenty-First Century." *Transition 56* 1992: 4-10. "Writing and Being." *New Contrast 78* (20.2) 1992: 6-13.

577. "A Thousand Days of the *Fatwa*: The Rushdie Affair Reconsidered." *Times Literary Supplement* 8 Nov.: 13.

H. REVIEWS BY GORDIMER

1958.   578. Rev. of *The Habit of Loving*, by Doris Lessing. *Africa South* (2.4): 124-26.

1960.   579. *"From the Third World." Rev. of *Drawn in Colour*, by Noni Jabavu. *Contact* 16 Apr.: 7.

1963.   580.   *"For Andrina Destiny Was Bitter." Rev. of *The Beadle*, by Pauline Smith. *New York Times Book Review* 16 June. Repr. in *Pauline Smith*. Southern African Literature Series, No 3. Ed. Dorothy Driver. Johannesburg: McGraw, 1983: 101-102.

1965.   581.   "A Wilder Fowl." Rev. of *Turbott Wolfe*, by William Plomer. *London Magazine* (5.3): 90-92. Repr. in *Atlas: The Magazine of the World Press* (10.5): 316-317. Also in *Turbott Wolfe: With Background Pieces by Roy Campbell, William Plomer, Laurens van der Post, Nadine Gordimer, Michael Herbert, Peter Wilhelm, David Brown and Stephen Gray*. By William Plomer. Ed. Stephen Gray. Johannesburg: Donker, 1980: 165-168.

1966.   582.   "Taking into Account." Rev. of *Force of Circumstance*, by Simone de Beauvoir. *London Magazine* (5.10): 73-77.

1967.   583.   "The Color of Want." Rev. of *The Race War*, by Ronald Segal. *The Nation* 6 Mar.: 313-315.

   584.   "The Dark Venus and the New Desdemona." Rev. of *The Literature and Thought of Modern Africa*, by Claude Wauthier. *London Magazine* (7.5): 71-76.

   585.   "'The Path and Not the Goal.'" Rev. of *The Literature and Thought of Modern Africa*, by Claude Wauthier. *The Nation* 26 June: 822-823.

1968.   586.   "The Onlooker and the Insider: A Look at Contemporary South Africa." Rev. of *The Separated People*, by Ellison Kahn Jr., and *The Long View*, by Alan Paton. *The Nation* 8 July: 21-22, 24-25. Extr. in *Modern Commonwealth Literature*. Ed. John H. Ferres and Martin Tucker. New York: Ungar, 1977: 94.

1971.   587.   "The Metaphor of Exile." Rev. of *Thoughts Abroad,* by John Bruin [pseud. Dennis Brutus]. *South African Outlook* Jan.: 12.

   588.   *Rev. of *Idanre and Other Poems*, by Wole Soyinka. *African Studies* (30.1): 64-65.

   589.   Rev. of *In a Free State*, by V. S. Naipaul. *New York Times Book Review* 17 Oct.: 5, 20.

1972. 590. "A Private Apprenticeship." Rev. of *The Mortgaged Heart*, by Carson McCullers. *London Magazine* (12.4): 134-137. [Incorrectly printed as (12.3).]

1974. 591. "Alberto Moravia's Africa." Rev. of *Which Tribe Do You Belong To?* by Alberto Moravia. *London Magazine* (14.4): 53-56.

592. "The Last Colonial Poet?" Rev. of *Lyric and Polemic: The Literary Personality of Roy Campbell*, by Rowland Smith. *London Magazine* (14.2): 115-118. Repr. *Snarl* (1.1): 1-2.

1975. 593. "At the Crossroads of Cultures." Rev. of *Morning Yet On Creation Day*, by Chinua Achebe. *Times Literary Supplement* 17 Oct.: 1227. Extr. in *Modern Black Writers*. Ed. Michael Popkin. New York: Ungar, 1978: 19-20.

594. "A Stinging Touch of Local Colour." Rev. of *Local Colour*, by Stephen Gray. *Rand Daily Mail* 29 Sept.: 17.

1977. 595. *"Reaching for Injustice." Rev. of *Love's Gravity*, by Per Wästberg. *Times Literary Supplement* 20 May: 604.

1978. 596. "A Brilliant Bigot." Rev. of *Sarah Gertrude Millin: A South African Life*, by Martin Rubin. *Times Literary Supplement* 15 Sept.: 1012.

1980. 597. "Death, Love and the Fruit Basket on Carmen Miranda's Head." Rev. of *Sergeant Getlio*, by Joao Ubaldo Ribeiro; *Sol*, by Mario Satz. *London Magazine* (20.3): 91-93.

598. "The Prison-House of Colonialism." Rev. of *Olive Schreiner: A Biography*, by Ruth First and Ann Scott. *Times Literary Supplement* 15 Aug.: 918. Repr. as "'The Prison-House of Colonialism': Review of Ruth First and Ann Scott's *Olive Schreiner*." *Olive Schreiner*. Ed. Cherry Clayton. Johannesburg: McGraw, 1983: 95-98. "Review of *Olive Schreiner: A Biography*, by Ruth First and Ann Scott." *Olive Schreiner and After: Essays on Southern African Literature*. Ed. Malvern van Wyk Smith and Don Maclennan. Cape Town: Philip, 1983: 14-19. "Afterword: 'The Prison House of Colonialism': Review of Ruth First and Ann Scott's *Olive Schreiner*." *An Olive Schreiner Reader: Writings on Women and South Africa*. Ed. and intro. Carol Barash. London: Pandora, 1987: 221-227.

1980.   599. Rev. of *Martyrs and Fanatics: South Africa and Human Destiny*, by Peter Dreyer. *The New Republic* 16 Aug.: 38-40.

1981.   600. "Seeing Things." Rev. of *The Visitation*, by Ahmed Essop. *The Daily News* 24 Feb.: 11.

1982.   601. "The Child Is the Man." Rev. of *Aké: The Years of Childhood*, by Wole Soyinka. *New York Review of Books* 21 Oct.: 3, 6.

602. "Mysterious Incest." Rev. of *Flaws in a Glass: A Self-Portrait*, by Patrick White. *New York Review of Books* 15 Apr.: 14-15.

603. "Unconfessed History." Rev. of *Ah, but Your Land Is Beautiful*, by Alan Paton. *The New Republic* 24 Mar.: 35-37.

1984.   604. "The Idea of Gardening." Rev. of *Life & Times of Michael K*, by J. M. Coetzee. *New York Review of Books* 2 Feb.: 3, 6. Abbr. in *Contemporary Literary Criticism*, Vol 33. Ed. Daniel G. Marowski and Jean C. Stine. Detroit: Gale: 109-111.

605. "New Notes from Underground." Rev. of *Mouroir*, by Breyten Breytenbach. *The Atlantic* July: 114-116.

606. "Satire Strikes Deep." Rev. of *The Emperor*, by Ahmed Essop. *The Star* 8 Aug.: 10M.

1985.   607. "The Just Cause." Rev. of *Move Your Shadow: South Africa, Black and White*, by Joseph Lelyveld. *New York Review of Books* 7 Nov.: 5-6, 8-10, 12, 14. Extr. as "The Screen That Hides Reality." *The Weekly Mail* 15-21 Nov.: 14-15.

608. "Victims Write Their Own Parts." Rev. of *We Came to Town*, ed. Caroline Kerfoot. *The Star* 23 July: 15. Repr. as "The Magic of Reading Taken for Granted." *The Friend* 26 July: 23.

1988.   609. "The Triumph of Memory: Images of the Faces That Were Sophiatown." Rev. of *Memory Is the Weapon*, by Don Mattera. *The Star* 8 Feb.: 10.

1990. 610. "International Books of the Year." Rev. of *The Love of Many Things: A Life of Vincent van Gogh*, by John Curtis; *Haroun and the Sea of Stories*, by Salman Rushdie; *On the Golden Porch*, by Tatyana Tolstaya. *Times Literary Supplement* 7-13 Dec.: 1333.

611. "Look Back and Shudder." Rev. of *The Mind of South Africa: The Story of the Rise and Fall of Apartheid*, by Allister Sparks. **Prime Time* (supp. to *The Sunday Star*) 20 May: 1, 2.

1991. 612. "A Race with Darkness." Rev. of *Hourglass*, by Danilo Kiss. Trans. Ralph Manheim. *The Observer* 6 Jan.: 47.

I. INTERVIEWS

1954. 613. "Miss Gordimer Was Excited: Spotlight on a New Best Seller." With Tom Macdonald. *Spotlight* Jan.: 24-25.

1958. 614. "'I'm Not So Observant' Says Nadine: But Johannesburg Sees Itself in Her Book." With The Man on the Reef. *The Star* 11 July: 15. Repr. in *Conversations with Nadine Gordimer*. Ed. Nancy Topping Bazin and Marilyn Dallman Seymour. Jackson: UP of Mississippi, 1990: 3-4. [*A World of Strangers*.]

1961. 615. Interview with Nadine Gordimer. With Bernard Sachs. *The Road to Sharpeville*. Johannesburg: Dial ; London: Dobson; New York: Liberty: 198-202. Repr. as "The Literary Scene: Nadine Gordimer" in *Conversations with Nadine Gordimer*: 5-8.

1963. 616. "Nadine Gordimer." With Studs Terkel. *Perspective on Ideas and the Arts* (12.5): 42-49. Repr. in *Conversations with Nadine Gordimer*: 12-32. [*The Lying Days*; *The Soft Voice of the Serpent*; "The Catch"; *Occasion for Loving*; "The Train from Rhodesia"; "Is There Nowhere Else Where We Can Meet?"]

617. "South Africa: Perplexities, Brutalities, Absurdities: The Author." With John Barkham. *Saturday Review* 21 Jan.: 63. Repr. as "Author: Nadine Gordimer" in *Conversations with Nadine Gordimer*: 9-11. [*Occasion for Loving*.]

1965.   618.   "A Writer in South Africa."   With Alan Ross.   *London Magazine* (5.2): 21-28. Based on series of conversations. Repr. in *Atlas: The Magazine of the World Press* July: 37-40. Also as "Nadine Gordimer: A Writer in South Africa" in *Conversations with Nadine Gordimer.* 33-42.   Extr. in *Contemporary Novelists.*   Ed. James Vinson.   London: St James, 1972: 501-502.

1969.   619.   *"'Nadine Gordimer."   With Catherine Stott.   *The Guardian* 30 May: 9.   *Repr. as "'I Must Stay and Fight.'"   *The Star* 13 June: 15.

620.   "Nadine Gordimer Talks to Andrew Salkey."   With Andrew Salkey.   *The Listener* 7 Aug.: 184-185.   Repr. in *Conversations with Nadine Gordimer.* 43-46.

1970.   621.   "Africa in the Eleventh Hour: An Interview with Nadine Gordimer."   With E. G. Burrows. *Michigan Quarterly Review* (9.4): 231-234.   Repr. in *Conversations with Nadine Gordimer.* 49-54.

622.   *"'Authors and Editors: Nadine Gordimer."   With Barbara A. Bannon.   *Publishers Weekly* 28 Dec.: 21-22.   Repr. in *Conversations with Nadine Gordimer.* 47-48.

1971.   623.   "Active Politics? Not for Me, Says Nadine Gordimer."   With Claude Lévi-Strauss.   *The Daily News* 13 Aug.: 10.

624.   "Nadine Gordimer: The Integrity of a Writer."   With Marshall Lee.   *The Star Literary Review* (supp. to *The Star*) 26 June: 3, 5.   Extr. as "Nadine Gordimer on Her New Book."   *Argus Literary Review* (supp. to *The Argus*) 7 July: 4.

1972.   625.   "Diamonds Are Polished—So Is Nadine."   With Diane Cassere. *Eve and TV Mail* (supp. to *Rand Daily Mail*) 27 July: 2, 4. Repr. in *Conversations with Nadine Gordimer.* 55-58. [*A Guest of Honour.*]

626.   "Nadine Gordimer the Angry Author."   With Margaret Wild. *Woman's Argus* (supp. to *The Argus*) 3 Aug.: 4. [*Livingstone's Companions.*]

627.   "Writing in Africa: Nadine Gordimer Interviewed."   With Stephen Gray and Phil du Plessis. *New Nation* Sept.: 2, 3, 5. Repr. in *Conversations with Nadine Gordimer.* 59-66. [*A Guest of Honour, Livingstone's Companions.*]

1973. 628. "Landmark in Fiction." With Stephen Gray. *Contrast 30* (8.2): 78-83. Repr. in *Conversations with Nadine Gordimer.* 67-72. [*A Guest of Honour.*]

1974. 629. "Interview with Nadine Gordimer, Michael Dues, James Matthews, Oswald Mtshali and James Polley about Black Poetry in South Africa." With Elaine Caulker and Clive Elliott. *BBC Arts and Africa* (10): 1-4.

1975. 630. "Book Awards Mean Nothing to Nadine." With Liz Brown. *The Daily News* 15 Mar.: 27. Repr. as "Top S A Writer Talks on Awards." *The Argus* 24 Mar.: 19. Exp. as "A Writer's Credo: Tell the Truth Without Cant: 'I Feel I'm a Witness, but Mustn't Be a Propagandist, even for the Angels.'" *The Star* 3 Apr.: 47. Adapt. as "Nadine Is Hardly Ecstatic over Award." *Pretoria News* 3 Apr.: 21. [Interview with Gordimer in New York after announcement of CNA Award for *The Conservationist.*]

631. "The Complex Nadine Gordimer." With Jim Mitchell. *Daily Dispatch* 23 July: 4.

632. "The Controversialist." With June Vigor. *The Daily News* 10 Sept.: 24. Repr. in *The Argus* 16 Sept.: 7. Abbr. in *The Star* 8 Oct.: 3.

633. "Gordimer: Critical Conscience of Our Society." With Kerry Swift. *TV Times and Colour Magazine* (supp. to *Sunday Times*) 11 May: 19-21.

1976. 634. "Gordimer: Creative Spirit in a Literary Wasteland." With Patricia Williams. *The Argus* 6 Feb.: 4.

635. "Nadine Gordimer: The Solitude of a White Writer." With Melvyn Bragg. *The Listener* 21 Oct.: 514. Repr. in *Conversations with Nadine Gordimer.* 73-77.

1977. 636. "Interview: Pat Schwartz Talks to Nadine Gordimer." With Pat Schwartz. *New South African Writing.* Johannesburg: Lorton: 74-81. Repr. in *Conversations with Nadine Gordimer.* 78-83.

1978. 637. "In Black and White." With Nesta Wyn Ellis. *Harpers & Queen* Nov.: 296-298. Repr. in *Conversations with Nadine Gordimer.* 87-95.

1978. 638. "The Writers Who Are Hardest Hit." With Carol Dalglish. *Rand Daily Mail* 3 May: 11. Repr. in *Conversations with Nadine Gordimer*. 84-86.

1979. 639. "Elke keer erger as jou boeke verbied word. . . ." With Elsa Krüger. *Beeld* 13 July: 7.

640. "Nadine Gordimer in Interview." With Ronald Hayman. *Books & Bookmen* July: 37-38. [*Burger's Daughter.*]

641. *"Nadine Gordimer: une Africaine blanche contre l'apartheid." With Claude Servan-Schreiber. *F Magazine* (21): 24+. Trans. Nancy Topping Bazin as "Nadine Gordimer: A White African against Apartheid" in *Conversations with Nadine Gordimer*: 108-121. [*A World of Strangers.*]

642. "Nadine Gordimer, Woman of Fiery Conviction." With Sammy Adelman. Part 3 of South African Writers Series. *Wits Student* (31.19): 18.

643. "Nadine Lays It on Line about Reds." With Hugh Herbert. *The Star* 22 June: 6.

644. "South African Writers Talking: Nadine Gordimer, Es'kia Mphahlele, and André Brink." With André de Villiers. *English in Africa* (6.2): 1-23.

645. *"South Africa's Nadine Gordimer: Novelist with a Conscience." With Diana Loercher. *Christian Science Monitor* 27 Nov.: B6+. Repr. in *Conversations with Nadine Gordimer*. 96-100. [*Burger's Daughter.*]

1980. 646. *"Learning to Live with Injustice." With Claude Servan-Schreiber. *World Press Review* Jan.: 30-34.

647. "Nadine Gordimer: Interview." With Johannes Riis. *Kunapipi* (2.1): 20-26. Repr. in *Conversations with Nadine Gordimer*. 101-107. [*The Late Bourgeois World*; *Occasion for Loving*; "The Amateurs"; "Which New Era Would That Be?"; "Africa Emergent".]

1981. 648. "Gordimer One of Six on BBC." With Rose Korber. *The Argus* 23 June: 6.

649. "Gordimer Still Clings to a Sense of Wonder." With Pat Schwartz. *Rand Daily Mail* 24 July: 11.

1981. 650. *Interview. With Susan McGregor. Broadcast on BBC African Service, "Arts and Africa" programme, 20 Sept.

651. "An Interview with Nadine Gordimer." With Ian Fullerton and Glen Murray. *Cencrastus* (6): 2-5.

652. "An Interview with Nadine Gordimer." With Stephen Gray. *Contemporary Literature* (22.3): 263-71. Repr. in *Interviews with Contemporary Writers: Second Series, 1972-1982*. Ed. L. S. Dembo. Madison, WI: U of Wisconsin P, 1983: 339-347. Repr. in *Conversations with Nadine Gordimer*: 176-184. [*Burger's Daughter, The Conservationist*.]

653. "'n Onderhoud met Nadine Gordimer." With Gerrit Olivier. *Die Vaderland* Sept.

654. "Nadine Gordimer: Prophet of Black Revolution." With Jane Taylor. *Sunday Times Magazine* (supp. to *Sunday Times*) 30 Aug.: 16, 18, 21, 43. [Profile based on interview; discusses *July's People*.]

655. "Nadine Gordimer, South African Witness." With Michiko Kakutani. *New York Times* 28 Dec.: C11.

656. "'A Story for This Place and Time': An Interview with Nadine Gordimer about *Burger's Daughter*." With Susan Gardner. *Kunapipi* (3.2): 99-113. Repr. in *Conversations with Nadine Gordimer*: 161-175.

657. "A Visit with Nadine Gordimer." With Edmund Morris. *New York Times Book Review* 7 June: 26-27.

1982. 658. "Deux voix contre l'apartheid." André Brink and Nadine Gordimer interviewed by Charles-Philippe Dulac and Tony Cartano. *magazine littéraire* July: 74-81.

659. "'The Future Is with the Blacks': Interview: Nadine Gordimer." With Spencer Reiss. *Newsweek* 8 Nov.: 56. Slightly altered version pub. as "'The Future Will Be with SA's Blacks.'" in *Sunday Times* 14 Nov.: 31. [For criticism by Gordimer of these alterations, see "Start Democracy from Scratch." *Sunday Times* 21 Nov.: 31.]

660. *Nadine Gordimer in discussion with James Matthews, Wally Serote, Gavin Jantes and Dollar Brand. With Alex Tetteh-Lartey. Broadcast on BBC African Service, "Arts and Africa" programme No 450G, on 8 Aug.

1982.   661. *"South Africa's Daughter." With Ann Collins. *City Woman* (holiday supp.): 15-18, 22, 24-26, 28-30.

662. "'White African' Nadine on Change." With Dirk de Villiers. *The Star* 8 Nov.: 17. Exp. as "'A White African', Gordimer." *The Friend* 10 Nov.: 11. "Gordimer: 'I Pen Imbalances.'" *Pretoria News* 11 Nov.: 16.

1983.   663. "The Art of Fiction LXXVII: Nadine Gordimer." With Jannika Hurwitt. *The Paris Review* (88): 82-127. Repr. in *Writers at Work: The Paris Review Interviews. Sixth Series.* Ed. George Plimpton. New York: Viking Penguin, 1984; Harmondsworth: Penguin, 1985: 239-279. *Women Writers at Work: The Paris Review Interviews.* Ed. George Plimpton. New York: Viking Penguin; Harmondsworth: Penguin, 1989: 225-261. *Conversations with Nadine Gordimer.* 127-160. [*A Guest of Honour, Burger's Daughter, The Conservationist, A World of Strangers.*]

664. "The Clash." With Diana Cooper-Clark. *London Magazine* (22.11): 45-59. Repr. in *Interviews with Contemporary Novelists.* London: Macmillan, 1986: 74-88. *Conversations with Nadine Gordimer.* 215-228. [*July's People; Burger's Daughter, A Guest of Honour, The Conservationist.*]

665. "A Lifetime of Mining for the Truth." With George Brock. *The Times* 18 Nov.: 13. Slightly different version as "After 40 Years of Writing: Looking Ahead . . . Looking Back." *The Star* 28 Nov.: 3. Repr. as "Gordimer at Sixty." *Sunday Tribune* 4 Dec.: 10.

1984.   666. "Changing Words in the Short Story of South Africa." With Pat Schwartz. *Rand Daily Mail* 2 June: 7. Repr. as "Gordimer's New World." *Eastern Province Herald* 13 June: 12. [*Something Out There.*]

667. "A Conversation with Nadine Gordimer." With Robert Boyers, Clark Blaise, Terence Diggory, Jordan Elgrably. *Salmagundi* (62): 3-31. Repr. in *Conversations with Nadine Gordimer.* 185-214. [*Burger's Daughter, The Conservationist, A Guest of Honour, The Late Bourgeois World.*]

1984. 668. "Nadine Gordimer." With Beata Lipman. *We Make Freedom: Women in South Africa.* London: Pandora: 106-111. Repr. as "Nadine Gordimer: First Person Singular." *Fair Lady* 29 May 1985: 116-117.

669. "Nadine Gordimer: An Interview." *Momentum: On Recent South African Writing.* Ed. M. J. Daymond, J. U. Jacobs and Margaret Lenta. Pietermaritzburg: U of Natal P: 32-34. [Extr. from filmed interview with Dr Joachim Braun which supplemented the series of films based on seven of Gordimer's short stories, Profile Productions, 1981.]

670. *"Nadine Gordimer: An Interview." With Marilyn Powell. *Canadian Forum* (63): 17-21. Repr. in *Conversations with Nadine Gordimer:* 229-238. [*Burger's Daughter.*]

671. "Reborn in South Africa: Nadine Gordimer Talks to Desmond O'Grady." *The Tablet* 4 Aug.: 739-740.

1985. 672. "'Even the Most Private Aspects of Life Are Penetrated by Politics': Nadine Gordimer and Susan Sontag: In Conversation." *The Listener* 23 May: 16-17. [Transcript of interview on *Voices.* Channel 4, BBC-TV, June.] Reported by Vivien Horler as "Gordimer Sees Little Worth Preserving in SA." *Argus Tonight* (supp. to *The Argus*) 28 May: 3.

673. ",,Wir hoffen auf das Ende der Apartheid": WAZ-Gespräch mit der südafrikanischen Nelly-Sachs-Preisträgerin Nadine Gordimer in Dortmund." *Westdeutsche Allgemeine Zeitung* 25 Nov.

1986. 674. *"Die Afrikanerin: Nadine Gordimer." With Klaus Harpprecht. *Frankfurter Allgemeine Magazin* (supp. to *Frankfurter Allgemeine Zeitung*) 3 Oct.: 12-16, 18, 20, 78.

675. "Inside South Africa." With Daniel Voll. *Vanity Fair* Feb.: 84-87.

676. "Menschlichkeit contra Rassenhass: Die Schriftstellerin Nadine Gordimer und ihr Land." With Ulrike Spiller. *BuchJournal* (1): 8-11.

677. "Nadine Gordimer." With Junction Avenue Theatre Company. *Sophiatown Speaks.* Ed. Pippa Stein and Ruth Jacobson. Johannesburg: Junction: 25-30. Repr. in *Conversations with Nadine Gordimer:* 247-252.

1987. 678. "Con Nadine Gordimer." With Itala Vivan. *Alfabeta* (95): 4-6. Trans. Jean Baptiste Para as "Vers une culture commune?" in *Europe: Revue littéraire mensuelle* (66.708) 1988: 39-47.

679. "Interview: Kate Kellaway Talks to Nadine Gordimer." With Kate Kellaway. *The Literary Review* May: 43-44. [*A Sport of Nature.*]

680. "Love among the Madness." With Anthony Sampson. *The Observer Review* 29 Mar.: 21. Ed. as "In Search of a Way to Live." *The Sunday Star* 5 Apr.: 17.

681. "Nadine Gordimer." With Dieter Welz. *Writing Against Apartheid: Interviews with South African Authors.* NELM Interviews Series No. 2. Grahamstown: National English Literary Museum: 37-45.

682. "Nadine Gordimer." With Miriam Berkley. *Publishers Weekly* 10 Apr.: 80-81.

683. *"Nadine Gordimer: Choosing to Be a White African." With Carol Sternhell. *Ms* Sept.: 28, 30, 32. Repr. in *Conversations with Nadine Gordimer:* 275-280. [*A Sport of Nature*; *July's People.*]

684. "Om alle tings samanheng og frigjieringa av mitt land: Ein formiddag med Nadine Gordimer." With Jan Askelund. *Vinduet* (41.4): 2-7. Rev. version trans. Thomas F. Van Laan as "On Writing and the Liberation of My Country: A Morning with Nadine Gordimer." *Conversations with Nadine Gordimer:* 264-274. [*A Sport of Nature*; *Burger's Daughter*; *The Late Bourgeois World*; *The Black Interpreters.*]

685. *Unpublished interview on Gordimer's travel writing. With Stephen Clingman. Johannesburg, Mar. Cited in *The Essential Gesture*: 8, 259.

686. *"A Visit with Nadine Gordimer." With Edmund Morris. *New York Times* 7 June.

687. *"A Voice from a Troubled Land: A Conversation with Nadine Gordimer." With Peter Marchant, Judith Kitchen and Stan Sanvel Rubin. Ed. Earl Ingersoll and Stan Sanvel

Rubin. *Ontario Review* (26): 5-14. Repr. in *Conversations with Nadine Gordimer.* 253-263. ["Sins of the Third Age"; *The Conservationist; July's People; A Guest of Honour.*]

1987. 688. "The Writer at the Walls of Jericho: Nadine Gordimer Talks about the World under Siege." With Pat Schwartz. *The Weekly Mail* 12-18 June: 22.

1988. 689. "A Country's Witness." With Elisabeth Dunn. *The Natal Mercury* 5 May: 3.

690. "Interview with Nadine Gordimer, Wednesday 27 January, 1988." With Karen Ruth Lazar. Appendix of "The Personal and the Political in Some of Nadine Gordimer's Short Stories." MA diss. U of the Witwatersrand: i-xiv. Pub. in *Between The Lines II.* Ed. Eva Hunter and Craig MacKenzie. Grahamstown, SA: NELM, 1993: 21-36. [*Selected Stories; Something Out There; Six Feet of the Country;* "A City of the Dead, A City of the Living"; *A Sport of Nature; The Conservationist;* "Something Out There"; "A Journey"; *Burger's Daughter.*]

1989. 691. *Interview in *Le nouvel Observateur* 22 Oct. Extr. as "Rightists Will Halt Power Sharing—Author." *Pretoria News* 24 Oct.: 10. Also in *The Star* 23 Oct.: 3. *Die Patriot* 3 Nov.: 11.

1990. 692. "Arts and Africa: An Interview with Nadine Gordimer." With Alex Tetteh-Lartey. *Conversations with Nadine Gordimer.* 281-284. [Transcript of broadcast on BBC African Service, "Arts and Africa" programme No. 694G.] [*A Sport of Nature.*]

693. *"Communist in Silk and Chiffon." With Lucy Hughes-Hallett. Supp. to *Independent on Sunday* 26 Aug.: 22.

694. *Conversations with Nadine Gordimer.* Ed. Nancy Topping Bazin and Marilyn Dallman Seymour. Jackson: UP of Mississippi.

> **Contents:**
> "'I'm Not So Observant,' Says Nadine—But Johannesburg Sees Itself in Her Book." With The Man on the Reef. 3-4.
> "The Literary Scene: Nadine Gordimer." With Bernard Sachs. 5-8.

"Nadine Gordimer: An Interview." With Marilyn Powell. 229-238.

"Talking to Writers: Nadine Gordimer." With Hermione Lee. 239-246.

"Nadine Gordimer." With the Junction Avenue Theatre Company. 247-252.

"A Voice from a Troubled Land: A Conversation with Nadine Gordimer." With Peter Marchant, Judith Kitchen and Stan Sanvel Rubin. 253-263.

"On Writing and the Liberation of My Country: A Morning with Nadine Gordimer." With Jan Askelund. 264-274.

"Nadine Gordimer: Choosing to Be a White African." With Carol Sternhell. 275-280.

"Arts and Africa: An Interview with Nadine Gordimer." With Alex Tetteh-Lartey. 281-284.

"Writers in Conversation." With Margaret Walters. 285-298.

"Off the Page: Nadine Gordimer." With Jill Fullerton-Smith. 299-305.

"Fresh Air: Nadine Gordimer." With Terry Gross. 306-313.

1990. 695. "Fresh Air: Nadine Gordimer." With Terry Gross. *Conversations with Nadine Gordimer.* 306-313. [Transcript of broadcast on WHYY-FM Philadelphia, "Fresh Air with Terry Gross" programme, 24 May 1989.]

696. "Love and Politics: Nadine Gordimer Talks to *The Bookseller* about Her New Novel, and about the Future for South Africa." *The Bookseller* 29 June: 2031, 2033. [*My Son's Story.*]

697. "Nadine Gordimer on BBC's 'Arts and Africa.'" With Alex Tetteh-Lartey. *Conversations with Nadine Gordimer.* 122-126. [Transcript of broadcast on BBC African Service, "Arts and Africa" programme No. 283, 1979.] [*The Black Interpreters.*]

698. "Nadine's Simple Truths: She Insists That She Is 'Just a Writer' but Gordimer Has Become a Voice Not Just for Well-Meaning South Africans, but for All People in a World That Is Trying to Merge Equality and Diversity into a New Whole." With Mark Muro. *Weekender* (supp. to *Weekend Argus*) 24 Nov.: 2.

1990.   699. "Off the Page: Nadine Gordimer." With Jill Fullerton-Smith. *Conversations with Nadine Gordimer*: 299-305. [Transcript of interview broadcast in the "Off the Page" series by Thames Television, 5 Jan. 1988.] [*The Late Bourgeois World*; *The Lying Days*; "The Termitary"; *Burger's Daughter*, *The Conservationist*; *A Sport of Nature*.]

700. "Sparks of Talent." With Ian Mayes. *Altered State: South Africa 1990*. London: Fourth Estate: 221-223.

701. "Talking to Writers: Nadine Gordimer." With Hermione Lee. *Conversations with Nadine Gordimer*: 239-246. [Transcript of broadcast on London Weekend Television, "Talking to Writers" programme, 15 Oct. 1986.] [*Burger's Daughter, The Lying Days*; *Lifetimes: Under Apartheid*; *July's People*.]

702. "'Vita ska inte bestämma kursen': Författeren Nadine Gordimer är optimistisk om Sydafrikas framtid, trots förtryck och våld." With Klas Nordström. *Dagens Nyheter* 28 Dec.: B1, B7.

703. "Writers in Conversation: Nadine Gordimer." With Margaret Walters. *Conversations with Nadine Gordimer*: 285-298. [Typescript of video interview No. 62 of the Institute of Contemporary Arts in the "Writer's Talk" series, 1987.] [*The Conservationist*; *The Lying Days*; *Occasion for Loving*; *The Late Bourgeois World*; *Burger's Daughter, A Sport of Nature*; *July's People*.]

1991.   704. "Mike Nicol / Nadine Gordimer." With Mike Nicol. *South African Literary Review* (1.2): 4-10. Extr. as "Gordimer: More than 'Just a Writer.'" *The Weekly Mail Review/Books* (supp. to *The Weekly Mail*) 22-28 Feb.: 11. [*The Conservationist*; *My Son's Story*.]

705. "Nadine Gordimer." With Duncan Brown and Bruno van Dyk. *Exchanges: South African Writing in Transition*. Ed. Brown and van Dyk. Pietermaritzburg: U of Natal P: 26-28. [Interview about the debate generated by Albie Sach's paper "Preparing Ourselves for Freedom."]

706. "Nadine Gordimer, årets Nobelpristagare i litteratur: —Jag skriver som om censuren inte existerar." With Collette van Luik. *Kvinna Nu* (10): 8-12.

1991.   707.   "Nadine Gordimer: Doyenne of South African Literature." With Paul Hotz. *The Daily News* 5 Sept.: 9.

708.   "Non amo le 'scalette' (e i giornalisti . . .)." With Franca Cavagnoli. *Millelibri* Nov.: 12-15.

709.   "The Power of a Well-Told Tale." With Paul Gray and Bruce W. Nelan. *Time* 14 Oct.: 70-71.

710.   "Skrywers & letterkunde: Ironie herstel ewewig." With Barrie Hough. *De Kat* Dec.: 81. [*Jump and Other Stories*; "The Moment before the Gun Went Off"; "Some Are Born to Sweet Delight."]

711.   "Sudafrica. La scelta di Nadine: 'La cosa più importante, oggi, è che non siamo più costretti a vivere nell'interregno.'" With Franca Cavagnoli. *Corriere Della Sera* 6 Jan.: 10.

1992.   712.   "Cosaw, Suitcase Libraries and The Responsible Laureate." With Gerrit Olivier. *Die Suid-Afrikaan* Feb./Mar.: 28-31.

713.   "Fragments of a Telephone Conversation with Nadine Gordimer." With Zbigniew Bialas. *Introducing South African Writing.* Ed. Bialas and Ktzysztof Kowalczyk. Cieszyn: Proart: 45-48.

714.   "The Future Is Another Country." With Stephen Clingman. *Transition 56*: 132-150. [Mentions *July's People*; *A Guest of Honour*; *The Conservationist*; *Burger's Daughter*; *My Son's Story*; "Living in the Interregnum."]

715.   "Prize and Prejudice." With Duncan Fallowell. *Woman's Journal* Mar.: 124-126, 128.

716.   "A Voice against Racism." With Karin Winegar. *Arts & Entertainment* (supp. to *Star Tribune*) 4 Oct.: 1F, 7F.

1993.   717.   "Nadine Gordimer: Interviewed by Robert Dorsman and Gitte Postel — Johannesburg, 10 July 1990." With Robert Dorsman and Gitte Postel. *Between the Lines II.* Ed. Eva Hunter and Craig MacKenzie. Grahamstown, SA: NELM: 37-52. [*July's People*; *The Conservationist*; "Living in the Interregnum"; "Relevance and Commitment"; "What Were You Dreaming?"]

BASIL MILLS

Nadine Gordimer autographs her books in NELM's collection, 1992.

WORKS OF CRITICISM ON GORDIMER

J. CRITICAL WRITING INCLUDING GORDIMER

1949.   718. Poyurs, A. "Nadine Gordimer's Moving Story." *Jewish Affairs* (4.1): 55, 57, 59. Repr. in *Novel Voices*. Poyurs. London: Macmillan, 1958: 33-35. ["The Defeated."]

1951.   719. Eglington, Charles. "S.A. English Culture: Reply to *Times* and *Burger*." *Trek* (15.10): 6-7.

720. Martin, David. "Nadine Gordimer and Doris Lessing." *Trek* (15.11): 26-27. [Response to "S.A. English Culture: Reply to *Times* and *Burger*" by Charles Eglington. *Trek* (15.10): 6-7.]

721. Sachs, Joseph. "The Short Stories of Gordimer, Lessing and Bosman." *Trek* (15.11): 15-16. Repr. in *Herman Charles Bosman As I Knew Him*. Sachs. *S.A. Opinion— Trek Anthology*. Ed. Sachs. Johannesburg: Dial, 1971: 138-142. [*Face to Face*.]

722. Talbot, B. "S.A. Short Story Writers." *Trek* (15.12): 22-23. [Letter in response to "The Short Stories of Gordimer, Lessing and Bosman" by Joseph Sachs. *Trek* (15.11): 15-16.]

1953.   723.   Delius, Anthony. "Danger from the Digit." *Standpunte 27* (7.3): 80-92. Repr. as "Danger from the Digit: *The Soft Voice of the Serpent*." *Critical Essays on Nadine Gordimer*. Ed. Rowland Smith. Boston: Hall, 1990: 23-25. [*The Soft Voice of the Serpent*.]

1954.   724.   Delius, Anthony. "The Next Instalment." *Standpunte* (8.3): 66-74. [*The Lying Days*.]

724.   725.   Walker, Oliver. "Post-War Boom in South African Literature." *South African P.E.N Year Book 1954*. Johannesburg: CNA: 5-10. Extr. as "Our Women Wear the Trousers — in Literature." *Milady: The Journal for Smart Women* July, 1955: 60-61.

726.   Webster, Mary Morison. "Trends in S.A. Literature." *The Forum* (3.6): 18-19. [*The Lying Days*.]

1957.   727.   Gardner, W. H. "Moral Somnambulism: A Study in Racial Contrasts." *The Month* (18.3): 160-169. ["Happy Event."]

1960.   728.   Bernstein, Edgar. "Fifty Years of the South African Novel: Fiction in English from Union to 1960." *P.E.N 1960: New South African Writing and a Survey of Fifty Years of Creative Achievement*. Johannesburg: P.E.N: 37-43 [Gordimer: 41-42].

729.   Girling, H. K. "Provincial and Continental: Writers in South Africa." *English Studies in Africa* (3.2): 113-118. Repr. as "Writers in South Africa: Provincial and Continental." *Queen's Quarterly* (69) Summer 1962: 237-243. [*A World of Strangers*.]

1961.   730.   Girling, H. K. "South African Novelists and Story Writers." *English Studies in Africa* (4.1): 80-86. ["A Horn of Plenty."]

731.   Sachs, Bernard. "Alan Paton and Nadine Gordimer." *The Road to Sharpeville*. Johannesburg: Dial; London: Dobson; New York: Liberty: 195-211 [Gordimer: 195-203].

1962.   732.   Woodward, Anthony G. "South African Writing: A New Play." *Contrast* (2.1): 45-50. [Refers briefly to influences on Gordimer's short-story writing.]

1963.   733.   *Magarey, Kevin. "The South African Novel and Race." *Southern Review* (1.1): 27-45. [*A World of Strangers*.]

1963. 734. Nakasa, Nathaniel. "Writing in South Africa." *The Classic* (1.1): 56-63. [Refers briefly to *A World of Strangers*.]

735. Nkosi, Lewis. "About Books." *South Africa: Information and Analysis* May: 8-11. [Briefly mentions *Occasion for Loving*.]

736. Pinchuck, I. "The South African Image." *Purple Renoster* (5): 72-84. ["Which New Era Would That Be?"; "Ah, Woe Is Me."]

737. *The Year's Work in English Studies Volume 41 1960.* Ed. Beatrice White. London: OUP, for The English Association: 15.

1964. 738. Gullason, Thomas H. "The Short Story: An Underrated Art." *Studies in Short Fiction* (2.1): 13-31. ["The Train from Rhodesia."]

[1965.] 739. Botha, Elize. "Nadine Gordimer en Joy Packer." *Suid-Afrikaanse skryfsters van die sestigerjare.* Cape Town: SABC: 30-32. [Orig. a series of Radio Talks on Radio Suid-Afrika in April and May.]

1965. 740. Nkosi, Lewis. "Les Grandes Dames." *Inkululeko* (1.3): 63. Also pub. in **The New African* (4.7): 163. [*Inkululeko* pub. to sidestep South Africa's banning of distribution of *The New African*.]

741. Partridge, A. C. "Recent Trends in South African English Writing." *English* (15.90): 235-237. [Briefly mentions *The Lying Days*.]

742. Staniland, Martin. "Apartheid and the Novel: Desperation and Stoicism in a Situation Which Frustrates." *The New African* (4.1): 15-17. [*A World of Strangers*; *Occasion for Loving*.]

1966. 743. *Rabkin, Lily. "Six Writers Whose Works May Live: Nadine Gordimer... Sharp Insight and Fine Detail." *Sunday Times Diamond Jubilee Review No. 2*: 5, 11.

1967. 744. Cronin, John F. "Writer Versus Situation: Three South African Novelists." *Studies* (56.221): 73-84. [*The Lying Days*; *A World of Strangers*; *Occasion for Loving*; *The Late Bourgeois World*.]

1967.   745. Tucker, Martin. *Africa in Modern Literature*. New York: Ungar: 221-223. Extr. in *Contemporary Literary Criticism, Vol 3*. Ed. Carolyn Riley. Detroit: Gale, 1975: 201. [*A World of Strangers*.]

1969.   746. Brutus, Dennis. "Protest against Apartheid: Alan Paton, Nadine Gordimer, Athol Fugard, Alfred Hutchinson and Arthur Nortje." *Protest and Conflict in African Literature*. Ed. Cosmo Pieterse and Donald Munro. London: Heinemann: 93-100. Extr. in *Modern Commonwealth Literature*. Ed. John H. Ferres and Martin Tucker. New York: Ungar, 1977: 47. [*The Late Bourgeois World*.]

1970.   747. Callan, Edward. "The Art of Nadine Gordimer and Alan Paton." *English Studies in Africa* (13.1): 291-292. [Introductory remarks to readings by Nadine Gordimer and Alan Paton.]

        748. Maclennan, Don. "The South African Short Story." *English Studies in Africa* (13.1): 105-123. ["Clowns in Clover"; "Happy Event"; "One Whole Year and Even More"; *The Late Bourgeois World*.]

        749. Sands, Raymond. "The South African Novel: Some Observations." *English Studies in Africa* (13.1): 89-104. [Refers briefly to *Occasion for Loving*.]

1971.   750. Klíma, Vladimír. *South African Prose Writing in English*. Prague: Oriental Institute: 95-101. [*The Late Bourgeois World*; *A World of Strangers*; "The Last Kiss."]

1972.   751. Beeton, D. R. "South African English Literature from the Perspective of the Seventies." *South African Libraries* (40.3): 148-157. [*The Lying Days*; *A Guest of Honour*.]

1973.   752. *"South African Culture in Chains." *Sechaba* (7.2): 15-17. [Problems faced by South African writers Peter Abrahams, Nadine Gordimer and Alan Paton.]

1974.   753. Gala. "Against Literary Apartheid." *African Communist* (58): 99-107. [*The Black Interpreters*.]

        754. Povey, John. "South Africa." *Literatures of the World in English*. Ed. Bruce King. London: Routledge: 154-171. ["Which New Era Would That Be?": 167-168.]

1975. 755. *Hedberg, Johannes. "Three Contemporary Novelists: Three Novels of 1974." *Moderna språk* (69): 107-120. [*The Conservationist*.]

1976. 756. *Breslin, J. B. "Inside South Africa." *America* Apr.: 344-346.

757. Hayman, Ronald. "Africa, White and Black: Nadine Gordimer . . Chinua Achebe . . Amos Tutuola . . Ayi Kwei Armah." *The Novel Today 1967-1975*. Hayman. Harlow, Essex: Longman, for The British Council: 46-49. [Briefly mentions *A Guest of Honour*; *The Conservationist*; *The Late Bourgeois World*.]

758. Smith, Rowland. "The Johannesburg *Genre*." *Exile and Tradition: Studies in African and Caribbean Literature.* Ed. Rowland Smith. Dalhousie African Studies Series. London: Longman; Dalhousie UP: 116-131. [*The Lying Days*; *A World of Strangers*.]

759. Smith, Rowland. "The Plot beneath the Skin: The Novels of C. J. Driver." *Aspects of South African Literature.* Ed. Christopher Heywood. London: Heinemann: 145-154. [*The Late Bourgeois World*.]

760. *The Year's Work in English Studies Volume 55 1974*. Ed. James Redmond. London: Murray, for The English Association: 25.

1977. 761. King, Bruce. "Recent Commonwealth Fiction." *The Sewanee Review* (Spring): 126-134. [*The Conservationist*; *Selected Stories*; "No Place Like"; "The Life of the Imagination"; "Is There Nowhere Else Where We Can Meet?"]

762. Spence, J. E. "Two Novels of Africa." *African Research and Documentation* (14): 3-10. [*A Guest of Honour*.] [Presidential Address at African Studies Association of the United Kingdom Symposium, Sept.]

763. Voss, A. E. "A Generic Approach to the South African Novel in English." *UCT Studies in English* (7): 110-119. [Orig. paper presented at a symposium on "The Criticism and Teaching of South African and African English Literature" at

a conference of university lecturers in English, U of Cape Town, 25 Jan.] [Refers briefly to *The Lying Days*; *A World of Strangers*; *The Conservationist*.]

1977. 764. *The Year's Work in English Studies* Volume 56 1975. Ed. James Redmond. London: Murray, for The English Association: 355.

1978. 765. Gerver, Elisabeth. "Women Revolutionaries in the Novels of Nadine Gordimer and Doris Lessing." *World Literature Written in English* (17.1): 38-50. [*The Lying Days*; *A World of Strangers*; *Occasion for Loving*; *The Late Bourgeois World*; *A Guest of Honour*; *The Conservationist*.]

766. Rabkin, David. "Ways of Looking: Origins of the Novel in South Africa." *Journal of Commonwealth Literature* (13.1): 27-44. [Refers to Gordimer's paper "The Novel and the Nation in South Africa."]

767. *The Year's Work in English Studies* Volume 57 1976. Ed. James Redmond. London: Murray, for The English Association: 316-317.

1979. 768. Cooke, John. "'A Hunger of the Soul': *Too Late the Phalarope* Reconsidered." *English Studies in Africa* (22.1): 37-43 [Gordimer: 37-38].

769. Gray, Stephen. *Southern African Literature: An Introduction.* Cape Town: Philip; London: Collins: 134, 136, 151-152, 154, 158, 181.

770. Jacobs, J. U. "The New Frontiersman: Some Recent South African Novels." *The AUETSA Papers 1979.* Proc. of a conference of the Association of University English Teachers of Southern Africa, U of Durban-Westville, July. [*Burger's Daughter*; *The Conservationist*.]

771. Marquard, Jean. "The Farm: A Concept in the Writing of Olive Schreiner, Pauline Smith, Doris Lessing, Nadine Gordomer [sic], and Bessie Head." *Dalhousie Review* (59.2): 293-307. [*The Conservationist*.]

772. *The Year's Work in English Studies* Volume 58 1977. Ed. James Redmond. London: Murray, for The English Association: 374. [*The Lying Days*.]

1980. 773. Essa, Ahmed. "Politics in South African Fiction." Paper presented at the twenty-third annual meeting of the African Studies Association, Philadelphia, Pennsylvania, 15-18 Oct. [*Burger's Daughter.*]

774. Roberts, Sheila. "Character and Meaning in Four Contemporary South African Novels." *World Literature Written in English* (19.1): 19-36. [*The Conservationist.*]

775. *The Year's Work in English Studies Volume 59 1978.* Ed. James Redmond. London: Murray, for The English Association: 351-352, 364. [*A Guest of Honour; The Late Bourgeois World.*]

1981. 776. Crosland, Margaret. *Beyond the Lighthouse: English Women Novelists in the Twentieth Century.* London: Constable: 141-144. [*Burger's Daughter; The Conservationist; The Late Bourgeois World.*]

777. King, Bruce. "Keneally, Stow, Gordimer and the New Literature." *The Sewanee Review* (89.3): 461-469. ["A Soldier's Embrace"; "Town and Country Lovers *One*"; *Burger's Daughter.*]

778. *The Year's Work in English Studies Volume 60 1979.* Ed. James Redmond. London: Murray, for The English Association: 354, 365. [*The Conservationist; A Guest of Honour; A World of Strangers.*]

1982. 779. Haarhoff, Dorian. "Two Cheers for Socialism: Nadine Gordimer and E. M. Forster." *English in Africa* (9.1): 55-64. [*A Guest of Honour.*]

780. *O'Hara, John D. "Reflections on Recent Prose." *New England Review* (4): 603-616.

781. Ravenscroft, Arthur. "African Novels of Affirmation." *The Uses of Fiction: Essays on the Modern Novel in Honour of Arnold Kettle.* Ed. Douglas Jefferson and Graham Martin. Milton Keynes: Open UP: 171-180. [*A Guest of Honour.*]

782. Rich, Paul. "Tradition and Revolt in South African Fiction: The Novels of André Brink, Nadine Gordimer and J. M. Coetzee." *Journal of Southern African Studies* (9.1): 54-73. [*The Conservationist*; refers briefly to *A World of Strangers*; *Burger's Daughter.*]

1982. 783. Roberts, Sheila. "South African Post-Revolutionary Fiction." *Standpunte 159* (35.3): 44-51. [*July's People.*]

784. *The Year's Work in English Studies Volume 61 1980.* Ed. James Redmond. London: Murray, for The English Association: 355. [*A World of Strangers.*]

1983. 785. Coetzee, J. M. "The Great South African Novel." *Leadership SA* (2.4): 74-75, 77, 79. [Briefly mentions *The Conservationist*; *Burger's Daughter*.]

786. *Gray, Stephen. "Interaction between English Literature and Other Language Experiences of Southern Africa." *Language and Literature in Multicultural Contexts.* Ed. Safendra Nandan. Suva, Fiji: U of South Pacific: 169-178. [Orig. paper presented at the Fifth Triennial Conference of the Association for Commonwealth Literature and Language Studies, U of the South Pacific, Suva, Fiji, 5 Jan. 1980.] [*Burger's Daughter*.]

787. Jones, Norman C. "Acculturation and Character Portrayal in Southern African Novels." *African Literature Today (13: Recent Trends in the Novel).* Ed. Eldred Durosimi Jones. London: Heinemann; New York: Africana: 180-200. [*The Conservationist*; *Burger's Daughter*.]

788. McEwan, Neil. "Outsiders? Nadine Gordimer and Laurens van der Post." *Africa and the Novel.* London: Macmillan: 128-160. [*July's People*; refers briefly to *The Late Bourgeois World*; *A Guest of Honour*, *The Conservationist*.]

789. Randall, Peter. "Publishing in South Africa: Challenges and Constraints." *African Book Publishing Record* (9.2/3): 105-108. [Refers briefly to Gordimer's comments on the South African publishing industry and censorship.]

790. Rich, Paul. "Liberal Realism in South African Fiction, 1948-1966." *The AUETSA Papers 1983.* Proc. of a conference of the Association of University English Teachers of Southern Africa, Grahamstown, July. Pub. in *English in Africa* (12.1): 47-81. [*A World of Strangers*; *Friday's Footprint*; *The Late Bourgeois World*.]

791. *Sheidley, William E. and Ann Charters. *Instructor's Manual to Accompany The Story and Its Writer: An Introduction to Short Fiction.* St. Martin's. ["A Chip of Glass Ruby."]

1983. 792. *Sirlin, Rhoda and David H. Richter. *Instructor's Manual for The Borzoi Book of Short Fiction*, ed. David H. Richter. Knopf. ["Is There Nowhere Else Where We Can Meet?"]

793. Smith, Rowland. "Allan Quatermain to Rosa Burger: Violence in South African Fiction." *World Literature Written in English* (22.2): 171-182. [*The Lying Days; Burger's Daughter.*]

794. Smith, Rowland. "The Seventies and After: The Inner View in White, English-Language Fiction." *Olive Schreiner and After: Essays on Southern African Literature in Honour of Guy Butler*. Ed. Malvern van Wyk Smith and Don Maclennan. Cape Town: Philip: 196-204. [*The Conservationist; Burger's Daughter; July's People.*]

795. Watson, Stephen. "The Fate of Liberalism in South Africa." *The History and Historiography of Commonwealth Literature*. Ed. Dieter Riemenschneider. Tübingen: Narr: 118-133. [Orig. paper presented at the EACLALS conference, U of Frankfurt, 1981; refers in general terms to Gordimer's place in the South African liberal tradition.]

1984. 796. Brink, André. "Writing against Big Brother: Notes on Apocalyptic Fiction in South Africa." *World Literature Today* (58.2): 189-194. [*July's People.*]

797. Chapman, Michael. "The Fiction-Maker: The Short Story in Literary Education." *The AUETSA Papers 1984*. Proc. of a conference of the Association of University English Teachers of Southern Africa, Rand Afrikaans U, July. Pub. in *Crux* (18.3&4): 3-20. ["The Train from Rhodesia."]

798. Jacobs, J. U. "Exile and the South African Novel." *The AUETSA Papers 1984*. Proc. of a conference of the Association of University English Teachers of Southern Africa, Rand Afrikaans U, July. [*Burger's Daughter.*]

799. Lindfors, Bernth. "Coming to Terms with the Apocalypse: Recent South African Fiction." *A Sense of Place: Essays in Post-Colonial Literatures*. Ed. Britta Olinder. Gothenburg: Gothenburg U: 196-203. [Proc. of the Gothenburg University Congress of Commonwealth Language and Literature, Sept. 1982.] [*July's People.*]

1984. 800. *Madden, David and Virgil Scott. *Instructor's Manual for Studies in the Short Story. 6th ed.* Holt. ["The Termitary."]

801. Rich, Paul. "Apartheid and the Decline of the Civilization Idea: An Essay on Nadine Gordimer's *July's People* and J. M. Coetzee's *Waiting for the Barbarians.*" *Research in African Literatures* (15.3): 365-393. [Orig. paper presented at History Workshop, U of the Witwatersrand, 1983.]

802. Rich, Paul. "Romance and the Development of the South African Novel." *Literature and Society in South Africa.* Ed. Landeg White and Tim Couzens. Cape Town: Miller Longman: 120-137. [*The Conservationist.*]

803. *The Year's Work in English Studies Volume 62 1981.* Ed. Laurel Brake. London: Murray; Atlantic Highlands, NJ: Humanities, for The English Association: 362, 393. [*The Conservationist; Burger's Daughter.*]

1985. 804. Merrett, Christopher. "The Academic Librarian and Political Censorship in South Africa: Victim or Collaborator?" *Wits Journal of Librarianship and Information Science* (3): 17-37. [Refers briefly to Gordimer and censorship; *Burger's Daughter.*]

805. Morphet, Tony. "In Defense of the Novelist: A Refutation of Heribert Adam's Concept of 'Literary Fallacy' or Pumpkins in the Interregnum." *Indicator South Africa: Perspectives* (2.4): 10-15. [A response to "Reflections on Gordimer's 'Interregnum'" by Heribert Adam. *Indicator South Africa: Perspectives* (1.3) 1984: 14-16.]

806. Roberts, Sheila. "A Questionable Future: The Vision of Revolution in White South African Writing." *Journal of Contemporary African Studies* (4.1/2): 215-223. [*July's People.*]

807. Scheub, Harold. "A Review of African Oral Traditions and Literature." *African Studies Review* (28.2/3): 1-72. [Refers briefly to *July's People.*]

808. *The Year's Work in English Studies Volume 63 1982.* Ed. Laurel Brake. London: Murray; Atlantic Highlands, NJ: Humanities, for The English Association: 476-477. [*The Conservationist; A Guest of Honour.*]

1986. 809. *Bonner, Charles H. *Instructor's Manual: Classic Short Fiction.* Prentice. ["The Train from Rhodesia."]

810. *Egner, Hanno. "Weisser Ausblicke auf südafrikanische Verhältnisse: Bücher von Nadine Gordimer und Christopher Hope." *Kommune* (1): 50-52.

811. Martin, Richard G. "Narrative, History, Ideology: A Study of *Waiting for the Barbarians* and *Burger's Daughter.*" *Ariel* (17.3): 3-21.

812. Viljoen, Hein. *Die Suid-Afrikaanse romansisteem anno 1981: 'n Vergelykende studie.* Potchefstroom, SA: Potchefstroom U for CHE: 278-357. [Pub. of PhD thesis submitted to Potchefstroom U for CHE, 1985. Summary pub. as "The System of the South African Novel *Anno* 1981" in *Literator* (6.3) 1985: 15-24. [*July's People.*]

813. Wade, Michael. "White South African Literature after World War II: English." *European-Language Writing in Sub-Saharan Africa.* Vol. 1. Ed. Albert S. Gérard. Budapest: Akadémiai Kiadó: 230-250. [*The Lying Days*; *The Late Bourgeois World*; *A Guest of Honour*; *The Conservationist*; *Burger's Daughter*; briefly refers to *A World of Strangers*; *Occasion for Loving.*]

814. *The Year's Work in English Studies Volume 64 1983.* Ed. Laurel Brake. London: Murray; Atlantic Highlands, NJ: Humanities, for The English Association: 422, 459, 532, 536-537, 546, 549. [*The Lying Days*; *Burger's Daughter*; *The Conservationist.*]

1987. 815. *Charters, Ann; William E. Sheidley and Martha Ramsey. *Instructor's Manual to Accompany The Story and Its Writer: An Introduction to Short Fiction, 2nd Edition, ed. Charters.* St. Martin's. ["Town and Country Lovers."]

816. Gorra, Michael. "The Sun Never Sets on the English Novel." *New York Times Book Review* 19 July: 1, 24-25. [*The Conservationist*; refers briefly to *Burger's Daughter.*]

817. Harlow, Barbara. *Resistance Literature.* New York: Methuen: 104, 177-181. [*July's People.*]

1987.   818.   Jacobs, Johan. "Writing in No Man's Land: Representation in Contemporary South African Literature." *SAVAL Papers VII*: 27-52. Proc. of a conference of the South African Society for General Literary Studies, Potchefstroom U for CHE, Mar. [*July's People.*]

819.   *The Year's Work in English Studies Volume 65 1984*. Ed. Laurel Brake. London: Murray; Atlantic Highlands, NJ: Humanities, for The English Association: 666, 677, 686, 688, 697-700. [*The Conservationist; Some Monday for Sure; Burger's Daughter; July's People; A World of Strangers.*]

1988.   820.   Clingman, Stephen. "Beyond the Limit: The Social Relations of Madness in Southern African Fiction." Paper presented at African Studies Seminar, U of the Witwatersrand, 3 Oct. [*The Conservationist.*]

821.   "Discussion." *Novel: A Forum on Fiction* (21.2 & 3): 345-359 [Gordimer: 348-355]. [Discussion at conference on "Why the Novel Matters: A Postmodern Perplex", Brown U, April 1987.]

822.   Glenn, Ian. "The Immorality Act and the Liberal Novel." *Africa Seminar: Collected Papers Volume 5: 1985*. Ed. Andrew D. Spiegel. Cape Town: Centre for African Studies, UCT: 108-123. [*Occasion for Loving.*]

823.   Hewson, Kelly. "Making the 'Revolutionary Gesture': Nadine Gordimer, J. M. Coetzee, and Some Variations on the Writer's Responsibility." *Ariel* (19.4): 55-72. [*The Conservationist; Burger's Daughter.*]

824.   Lenta, Margaret. "Fictions of the Future." *English Academy Review 5*: 133-145. [*July's People; A Sport of Nature; The Late Bourgeois World; Burger's Daughter.*]

825.   Lockett, Cecily. "The Black Woman in South African English Literature." *Journal of Literary Studies* (4.1): 21-37. [Refers briefly to *The Conservationist.*]

826.   *Masilela, Ntongela. "The White South African in Our National Situation." *Matatu* (1.3/4): 48-64.

1988. 827. Smith, Rowland. "Leisure, Law and Loathing: Matrons, Mistresses, Mothers in the Fiction of Nadine Gordimer and Jillian Becker." *World Literature Written in English* (28.1): 41-51. ["Ah, Woe Is Me"; *July's People*; *A Sport of Nature*.]

828. Wade, Michael. "Identity and the Mature Writer: Peter Abrahams: *The View from Coyaba* and Nadine Gordimer: *A Sport of Nature*." Paper presented at ALA conference, Pittsburgh, Apr.

829. *The Year's Work in English Studies Volume 66 1985*. Ed. Laurel Brake. London: Murray; Atlantic Highlands, NJ: Humanities, for The English Association: 648, 664-667. [*A World of Strangers*, *The Late Bourgeois World*; *A Guest of Honour*, *July's People*; *Burger's Daughter*, *The Conservationist*.]

1988/9. 830. Chapman, Michael. "Writing in a State of Emergency." *Southern African Review of Books* (2.2): 14. [Refers briefly to *A Sport of Nature*.]

1989. 831. Berthoud, Jacques. "Writing under Apartheid." *Current Writing* (1): 77-87. [*The Essential Gesture*.]

832. Breitinger, Eckhard. "Homeland or Life on the Border Line." *Nouvelles du Sud* (12): 131-139. [*July's People*.]

833. Henderson, Australia. "Women in Love and War in the Works of Flora Nwapa and Nadine Gordimer." Paper presented at the ALA conference, Dakar, Sénégal, Mar. [*The Lying Days*; *A Sport of Nature*; *Occasion for Loving*; *July's People*; *The Essential Gesture*.]

834. Jacobs, J. U. "The Colonial Mind in a State of Fear: The Psychosis of Terror in the Contemporary South African Novel." *North Dakota Quarterly* (57.3): 24-43. [*July's People*.]

835. Lenta, Margaret. "Intimate Knowledge and Wilful Ignorance: White Employers and Black Employees in South African Fiction." *Women and Writing in South Africa: A Critical Anthology*. Ed. Cherry Clayton. Johannesburg: Heinemann: 237-251. [*July's People*.]

836. Mazurek, Raymond A. "Gordimer's 'Something Out There' and Ndebele's *'Fools' and Other Stories*: The Politics of Literary Form." *Studies in Short Fiction* (26.1): 71-79.

1989.   837.   Nkosi, Lewis. "Vu de l'extérieur: La littérature d'Afrique du sud et la crise des représentations, écrivains noirs, écrivains blancs." *Nouvelles du Sud* (12): 155-158. Special ed. ent. *Afrique australe: Les situations et ses representations en litterature.* ["The Train from Rhodesia"; "A Smell of Death and Flowers"; *A Sport of Nature.*]

838.   Oboe, Annalisa. "The Colour of Fear: A Reading of Two South African Short Stories." *Nouvelles du Sud* (12): 27-35. ["The Train from Rhodesia."]

839.   Thorpe, Michael. "Calling the Kettle Black: Some Thoughts on 'Cultural Imperialism.'" *Encounter* Dec.: 40-44. [Discusses briefly "Living in the Interregnum", *Burger's Daughter, A Sport of Nature.*]

840.   Tremaine, Louis. "Divided Self and Unimagined Other in *July's People* and *Waiting for the Barbarians.*" Paper presented at the ALA Conference, Dakar, Sénégal, Mar.

841.   Wilkinson, Jane. "Feasting to Death: 'Garden Party' Variations." *Short Fiction in the New Literatures in English: Proceedings of the Nice Conference of the European Association for Commonwealth Literature & Language Studies, March 1988.* Ed. J. Bardolph. Nice: Faculté des Lettres et Sciences Humaines, Nice U: 23-30. ["A Company of Laughing Faces."]

842.   *The Year's Work in English Studies Volume 67 1986.* Ed. Laurel Brake. London: Murray; Atlantic Highlands, NJ: Humanities, for The English Association: 477, 717-718. [*Burger's Daughter.*]

1990.   843.   Anderson, Peter. "Essential Gestures: Gordimer, Cronin and Identity Paradigms in White South African Writing." *English in Africa* (17.2): 37-57. ["Spoils"; *The Essential Gesture.*]

844.   Attwell, David. "The Problem of History in the Fiction of J. M. Coetzee." *Rendering Things Visible: Essays on South African Literary Culture.* Ed. Martin Trump. Johannesburg: Ravan: 94-133. [Briefly mentions *Burger's Daughter.*]

845.   Brink, André. "Mutants of the Picaresque: *Moll Flanders* and *A Sport of Nature.*" *Journal of Literary Studies* (6.4): 261-274.

1990. 846. Clingman, Stephen. "Literature and History in South Africa." *Radical History Review* (46.7): 145-159. [*Burger's Daughter.*]

847. Clingman, Stephen. "Revolution and Reality: South African Fiction in the 1980s." *Rendering Things Visible: Essays on South African Literary Culture*: 41-60. [*July's People*; briefly mentions *The Conservationist*; *A Sport of Nature.*]

848. Engle, Lars. "'The Novel without the Police.'" *The AUETSA Papers 1990. Vol I: African and South African Themes.* Proc. of a conference of the Association of University English Teachers of Southern Africa, U of Stellenbosch, 3-7 July. Pub. in *Pretexts* (3.1-2) 1991: 105-117. [Briefly mentions *A Sport of Nature.*]

849. Gray, Rosemary. "Text and Context: A Reading of Elizabeth Charlotte Webster's *Ceremony of Innocence* and Nadine Gordimer's *The Conservationist.*" *Commonwealth Essays and Studies* (13.1): 55-67.

850. Gray, Stephen. "Women in South African Theatre." *SATJ* (4.1): 75-87. [Refers briefly to "The First Circle."]

851. Kearney, J. A. "John Conyngham's *The Arrowing of the Cane.*" *The AUETSA Papers 1990. Vol I: African and South African Themes.* Proc. of a conference of the Association of University English Teachers of Southern Africa, U of Stellenbosch, 3-7 July. [Refers briefly to *The Conservationist.*]

852. Lockett, Cecily. "Feminism(s) and Writing in English in South Africa." *Current Writing* (2.1): 1-21 [Gordimer: 10-13]. [Ed. version of paper presented at a conference of the Association of University English Teachers of Southern Africa, Pretoria U, July, 1989.]

853. Macaskill, Brian. "Interrupting the Hegemonic: Textual Critique and Mythological Recuperation from the White Margins of South African Writing." *Novel: A Forum on Fiction* (23.2): 156-181. [*The Conservationist.*]

854. Nkosi, Lewis. "A Country of Borders." *Southern African Review of Books* Aug./Oct.: 19, 20. [Page 19 incorrectly labelled June/July.] Extr. as "The Problem of the

'Cross-Border' Reader." *The Weekly Mail Review/Books* (supp. to *The Weekly Mail*) 26 Oct.-1 Nov.: 12. ["Africa Emergent."]

1990.   855.   Sarvan, Charles. "Bessie Head: Two Letters." *Wasafiri* (12): 11-15. [Head briefly comments on Gordimer.]

856.   Scherzinger, Karen. "The Problem of the Pure Woman: South African Pastoralism and Female Rites of Passage." *The AUETSA Papers 1990. Vol V: Feminism.* Proc. of a conference of the Association of University English Teachers of Southern Africa, U of Stellenbosch, 3-7 July. Rev. and pub. in *UNISA English Studies* (29.2) 1991: 29-35. [Refers briefly to *The Conservationist*.]

857.   Wade, Jean-Philippe. "The Allegorical Text and History: J. M. Coetzee's *Waiting for the Barbarians*." *Journal of Literary Studies* (6.4): 275-288 [Gordimer: 276-277].

858.   *The Year's Work in English Studies Volume 68 1987.* Ed. Laurel Brake. Oxford: Blackwell; Atlantic Highlands, NJ: Humanities, for The English Association: 507, 707, 717-718. [*Burger's Daughter*; *July's People*; *Something Out There*.]

1991.   859.   Bowker, Veronica and Bert Olivier. "A Dialogue on Reading and Writing in and out of Time: History as Co-Determinant in Literary-Theoretical Reception and Production." *The AUETSA Papers.* Proc. of a conference of the Association of University English Teachers of Southern Africa, U of Fort Hare, July. [*July's People*; briefly mentions *A Sport of Nature*.]

860.   Bradford, Helen. "'Her Body, Her Life': 150 Years of Abortion in South Africa." Paper No. 22 presented at a conference on "Women & Gender in Southern Africa" at U of Natal, Durban, 30 Jan.-2 Feb. ["Happy Event."]

861.   Clayton, Cherry. "Post-Colonial, Post-Apartheid, Post-Feminist: Family and State in Prison Narratives by South African Women." *Kunapipi* (13.1&2): 136-144. [*Burger's Daughter*.]

862.   Gray, Stephen. "An Author's Agenda: Re-Visioning Past and Present for a Future South Africa." *Kunapipi* (13.1&2): 23-31. ["Living in the Interregnum."]

1991. 863. Haarhoff, Dorian. *The Wild South-West: Frontier Myths and Metaphors in Literature Set in Namibia, 1760-1988.* Johannesburg: Witwatersrand UP: 99, 149, 194, 197, 201, 206-209, 226. [Briefly discusses "Oral History."]

864. MacKenzie, Craig. "Showing the Flag beyond the Internationale." *South African Literary Review* (1.2): 23-24. ["Teraloyna."]

865. Nuttall, Sarah. Rev. of *Colours of a New Day*, ed. Sarah Lefanu and Stephen Hayward. *Journal of Southern African Studies* (17.3): 570-573. ["Teraloyna."]

866. Petersen, Kirsten Holst. "South Africa." *The Commonwealth Novel since 1960.* Ed. Bruce King. London: Macmillan: 125-141. [*The Late Bourgeois World*; *The Conservationist*; *July's People*; *Burger's Daughter*; *A Sport of Nature*; briefly mentions *The Lying Days*; *A World of Strangers*; *Occasion for Loving*.]

867. Smith, Malvern van Wyk. "Waiting for Silence; or, the Autobiography of Metafiction in Some Recent South African Novels." *Current Writing* (3.1): 91-104. [*My Son's Story*.]

868. Wood, Felicity. "Subversive, Undisciplined and Ideologically Unsound or Why Don't South Africans Like Fantasy." *The AUETSA Papers.* Proc. of a conference of the Association of University English Teachers of Southern Africa, U of Fort Hare, July. [Briefly mentions *Burger's Daughter*; "The Essential Gesture."]

869. *The Year's Work in English Studies Volume 69 1988.* Ed. Laurel Brake and Gordon Campbell. Oxford: Blackwell; Atlantic Highlands, NJ: Humanities, for The English Association: 519, 681, 686, 687, 696-697. [*The Essential Gesture*; *Burger's Daughter*; *A Sport of Nature*; *A World of Strangers*; *The Lying Days*; *July's People*; *A Guest of Honour*; *The Conservationist*.]

1992. 870. Alfred, Luke. "Gordimer, Brink and Goldblatt in New Granta." Rev. of *Granta 40: The Womaniser*. *Review/ Books* (supp. to *The Weekly Mail*) 25 Sept.-1 Oct.: 3. ["Look-Alikes."]

1992.   871. Bjornson, Richard. "UNESCO Symposium on the Main Issues in African Fiction and Poetry on the Threshold of the Twenty-First Century." *ALA Bulletin* (18.2): 13-21.

872. Brink, André. "Reinventing the Real: English South African Fiction Now." Address given at the Winter School, Standard Bank National Festival of the Arts, Grahamstown, July. Pub. in *New Contrast 81* (21.1) 1993: 44-55. [*July's People*; *A Sport of Nature*; *Burger's Daughter*; *My Son's Story*.]

873. Ergas, Zeki. "Op soek na metafore vir die Onrus." Jan Rabie, Marjorie Wallace and Hermien Dommisse in discussion with Zeki Ergas. *Die Suid-Afrikaan* (41): 39-40. [Briefly discusses work of Brink, Coetzee, Gordimer, Serote and Kuzwayo.]

874. Henley, Ann. "'Space for Herself': Nadine Gordimer's *A Sport of Nature* and Josephine Humphreys' *Rich in Love*." *Frontiers: A Journal of Women Studies* (13.1): 81-89.

875. Peck, Richard. "Condemned to Choose, but What? Existentialism in Selected Works by Fugard, Brink and Gordimer." *Research in African Literatures* (23.3): 67-84. [*Burger's Daughter*; briefly mentions *July's People*; *A Sport of Nature*.]

876. *Perspectives on South African English Literature.* Ed. Michael Chapman, Colin Gardner and Es'kia Mphahlele. Johannesburg: Donker: 272-292, 353, 422, 424-425, 457, 469, 477, 486, 488, 491, 515, 525.

877. Voss, A. E. "Reading and Writing in the New South Africa." *Current Writing* (4): 1-9. [Briefly mentions *My Son's Story*; *A Sport of Nature*; *The Late Bourgeois World*.]

878. *The Year's Work in English Studies Volume 70 1989.* Ed. Gordon Campbell. Oxford: Blackwell; Atlantic Highlands, NJ: Humanities, for The English Association: 51-52, 695, 702, 704-705, 780. [*Burger's Daughter*; "The African Magician"; *The Essential Gesture*; "A Company of Laughing Faces."]

1993.   879. Hunter, Eva. Introduction. *Between the Lines II*. Ed. Hunter and Craig MacKenzie. Grahamstown, SA: NELM: 3-19. [*Burger's Daughter*; *July's People*; *A Sport of Nature*.]

1993. 880. Wade, Michael. *White on Black in South Africa: A Study of English-Language Inscriptions of Skin Colour.* New York: St. Martin's: x, 39, 75, 84, 86-129, 151, 158, 162. [*A Sport of Nature*; *A World of Strangers*; *Burger's Daughter*; *Face to Face*; "Friday's Footprint"; "Good Climate, Friendly Inhabitants"; "Happy Event"; "Is There Nowhere Else Where We Can Meet?"; *July's People*; *Not for Publication*; *Occasion for Loving*; *Six Feet of the Country*; "Some Monday for Sure"; *The Conservationist*; *The Late Bourgeois World*; *The Lying Days*; *The Soft Voice of the Serpent*; "The Train from Rhodesia."]

K. CRITICAL WRITING SPECIFICALLY ON GORDIMER

1953. 881. Rabkin, Lily. "The Art of Nadine Gordimer." *The Forum* (2.8): 40-42. [*The Lying Days.*]

1956. 882. Abramovitz, Arnold. "Nadine Gordimer and the Impertinent Reader." *Purple Renoster* (1): 13-17.

1959. 883. Sachs, Bernard. "Nadine Gordimer: Writer with the Eye of a Camera." *South African Personalities and Places.* Johannesburg: Kayor: 83-89. [*The Lying Days*; *A World of Strangers.*]

884. Ulman, Ruth. "Nadine Gordimer." *Wilson Library Bulletin* (33.9): 616. [*The Lying Days; Six Feet of the Country*; *A World of Strangers.*]

1960. 885. Abrahams, Lionel. "Nadine Gordimer: The Transparent Ego." *English Studies in Africa* (3.2): 146-151. Repr. in *Critical Essays on Nadine Gordimer.* Ed. Rowland Smith. Boston: Hall, 1990: 26-30. [Briefly mentions *A World of Strangers*; *The Lying Days*; "The Defeated"; "The Last Kiss"; "A Style of Her Own"; "The Gentle Art"; "Check Yes or No."]

1961. 886. Van Heyningen, Christina. "Nadine Gordimer: A Letter." *Theoria* (17): 34-37. [Letter in response to Woodward's article below.]

887. Woodward, Anthony G. "Nadine Gordimer." *Theoria* (16): 1-12. [*The Lying Days*; *The Soft Voice of the Serpent*; "A Present for a Good Girl"; "A Watcher of the Dead."]

1963. 888. Snyman, J. P. L. "South African Writers—III: Nadine Gordimer." *Femina & Woman's Life* 4 July: 61. [Briefly mentions *Face to Face*; *Six Feet of the Country*; "Happy Event"; *The Lying Days*; *A World of Strangers*; *Occasion for Loving*.]

1965. 889. McGuinness, Frank. "The Novels of Nadine Gordimer." *London Magazine* (5.3): 97-102. [*The Lying Days*; *Not for Publication*.]

1967. 890. Nkosi, Lewis. "Miss Gordimer and *The Classic*." *South Africa: Information and Analysis* (52): 2-4.

1968. 891. Nkosi, Lewis. "Politics: A Dirtier Word than Sex!" *South Africa: Information and Analysis* (65): 1-4. [Response to Gordimer's essay "Politics: A Dirtier Word than Sex!" *Solidarity* (3.11): 69-71.]

1972. 892. Laredo, Ursula. "Gordimer, Nadine." *Contemporary Novelists*. Ed. James Vinson. London: St. James: 502-503. [Briefly mentions *The Late Bourgeois World*; *A Guest of Honour*; *The Lying Days*; *A World of Strangers*; *Occasion for Loving*.]

[1973.] 893. Laredo, Ursula. "Gordimer, Nadine." *English and South Africa*. Ed. Alan Lennox-Short. Nasou: 56-58. [Briefly mentions *The Lying Days*; *A World of Strangers*; *Occasion for Loving*; *The Late Bourgeois World*; *A Guest of Honour*.]

1973. 894. Laredo, Ursula. "African Mosaic: The Novels of Nadine Gordimer." *Journal of Commonwealth Literature* (8.1): 42-53. [*A World of Strangers*; *A Guest of Honour*; *The Late Bourgeois World*; *The Soft Voice of the Serpent*; *The Lying Days*; *Occasion for Loving*.]

895. Neville, Jill. "In Black and White." *Harpers & Queen* Nov.: 297-298. [Briefly mentions *The Late Bourgeois World*; *The Conservationist*; *The Lying Days*; *Occasion for Loving*.]

1974. 896. Haugh, Robert F. *Nadine Gordimer*. Twayne's World Author Series No. 315. New York: Twayne. Extr. in *Contemporary Literary Criticism, Vol 18*. Ed. Sharon R. Gunston. Detroit: Gale, 1981: 184-187. ["Ah, Woe Is Me"; "The Amateurs"; "Another Part of the Sky"; "A Bit of Young Life"; "The Catch"; "Charmed Lives"; "Check Yes or No"; "The Defeated"; "Enemies"; "Face from Atlantis"; *Face to*

Face; *Friday's Footprint*; "The Gentle Art"; *A Guest of Honour*; "Happy Event"; "The Hour and the Years"; "Horn of Plenty"; "An Image of Success"; "Is There Nowhere Else Where We Can Meet?"; "The Kindest Thing to Do"; *The Late Bourgeois World*; "La Vie Bohème"; "Livingstone's Companions"; *Livingstone's Companions*; *The Lying Days*; "Monday Is Better than Sunday"; "No Place Like"; *Not for Publication*; *Occasion for Loving*; "Our Bovary"; "Out of Season"; "The Prisoner"; "A Satisfactory Settlement"; "Six Feet of the Country"; *Six Feet of the Country*; *The Soft Voice of the Serpent*; "A Style of Her Own"; "Tenants of the Last Tree-House"; "A Third Presence"; "The Train from Rhodesia"; "The Umbilical Cord"; "A Watcher of the Dead"; "Which New Era Would That Be?"; "The White Goddess and the Mealie Question"; *A World of Strangers*; "Why Haven't You Written."]

1974. 897. Magarey, Kevin. "Cutting the Jewel: Facets of Art in Nadine Gordimer's Short Stories." *Southern Review* (7.1): 3-28. Repr. in *Critical Essays on Nadine Gordimer*: 45-74. ["The Soft Voice of the Serpent"; "The Catch"; "Check Yes or No"; "A Style of Her Own"; "Message in a Bottle"; "Friday's Footprint"; briefly mentions *A Guest of Honour*; "Some Monday for Sure."]

1975. 898. Hope, Christopher. "Out of the Picture: The Novels of Nadine Gordimer." *London Magazine* (15.1): 49-55. [*The Lying Days*; *A World of Strangers*; *A Guest of Honour*; *The Conservationist*.]

899. O'Sheel, P. "Nadine Gordimer's *The Conservationist*." *World Literature Written in English* (14.2): 514-519.

900. *Swift, Kerry. "Gordimer: Critical Conscience of Our Society." *Sunday Times TV Times and Colour Magazine* (supp. to *Sunday Times*) 11 May: 19-21.

901. Wauthier, Claude. "Nadine Gordimer ou le refus de l'exil." *L'Afrique Littéraire et Artistique* (36): 12-14. [Briefly mentions *A World of Strangers*; *The Late Bourgeois World*; *Occasion for Loving*; *A Guest of Honour*; *The Conservationist*.]

1976.   902. Lomberg, Alan. "Withering into the Truth: The Romantic Realism of Nadine Gordimer." *English in Africa* (3.1): 1-12. Repr. in *Critical Essays on Nadine Gordimer*: 31-45. [*The Lying Days*; *The Late Bourgeois World*; *A World of Strangers*; *Occasion for Loving*; *A Guest of Honour*.]

1977.   903. Green, Robert J. "Nadine Gordimer: 'The Politics of Race.'" *World Literature Written in English* (16.2): 256-262. [*The Conservationist*; refers briefly to *A Guest of Honour*; *The Lying Days*; *The Late Bourgeois World*.]

904. Green, Robert J. "Nadine Gordimer's *A Guest of Honour*." *World Literature Written in English* (16.1): 55-66.

905. *Ogungbesan, Kolawole. "The Liberal Expatriate and African Politics: Nadine Gordimer's *A Guest of Honour*." *Nigerian Journal of the Humanities* (1.1): 29-41. *Repr. as "Nadine Gordimer's *A Guest of Honour*: Politics, Fiction and the Liberal Expatriate." *Southern Review* (12.2) 1979: 108-123.

906. Ogungbesan, Kolawole. "The Way Out of South Africa: Nadine Gordimer's *The Lying Days*." *Theoria* (49): 45-59. Repr. in *Ba Shiru* (9.1&2) 1978: 48-62.

1978.   907. Cooke, John. "African Landscapes: The World of Nadine Gordimer." *World Literature Today* (52.4): 533-538. [*The Lying Days*; "Is There Nowhere Else Where We Can Meet?"; "The Bridegroom"; "The Life of the Imagination"; *A World of Strangers*; *Occasion for Loving*; *The Black Interpreters*; *A Guest of Honour*; *The Conservationist*.]

908. Fido, Elaine. "*A Guest of Honour*: A Feminine View of Masculinity." *World Literature Written in English* (17.1): 30-37. Repr. in *Critical Essays on Nadine Gordimer*: 97-104.

909. *Nazareth, Peter. "The White Stranger in a Modest Place of Honour." *The Third World Writer: His Social Responsibility*. Nairobi: Kenya Literature Bureau.

910. *Ogungbesan, Kolawole. "Nadine Gordimer's *The Conservationist*: A Touch of Death." *International Fiction Review* (5): 109-115.

911. Ogungbesan, Kolawole. "Nadine Gordimer's *The Late Bourgeois World*: Love in Prison." *Ariel* (9.1): 31-49.

1978. 912. Parker, Kenneth. "Nadine Gordimer and the Pitfalls of Liberalism." *The South African Novel in English: Essays in Criticism and Society*. Ed. Parker. New York: Africana. London: Macmillan: 114-130. [*A World of Strangers*; *Occasion for Loving*; *The Late Bourgeois World*.]

913. Wade, Michael. *Nadine Gordimer*. Modern African Writers Series. London: Evans. [*The Lying Days; A World of Strangers*; *Occasion for Loving*; *The Late Bourgeois World*; *A Guest of Honour*; *The Conservationist*.]

914. Wade, Michael. "Nadine Gordimer and Europe-in-Africa." *The South African Novel in English: Essays in Criticism and Society*: 131-163. [*A Guest of Honour*, briefly mentions *The Late Bourgeois World*; *The Lying Days*; *A World of Strangers*; *Occasion for Loving*.] [Abbr. from PhD diss.]

1979. 915. Anniah Gowda, H. H. "The Design and the Technique in Nadine Gordimer's *The Conservationist*." *The Literary Half-Yearly* (20.2): 3-10. [Also mentions *The Lying Days*; *A World of Strangers*; *Occasion for Loving*; *The Late Bourgeois World*; *A Guest of Honour*.]

916. Green, Robert. "Nadine Gordimer's *A World of Strangers*: Strains in South African Liberalism." *English Studies in Africa* (22.1): 45-54. Repr. in *Critical Essays on Nadine Gordimer*: 74-86. Longer version given as "Literature and Political History: The Case of Gordimer's *A World of Strangers*." *Chancellor College Staff Seminar Paper, No. 1*. U of Malawi.

1980. 917. Christie, Sarah; Geoffrey Hutchings and Don Maclennan. "Nadine Gordimer: *The Late Bourgeois World* (1966)." *Perspectives on South African Fiction*. Johannesburg: Donker: 145-157.

918. Ogungbesan, Kolawole. "Reality in Nadine Gordimer's *A World of Strangers*." *English Studies: A Journal of English Language and Literature* (61.2): 142-155.

919. *Smith, Rowland. "Living for the Future: Nadine Gordimer's *Burger's Daughter*." *World Literature Written in English* (19.2): 163-173.

1980.   920. Wettenhall, Irene. "Liberalism and Radicalism in South Africa since 1948: Nadine Gordimer's Fiction." *New Literature Review* (8): 36-44. [*A World of Strangers*; *Occasion for Loving*; *The Lying Days*; *The Late Bourgeois World*; *A Guest of Honour.*]

921. Wilhelm, Peter. "Savage Fiction." *The Bloody Horse* (2): 89-93. [*Burger's Daughter.*]

1981.   922. Clingman, Stephen. "History from the Inside: The Novels of Nadine Gordimer." *Journal of Southern African Studies* (7.2): 165-193. [*The Lying Days*; *A World of Strangers*; *Occasion for Loving*; *The Late Bourgeois World*; *A Guest of Honour*; *The Conservationist*; *Burger's Daughter.*]

923. Daymond, Margaret. "Disintegration, Isolation, Compassion." *The Bloody Horse* (4): 91-94. [*A Soldier's Embrace*; "Town and Country Lovers"; "Siblings"; "A Need for Something Sweet"; "A Soldier's Embrace"; briefly mentions "Time Did"; "A Hunting Accident"; "Oral History"; "Is There Nowhere Else Where We Can Meet?"; "The Catch"; "The Life of the Imagination"; "A Company of Laughing Faces"; "Rain-Queen"; "A Chip of Glass Ruby"; "Something for the Time Being."]

924. *De Santana, H. "Sensing the Earthquakes in Society." *Maclean's* (94): 21-22.

925. Githii, Ethel W. "Nadine Gordimer's *Selected Stories*." *Critique: Studies in Modern Fiction* (22.3): 45-54. ["The Soft Voice of the Serpent"; "The Catch"; "Horn of Plenty"; "The Kindest Thing to Do"; "A Commonplace Story"; "La Vie Bohème"; "Ah, Woe Is Me"; "The Train from Rhodesia"; "A Present for a Good Girl"; "A Bit of Young Life"; "Is There Nowhere Else Where We Can Meet?"; *A World of Strangers.*]

926. Green, Robert. "Nadine Gordimer's *Burger's Daughter*: Censors and Authors, Narrators and Narratees." Paper delivered at a conference on "Literature and Society in Southern Africa", Centre for Southern African Studies, U of York, 8-11 Sept. Also delivered as *Chancellor College Staff Seminar Paper, No. 16.* U of Malawi.

927. Haarhoff, D. "White Africans: Nadine Gordimer's *A Guest of Honour*." *Logos* (1.1): 13-14.

1981. 928. Moss, Rose. "Hand in Glove: Nadine Gordimer: South African Writer." *African Writing Today.* Ed. Peter Nazareth. Hamilton, New Zealand: Outrigger: 106-122. Special issue of *Pacific Moana Quarterly* (6.3/4). ["Six Feet of the Country"; "Happy Event"; "Enemies"; *The Lying Days*; *A World of Strangers*; *Occasion for Loving*; *The Conservationist*.]

929. Newman, Judie. "Gordimer's *The Conservationist*: 'That Book of Unknown Signs.'" *Critique: Studies in Modern Fiction* (22.3): 31-44. Rev. as "Realism Deconstructed" in *Nadine Gordimer*. Newman. Contemporary Writers Series. London: Routledge, 1988: 55-67.

930. Roberts, Sheila. "South African Censorship and the Case of *Burger's Daughter.*" *World Literature Written in English* (20.1): 41-48.

931. Taylor, Jane. "Nadine Gordimer: Prophet of Black Revolution." *Sunday Times Magazine* (supp. to *Sunday Times*) 30 Aug.: 16, 18, 21, 43. [Profile based on interview; *July's People*.]

1982. 932. Cooke, John. "Out of the Garden: Nadine Gordimer's Novels." *Design and Intent in African Literature.* Ed. David F. Dorsey, Phanuel A. Egejuru and Stephen H. Arnold. Washington: Three Continents: 17-27. [*The Lying Days, Occasion for Loving, The Conservationist*.]

933. Gardner, Susan. "Still Waiting for the Great Feminist Novel: Nadine Gordimer's *Burger's Daughter.*" *Hecate* (8.1): 61-76. Rev. version of paper "Nadine Gordimer's *Burger's Daughter*: A 'Metapatriarchal' Novel?" presented at English Department Seminar, U of Natal, Durban, May.

934. Heinemann, Margot. "*Burger's Daughter*: The Synthesis of Revelation." *The Uses of Fiction: Essays on the Modern Novel in Honour of Arnold Kettle.* Ed. Douglas Jefferson and Graham Martin. Milton Keynes: Open UP: 181-197.

935. Holland, Roy. "The Critical Writing of Nadine Gordimer." *Communiqué* (7.2): 7-37. [*The Black Interpreters*; "South Africa: Towards a Desk Drawer Literature"; "Origins and Directions in African Literature"; "White Proctorship and Black Disinvolvement"; "Some Political Novels in Africa";

"English Language Literature and Politics in South Africa"; "Some Notes on African Writing"; "Themes"; *A Guest of Honour.*]

1982.   936. Hughes, Bren. *"Burger's Daughter,* and Literary Studies in Southern Africa." *The AUETSA Papers 1982*: 260-274. Proc. of a conference of the Association of University English Teachers of Southern Africa, U of Natal, June/July.

937. Mutch, Ronnie. "Growing Up with Gordimer." *The Literary Review* Jan.: 44-45. [*The Lying Days; Burger's Daughter; July's People.*]

938. Rhedin, Folke. "Nadine Gordimer's Novels." *Report of Workshop on World Literatures Written in English outside Great Britain and the USA.* Umeå Papers in English No. 2. Ed. Raoul Granqvist. Umeå, Sweden: Dept. of English, U of Umeå: 45-48.

939. Richards, Antonia. "Nadine Gordimer." Letter. *The Literary Review* Feb. [Response to Ronnie Mutch's article "Growing Up With Gordimer" in *The Literary Review* Jan.: 44-45.]

940. Van Donge, Jan Kees. "Nadine Gordimer's *A Guest of Honour.* A Failure to Understand Zambian Society." *Journal of Southern African Studies* (9.1): 74-92. [Orig. paper "Fiction, Reality, Truth and Falsehood: Nadine Gordimer's *A Guest of Honour.* A Failure to Understand Zambian Society" presented at a conference on "Literature and Society in Southern Africa", Centre for Southern African Studies, U of York, 8-11 Sept., 1981.

[1983.]   941. Adam, Heribert. *Reflections on Gordimer's Interregnum.* Occasional Papers Series 1. Bellville: Centre for Research on Africa, U of Western Cape. Repr. as "Reflections on Gordimer's 'Interregnum.'" *Indicator South Africa: Perspectives* (1.3) 1984: 14-16. [Response to Gordimer's "Living in the Interregnum." *New York Review of Books* 20 Jan., 1983: 21-22, 24-29.]

1983.   942. Bailey, Paul. Introduction. *Occasion for Loving.* London: Virago: vii-x.

943. Bailey, Paul. Introduction. *The Lying Days.* London: Virago: xi-xiv.

1983. 944. Driver, Dorothy. "Nadine Gordimer: The Politicization of Women." *The AUETSA Papers 1983*. Proc. of a conference of the Association of University English Teachers of Southern Africa, Rhodes U, July. Pub. in *English in Africa* (10.2): 29-54. Repr. in *Critical Essays on Nadine Gordimer*. 180-204. [*The Lying Days*; *A World of Strangers*; *Occasion for Loving*; *The Late Bourgeois World*; *A Guest of Honour*; *The Conservationist*; *Burger's Daughter*; *July's People*; "The Smell of Death and Flowers"; "Six Feet of the Country"; "Friday's Footprint"; "The Life of the Imagination"; "Rain-Queen"; "The Train from Rhodesia"; "The Bridegroom"; "An Intruder"; "Happy Event"; "Which New Era Would That Be?"; "A City of the Dead, A City of the Living".] [Pilot version presented as "Nadine Gordimer's Women: The Place Where Politics Occur" at the English Association, Cape Town; also presented at The Africa Seminar Programme, Centre for African Studies, U of Cape Town.]

945. Heywood, Christopher. *Nadine Gordimer*. Writers and Their Work, No 281. Windsor: Profile. Extr. in *Contemporary Literary Criticism, Vol 33*. Ed. Daniel G. Marowski and Jean C. Stine. Detroit: Gale, 1985: 182-183. [*The Lying Days*; *A World of Strangers*; *Occasion for Loving*; *The Late Bourgeois World*; *A Guest of Honour*; *The Conservationist*; *Burger's Daughter*; *July's People*; "Some Monday for Sure"; "A Chip of Glass Ruby"; "Which New Era Would That Be?"; "Not for Publication"; "Africa Emergent"; "The African Magician"; "The Bridegroom"; *The Black Interpreters*.]

946. JanMohamed, Abdul R. "Nadine Gordimer: The Degeneration of the Great South African Lie." *Manichean Aesthetics: The Politics of Literature in Colonial Africa*. Amherst: U of Massachusetts P: 79-149; 291-294. Extr. as "The Degeneration of the Great South African Lie: *Occasion for Loving*" in *Critical Essays on Nadine Gordimer*. 90-96. ["Is There Nowhere Else Where We Can Meet?"; *The Lying Days*; *A World of Strangers*; *Occasion for Loving*; *The Late Bourgeois World*; *A Guest of Honour*; *The Conservationist*; *Burger's Daughter*; *July's People*.]

1983.   947. King, Michael. "Race and History in the Stories of Nadine Gordimer." *Africa Insight* (13.3): 222-226. ["The Amateurs"; "Ah, Woe Is Me"; "Six Feet of the Country"; "Something for the Time Being"; "The Smell of Death and Flowers"; "Is There Nowhere Else Where We Can Meet?"; "Monday Is Better than Sunday"; "Horn of Plenty"; "Some Monday for Sure"; "A Chip of Glass Ruby"; "The Pet"; "Open House"; "Africa Emergent"; "Town and Country Lovers"; *A Guest of Honour; Occasion for Loving.*]

948. Roberts, Sheila. "Nadine Gordimer's 'Family of Women.'" *Theoria* (60): 45-57. Repr. in *Critical Essays on Nadine Gordimer:* 167-179. [*The Lying Days; Occasion for Loving; The Late Bourgeois World; Burger's Daughter.*]

949. Thorpe, Michael. "The Motif of the Ancestor in *The Conservationist.*" *Research in African Literatures* (14.2): 184-192. Repr. in *Critical Essays on Nadine Gordimer:* 116-123.

1984.   950. *Adams, Adrian. "La valise dans le cercueil: L'Afrique et l'avenir des Européens dans le romans de Nadine Gordimer." *Cahiers d'études africaines* (24.3): 363-370. *Repr. in *Nouvelles du Sud* (5) 1986: 113-122.

951. Bailey, Nancy. "Living without the Future: Nadine Gordimer's *July's People.*" *World Literature Written in English* (24.2): 215-224.

952. Boyers, Robert. "Public and Private: On *Burger's Daughter.*" *Salmagundi* (62): 62-92.

953. Clingman, Stephen. "Multi-Racialism, or *A World of Strangers.*" *Salmagundi* (62): 32-61. Rev. as "Social Commitment: *A World of Strangers*" in *The Novels of Nadine Gordimer: History from the Inside.* Clingman. Johannesburg: Ravan, 1986: 45-71.

954. Clingman, Stephen. "Writing in a Fractured Society: The Case of Nadine Gordimer." *Literature and Society in South Africa.* Ed. Landeg White and Tim Couzens. London: Longman: 161-174. [Orig. paper presented at a conference on "Literature and Society in Southern Africa", Centre for Southern African Studies, U of York, 8-11 Sept., 1981.] Rev. as "Deep History" in *The Novels of Nadine Gordimer:*

History from the Inside: 205-222. [*The Conservationist*; *A World of Strangers*; *Occasion for Loving*; *Burger's Daughter*; *The Lying Days*; *July's People*.]

1984. 955. Daymond, M. J. "*Burger's Daughter*. A Novel's Reliance on History." *Momentum: On Recent South African Writing.* Ed. Daymond, J. U. Jacobs and Margaret Lenta. Pietermaritzburg: U of Natal P: 159-170.

956. *De Angelis, Maria Pia. "Nadine Gordimer: Impegno/ Impasse del 'White Liberal.'" *Quaderni di Filologia Germanica della Facolta di Lettere e Filosofia dell'Universita di Bologna* (3): 71-88.

957. Goodheart, Eugene. "The Claustral World of Nadine Gordimer." *Salmagundi* (62): 108-117. [*Occasion for Loving*; *A Guest of Honour*; *The Conservationist*; *July's People*.]

958. Hardwick, Elizabeth. "Somebody Out There." *New York Review of Books* 16 Aug.: 3-4, 6-7. ["Something Out There"; *The Conservationist*; *Burger's Daughter*, *July's People*.]

959. "Nadine Gordimer: *Some Monday for Sure*." *A Teacher's Guide to African Literature: Prose Texts*. Comp. H. L. B. Moody, Elizabeth Gunner and Edward Finnegan. London: Macmillan: 144-148.

960. Smith, Rowland. "Masters and Servants: Nadine Gordimer's *July's People* and the Themes of Her Fiction." *Salmagundi* (62): 93-107. Repr. in *Critical Essays on Nadine Gordimer*: 140-152. [*July's People*; briefly mentions "Is There Nowhere Else Where We Can Meet?"; *The Conservationist*; *The Late Bourgeois World*; "Ah, Woe Is Me"; *Occasion for Loving*; "Africa Emergent"; *Burger's Daughter*.]

961. Wieseltier, Leon. "Afterword." *Salmagundi* (62): 193-196. ["Something Out There."]

1985. 962. Clingman, Stephen. "Introduction to *History from the Inside: The Novels of Nadine Gordimer*." *The AUETSA Papers 1985*. Proc. of a conference of the Association of University English Teachers of Southern Africa, U of Cape Town, July. Pub. as "Introduction: History from the Inside" in *The Novels of Nadine Gordimer: History from the Inside*: 1-20.

1985. 963. Clingman, Stephen. "Writing Out There." *English Academy Review 3*: 191-201. [*Something Out There*; "At the Rendezvous of Victory"; "Something Out There"; "A City of the Dead, A City of the Living"; "Crimes of Conscience"; "Letter from His Father"; "Sins of the Third Age"; "Rags and Bones"; "Terminal"; "A Correspondence Course"; "Blinder"; "Is There Nowhere Else Where We Can Meet?"; *The Lying Days*; *A World of Strangers*; *July's People*; *The Late Bourgeois World*; *Burger's Daughter*; *The Conservationist*.] [Modified version of a paper "Reading *Something Out There*" presented at the launch of *Something Out There* by Ravan Press in 1984.]

964. Cooke, John. *The Novels of Nadine Gordimer: Private Lives/Public Landscapes*. Baton Rouge: Louisiana State UP. Extr. as "Landscapes Inhabited in Imagination: *A Guest of Honour*" in *Critical Essays on Nadine Gordimer*: 104-116. [*The Lying Days*; *Occasion for Loving*; *Burger's Daughter*; *A Guest of Honour*; *July's People*.]

965. *David, Catherine. "Nadine Gordimer contre les privileges." *Le nouvel Observateur* 28 June-4 July: 68.

966. Eckstein, Barbara. "Pleasure and Joy: Political Activism in Nadine Gordimer's Short Stories." *World Literature Today* (59.3): 343-346. ["Is There Nowhere Else Where We Can Meet?"; "The Smell of Death and Flowers"; "A Soldier's Embrace"; "A Chip of Glass Ruby"; "Something Out There."]

967. Greenstein, Susan M. "Miranda's Story: Nadine Gordimer and the Literature of Empire." *Novel: A Forum on Fiction* (18.3): 227-242. [*Burger's Daughter*; *July's People*.]

968. *Leeuwenburg, Rina. "Nadine Gordimer's *Burger's Daughter*: Why Does Rosa Go Back?" *New Literature Review* (14): 23-31. [Orig. paper presented at African Studies Association of Australia and the South Pacific Conference, Melbourne U.]

969. "Nadine Gordimer 1923- ." *Contemporary Literary Criticism, Vol 33*. Ed. Daniel G. Marowski and Jean C. Stine. Detroit: Gale: 176.

970. Newman, Judie. "Prospero's Complex: Race and Sex in Nadine Gordimer's *Burger's Daughter*." *Journal of Commonwealth Literature* (20.1): 81-99. Repr. in *Critical*

Essays on Nadine Gordimer. 124-140. Rev. and exp. to include comments on *July's People* as "Prospero's Complex" in *Nadine Gordimer.* Contemporary Writers Series: 68-92. [Orig. paper "Prospero's Complex: Race and Sex in *Burger's Daughter*" presented at a conference on "History and Ideology of Anglo-Saxon Racial Attitudes, c 1870-1970", Research Unit on Ethnic Relations, U of Aston in Birmingham, 13-15 Sept., 1982.]

1985. 971. Ngara, Emmanuel. "The Dilemma of a South African Liberal: Nadine Gordimer's *The Late Bourgeois World.*" *Art and Ideology in the African Novel: A Study of the Influence of Marxism on African Writing.* London: Heinemann: 99-107.

972. Ngara, Emmanuel. "Liberalism and Realism: Nadine Gordimer." *Art and Ideology in the African Novel*: 110.

973. Smyer, Richard I. "Africa in the Fiction of Nadine Gordimer." *Ariel* (16.2): 15-29. [*A World of Strangers*; *Occasion for Loving*; *The Soft Voice of the Serpent*; *Six Feet of the Country*; *A Guest of Honour*; *The Conservationist*; *The Lying Days*; *Burger's Daughter*; *A Soldier's Embrace*; *July's People*; *Not for Publication*; *Friday's Footprint*; "Livingstone's Companions"; "The Defeated"; "Charmed Lives"; "La Vie Bohème"; "The Hour and the Years"; "One Whole Year, and Even More"; "For Dear Life"; "Is There Nowhere Else Where We Can Meet?"; "The Worst Thing of All"; "A Company of Laughing Faces"; "The Bridegroom"; "The African Magician"; "The Talisman"; "Native Country"; "Vital Statistics"; "The White Goddess and the Mealie Question"; "Town and Country Lovers *One*"; "Siblings"; "The Termitary"; "The Path of the Moon's Dark Fortnight"; "Six Feet of the Country"; "Horn of Plenty."]

974. Smyer, Richard I. "Risk, Frontier, and Interregnum in the Fiction of Nadine Gordimer." *Journal of Commonwealth Literature* (20.1): 68-80. [*The Lying Days*; *A Guest of Honour*; *A World of Strangers*; *Occasion for Loving*; *The Conservationist*; *Burger's Daughter*; *July's People*; "The Life of the Imagination"; refers briefly to "The Bride of Christ"; "The Worst Thing of All"; "The Smell of Death and Flowers";

"The Need for Something Sweet"; "Town and Country Lovers *Two*"; "Open House"; "The Night the Favourite Came Home."]

1985.   975.   Toolan, Michael. "Taking Hold of Reality: Politics and Style in Nadine Gordimer." *ACLALS Bulletin* (7.1): 76-88. [*The Conservationist*; "A Correspondence Course"; briefly mentions *July's People*; "Something Out There"; "Some Monday for Sure"; "Livingstone's Companions"; "The Bride of Christ"; "A City of the Dead, A City of the Living."]

976.   Viola, André. "Conservateurs, progressistes et révolutionnaires dans les romans d'André Brink et de Nadine Gordimer." *L'Afrique Littéraire* (75): 69-89. [*The Late Bourgeois World*; *The Conservationist*; *July's People*; *The Lying Days*; *Occasion for Loving*; *A World of Strangers*; *A Guest of Honour*; *Burger's Daughter*; "A Chip of Glass Ruby"; "Some Monday for Sure"; *Something Out There*.]

1986.   977.   Clingman, Stephen. *The Novels of Nadine Gordimer: History from the Inside*. Johannesburg: Ravan; London: Allen. Chapter 7 "Deep History" repr. in *Critical Essays on Nadine Gordimer*: 205-222. [*The Lying Days*; *A World of Strangers*; *Occasion for Loving*; *The Late Bourgeois World*; *A Guest of Honour*; *The Conservationist*; *Burger's Daughter*; *July's People*; *Face to Face*; *The Soft Voice of the Serpent*; "A Commonplace Story"; "A Lion on the Freeway"; "A Soldier's Embrace"; "Africa Emergent"; "Ah, Woe Is Me"; "Come Again Tomorrow"; "Is There Nowhere Else Where We Can Meet?"; "Monday Is Better than Sunday"; "Oral History"; "Six Feet of the Country"; "Sweet Dreams Selection"; "The Amateurs"; "The Battlefield at No. 29"; "The Defeated"; "The Train from Rhodesia."]

978.   De Kock, Leon. "Gordimer, Nadine." *Contemporary Novelists*. Ed. D. L. Kirkpatrick and James Vinson. Fourth ed. New York: St. Martin's: 355-366. [Briefly mentions *The Lying Days*; *Occasion for Loving*; *The Late Bourgeois World*; *A World of Strangers*; *A Guest of Honour*; *The Conservationist*; *July's People*.]

1986. 979. Nowak, Helena. "Soviet Literary Critics on Nadine Gordimer." *Contrast 62* (16.2): 65-68. [*A World of Strangers*; *Occasion for Loving*; *The Soft Voice of the Serpent*; *Six Feet of the Country*; *Friday's Footprint*; *Not for Publication*.]

980. Schroth, Evelyn. "Nadine Gordimer's 'A Chip of Glass Ruby': A Commentary on Apartheid Society." *Journal of Black Studies* (17.1): 85-90.

981. Trump, Martin. "The Short Fiction of Nadine Gordimer." *Research in African Literatures* (17.3): 341-369. ["Is There Nowhere Else Where We Can Meet?"; "The Train from Rhodesia"; "Six Feet of the Country"; "Good Climate, Friendly Inhabitants"; "Something for the Time Being"; "Some Monday for Sure"; "Open House"; "Africa Emergent"; *A Soldier's Embrace*; *Something Out There*.]

982. Wade, Michael. "Nadine Gordimer." *Essays on Contemporary Post-Colonial Fiction*. Ed. Hedwig Bock and Albert Wertheim. München: Huebeck: 115-148. [*The Lying Days*; *A World of Strangers*; *Occasion for Loving*; *The Late Bourgeois World*; *A Guest of Honour*; *The Conservationist*; *Burger's Daughter*; *July's People*.]

1987. 983. Arnold, Rainer. "Nadine Gordimer: *Julys Leute*." *Weimarer Beiträge: Zeitschrift für Literaturwissenschaft, Ästhetik und Kulturtheorie* (33.1): 130-138.

984. *Burton, Robert S. "The Composition of Identity in Nadine Gordimer's *Burger's Daughter*." *Notes on Contemporary Literature* (17.5): 6-7.

985. Gordon, Jennifer. "Dreams of a Common Language: Nadine Gordimer's *July's People*." *Women in African Literature Today (African Literature Today 15)*. Ed. Eldred Durosimi Jones. London: Currey; Trenton, NJ: Africa: 102-108.

986. Hagena, Antje. *Nadine Gordimers neuere Romane: Eine Untersuchung in Thematik und Erzählstrategie*. Essen: Eule. [*The Conservationist*; *Burger's Daughter*; *July's People*.]

1987.   987. Jacobs, J. U. "Living Space and Narrative Space in Nadine Gordimer's *Something Out There.*" *The AUETSA Papers 1987.* Proc. of a conference of the Association of University English Teachers of Southern Africa, Rhodes U, July. Pub. in *English in Africa* (14.2): 31-43.

988. Lamarra, Annamaria. "Nadine Gordimer." *Belfagor: Rassegna di varia Umanita* 30 Nov. (42.6): 657-668.

989. Liscio, Lorraine. *"Burger's Daughter:* Lighting a Torch in the Heart of Darkness." *Modern Fiction Studies* (33.2): 245-261.

990. *Llosa, Maria Vargos. "Gordimer's Dilemma." *Vanity Fair* May: 40-42.

991. *Mariani, Gigliola Sacerdoti. "L'impegno politico di Nadine Gordimer, 'Africa bianca.'" *Nuova antologia* (122.2161): 134-144. [*A Guest of Honour.*]

992. Viola, André. "Communication and Liberal Double Bind in *July's Children* [sic] by Nadine Gordimer." *Commonwealth Essays and Studies* (9.2): 52-58.

1988.   993. *Alexander, Peter F. "Political Attitudes in Nadine Gordimer's Fiction." *AUMLA: Journal of the Australasian Universities' Language and Literature Association* (70): 220-238.

994. Donaghy, Mary. "Double Exposure: Narrative Perspective in Gordimer's *A Guest of Honour.*" *Ariel* (19.4): 19-32.

995. Gray, Stephen. "Gordimer's *A World of Strangers* as Memory." *Ariel* (19.4): 11-16. Repr. in *Critical Essays on Nadine Gordimer:* 86-90.

996. *Green, Robert. "From *The Lying Days* to *July's People*: The Novels of Nadine Gordimer." *Journal of Modern Literature* (14.4): 543-563. *Repr. as "The Novels of Nadine Gordimer." *Perspectives on South African English Literature.* Ed. Michael Chapman, Colin Gardner and Es'kia Mphahlele. Johannesburg: Donker, 1992: 272-291. [*The Lying Days*; *A World of Strangers*; *Occasion for Loving*; *The Late Bourgeois World*; *A Guest of Honour*; *The Conservationist*; *Burger's Daughter*; *July's People.*]

1988. 997. Newman, Judie. *Nadine Gordimer.* Contemporary Writers Series. London: Routledge. [*The Lying Days*; *A World of Strangers*; *Occasion for Loving*; *The Late Bourgeois World*; *A Guest of Honour*; *The Conservationist*; *Burger's Daughter*; *July's People*; *A Sport of Nature.*]

998. Peck, Richard. "What's a Poor White to Do? White South African Options in *A Sport of Nature.*" *Ariel* (19.4): 75-93. Repr. in *Critical Essays on Nadine Gordimer*: 153-167. [*Burger's Daughter*; *A Sport of Nature.*]

999. Smith, Rowland. "Inside and Outside: Nadine Gordimer and the Critics." *Ariel* (19.4): 3-9. [Introduction to special issue of *Ariel* on Nadine Gordimer in which Smith reviews the contributions.]

1000. Temple-Thurston, Barbara. "Madam and Boy: A Relationship of Shame in Gordimer's *July's People.*" *World Literature Written in English* (28.1): 51-58.

1001. Viola, André. "The Irony of Tenses in Nadine Gordimer's *The Conservationist.*" *Ariel* (19.4): 45-54.

1002. Visel, Robin. "A Half-Colonization: The Problem of the White Colonial Woman Writer." *Kunapipi* (10.3): 39-45. [*The Lying Days*; *Burger's Daughter.*]

1003. Visel, Robin. "Othering the Self: Nadine Gordimer's Colonial Heroines." *Ariel* (19.4): 33-42. [*Burger's Daughter*; *The Conservationist*; *Occasion for Loving*; *The Late Bourgeois World*; *July's People*; *A Sport of Nature.*]

1989. 1004. Abrahams, Lionel. "Revolution, Style and Morality: Reflections around Nadine Gordimer's *A Sport of Nature.*" *Sesame* (12): 27-30.

1005. *Engle, Lars. "The Political Uncanny: The Novels of Nadine Gordimer." *Yale Journal of Criticism: Interpretation in the Humanities* (2.2): 101-127. [*Burger's Daughter*; *July's People.*]

1006. Gray, Rosemary. "Nadine Gordimer's *July's People*: An Apocalyptic Vision." *Nouvelles du Sud* (12): 87-101.

1007. *July's People by Nadine Gordimer.* Guidelines Study Aids. Craighall, SA: Guidelines.

1989.   1008. Link, Viktor. "The African Magician and His Western Audience: Norms in Nadine Gordimer's 'The African Magician.'" *Commonwealth Essays and Studies* (11.2): 104-109.

1009. Maclennan, Don. "The Vacuum Pump: The Fiction of Nadine Gordimer." *Upstream* (7.1): 30-33. [Briefly mentions *A World of Strangers*; *Occasion for Loving*; *The Late Bourgeois World*; *The Conservationist*; *Burger's Daughter*.]

1010. Meese, Elizabeth A. "The Political Is the Personal: The Construction of Identity in Nadine Gordimer's *Burger's Daughter*." *Feminism and Institutions: Dialogues on Feminist Theory*. Ed. Linda Kauffman. Cambridge, MA: Blackwell: 253-275.

1011. "Nadine Gordimer 1923- ." *Contemporary Literary Criticism, Vol 51*. Ed. Daniel G. Marowski and Roger Matuz. Detroit: Gale: 155-156.

1012. Parker, Kenneth. "Imagined Revolution: Nadine Gordimer's *A Sport of Nature*." *Women and Writing in South Africa: A Critical Anthology*. Ed. Cherry Clayton. Johannesburg: Heinemann: 209-223. Trans. as "Une révolution imaginaire: *A Sport of Nature*, de Nadine Gordimer." *Nouvelles du Sud* (12): 15-25.

1013. Peck, Richard. "One Foot before the Other into an Unknown Future: The Dialectic in Nadine Gordimer's *Burger's Daughter*." *World Literature Written in English* (29.1): 26-43.

1014. Radhakrishan, R. "Negotiating Subject Positions in an Uneven World." *Feminism and Institutions: Dialogues on Feminist Theory*: 276-290. [*Burger's Daughter*, also discusses Meese's article "The Political Is the Personal: The Construction of Identity in Nadine Gordimer's *Burger's Daughter*" in *Feminism and Institutions: Dialogues on Feminist Theory*: 253-275.]

1015. "Treasures of the Sea — Nadine Gordimer." *Stories South Africa: A Study Guide*. Craighall, SA: Guidelines: 21-23.

1989. 1016. Trump, Martin. "What Time Is This for a Woman? An Analysis of Nadine Gordimer's Short Fiction." *Women and Writing in South Africa*: 183-208. ["Is There Nowhere Else Where We Can Meet?"; "The Train from Rhodesia"; "Six Feet of the Country"; "The Smell of Death and Flowers"; "Good Climate, Friendly Inhabitants"; "Something for the Time Being"; "Some Monday for Sure"; "A Chip of Glass Ruby"; "Open House"; "A Soldier's Embrace."]

1017. Wagner, Kathrin. "'Both As Citizen and As a Woman?' Women and Politics in Some Gordimer Novels." Paper presented at the ACLALS Triennial Conference, Canterbury, Aug. To be pub. in *From Commonwealth to Post-Colonial: Critical Essays*. Ed. Anna Rutherford. Dangaroo Press, c. 1993. [*Burger's Daughter*; *July's People*; briefly mentions *The Conservationist*; *The Late Bourgeois World*; *A Sport of Nature*.]

1018. Ward, David. "Nadine Gordimer: The Novels." *Chronicles of Darkness*. London: Routledge: 112-135. [*The Lying Days*; *A World of Strangers*; *Occasion for Loving*; *The Late Bourgeois World*; *A Guest of Honour*; *The Conservationist*; *Burger's Daughter*; *July's People*; *A Sport of Nature*.]

1019. Ward, David. "Nadine Gordimer: The Short Stories." *Chronicles of Darkness*: 101-111. ["The Soft Voice of the Serpent"; "The Catch"; "The Kindest Thing to Do"; "A Company of Laughing Faces"; "Treasures of the Sea"; "Is There Nowhere Else Where We Can Meet?"; "A Hunting Accident"; "A Lion on the Freeway"; "Something Out There."]

1990. 1020. Cooper, Brenda. "New Criteria for an 'Abnormal Mutation'? An Evaluation of Gordimer's *A Sport of Nature*." *Rendering Things Visible: Essays on South African Literary Culture*. Ed. Martin Trump. Johannesburg: Ravan: 68-93.

1021. *Critical Essays on Nadine Gordimer*. Ed. Rowland Smith. Boston: Hall. [*Burger's Daughter*; *The Conservationist*; *The Essential Gesture*; *Face to Face*; *Friday's Footprint*; *A Guest of Honour*; *July's People*; *The Late Bourgeois World*; *Livingstone's Companions*; *The Lying Days*; *Not for Publication*; *Occasion for Loving*; *Selected Stories*; *Six Feet of the Country*; *The Soft Voice of the Serpent*; *The Soldier's*

Embrace; *Something Out There*; *A Sport of Nature*; *A World of Strangers*; "Living in the Interregnum"; "Relevance and Commitment"; "The African Magician"; "Ah, Woe Is Me"; "The Amateurs"; "Another Part of the Sky"; "At the Rendezvous of Victory"; "The Bridegroom"; "The Catch"; "Charmed Lives"; "Check Yes or No"; "A Chip of Glass Ruby"; "The Cicatrice"; "A City of the Dead, A City of the Living"; "Clowns in Clover"; "A Commonplace Story"; "The Defeated"; "The End of the Tunnel"; "Enemies"; "Friday's Footprint"; "The Gentle Art"; "Happy Event"; "An Image of Success"; "An Intruder"; "Is There Nowhere Else Where We Can Meet?"; "The Kindest Thing to Do"; "The Last Kiss"; "The Life of the Imagination"; "Message in a Bottle"; "Monday Is Better than Sunday"; "My First Two Women"; "Native Country"; "The Night the Favourite Came Home"; "Out of Season"; "Present for a Good Girl"; "Rags and Bones"; "Rain-Queen"; "Siblings"; "Sins of the Third Age"; "Six Feet of the Country"; "The Smell of Death and Flowers"; "The Soft Voice of the Serpent"; "Some Monday for Sure"; "Something Out There"; "A Style of Her Own"; "The Talisman"; "Tenants of the Last Tree-House"; "Terminal"; "A Thing of the Past"; "Through Time and Distance"; "Time Did"; "The Train from Rhodesia"; "A Watcher of the Dead"; "Which New Era Would That Be?"; "The Worst Thing of All."]

1990. 1022. Devoize, Jeanne. "Elements of Narrative Technique in Nadine Gordimer's 'Is There Nowhere Else Where We Can Meet?'" *Journal of the Short Story in English* (15): 11-16.

1023. Head, Dominic. "Positive Isolation and Productive Ambiguity in Nadine Gordimer's Short Stories." *Journal of the Short Story in English* (15): 17-30. ["The Catch"; "Some Monday for Sure"; *Selected Stories*; "Crimes of Conscience."]

1024. Lazar, Karen. "Feminism as 'Piffling'?: Ambiguities in Some of Nadine Gordimer's Short Stories." *Current Writing* (2): 101-116. ["The Third Presence"; "Happy Event"; "Good Climate, Friendly Inhabitants"; "Blinder"; "A Chip of Glass Ruby"; "An Intruder"; "The Termitary."]

1025. Link, Viktor. "The Unity of 'Something Out There.'" *Journal of the Short Story in English* (15): 31-40.

1990. 1026. Louvel, Liliane. "Divided Space, a Reading of Nadine Gordimer's Short Story 'The Termitary.'" *Journal of the Short Story in English* (15): 41-54.

1027. Mariën, Wim. "White Commitment in Africa. Decision-Making in Some of Gordimer's Novels." *Crisis and Conflict: Essays on Southern African Literature: Proceedings of the XIth Annual Conference on Commonwealth Literature and Language Studies in German-Speaking Countries, Aachen-Liège, 16—19 June, 1988.* Ed. Geoffrey V. Davis. Essen: Eule: 109-116. [*A Guest of Honour; Burger's Daughter.*]

1028. Neill, Michael. "Translating the Present: Language, Knowledge, and Identity in Nadine Gordimer's *July's People.*" *Journal of Commonwealth Literature* (25.1): 71-97.

1029. Newman, Judie. "Nadine Gordimer and the Naked Southern Ape: 'Something Out There.'" *Journal of the Short Story in English* (15): 55-74.

1030. Visser, Nicholas. "Beyond the Interregnum: A Note on the Ending of *July's People.*" *Rendering Things Visible: Essays on South African Literary Culture*: 61-67.

1031. Wagner, Kathrin M. "'History from the Inside'? Text and Subtext in Some Gordimer Novels." *Crisis and Conflict: Essays on Southern African Literature*: 89-107. [*The Late Bourgeois World; Burger's Daughter; July's People; The Conservationist; A Sport of Nature.*]

1032. Weinhouse, Linda. "The Deconstruction of Victory: Gordimer's *A Sport of Nature.*" *Research in African Literatures* (21.2): 91-100. [Also mentions *July's People.*]

1033. Wheeler, Kathleen. "Nadine Gordimer: Irony and the Politics of Style." *Journal of the Short Story in English* (15): 75-93. ["The Train from Rhodesia"; "Is There Nowhere Else Where We Can Meet?"; briefly mentions *Some Monday for Sure; Selected Stories.*]

1991. 1034. Gorak, Irene. "Libertine Pastoral: Nadine Gordimer's *The Conservationist.*" *Novel: A Forum on Fiction* (24.3): 241-256. [Also briefly mentions *A Sport of Nature; The Late Bourgeois World*; "Six Feet of the Country."]

1991. 1035. "Gordimer, Nadine 1923-." *Major 20th-Century Writers: Vol 2: E-K.* Ed. Bryan Ryan. Detroit: Gale: 1218-1223.

1036. Jacobs, J. U. "Nadine Gordimer's Intertextuality." *The AUETSA Papers.* Proc. of a conference of the Association of University English Teachers of Southern Africa, U of Fort Hare, July. [*Selected Stories*; *The Lying Days*; *A World of Strangers*; *Occasion for Loving*; *The Late Bourgeois World*; *Burger's Daughter*; *July's People*; *A Sport of Nature*; *My Son's Story*; *The Conservationist*; briefly mentions *A Guest of Honour*; *Something Out There*.]

1037. Kanga, Firdaus. "A Question of Black and White: Nadine Gordimer's Political Novels and Stories." *Times Literary Supplement* 11 Oct.: 14. [Briefly mentions "The Soft Voice of the Serpent"; *A World of Strangers*; *Occasion for Loving*; *A Sport of Nature*; *Burger's Daughter*; "The Ultimate Safari"; "The Journey"; "Teraloyna"; "Spoils"; "Home"; "The Moment before the Gun Went Off"; "Keeping Fit"; "Once upon a Time."]

1038. Kohler, Peter. "Gordimer's Son (or the Late Gordimer World)." *South African Literary Review* (1.2): 4-12. [*My Son's Story*.]

1039. Petersen, Kirsten Holst. "The Search for a Role for White Women in a Liberated South Africa: A Thematic Approach to the Novels of Nadine Gordimer." *Kunapipi* (13.1&2): 170-177. [*Burger's Daughter*; *A Sport of Nature*; briefly mentions *The Lying Days*; *A World of Strangers*; *The Late Bourgeois World*; *Occasion for Loving*; *The Conservationist*; *July's People*.]

1040. Rowe, Margaret Moan. "Mapping Away 'to Offer One's Self': Nadine Gordimer's *Burger's Daughter*." *Commonwealth Novel in English* (4.2): 45-54.

1041. Smith, Rowland. "Nadine Gordimer: Truth, Irony and Commitment." *International Literature in English: Essays on Modern Writers.* Ed. Robert L. Ross. New York: Garland: 171-180. [*Burger's Daughter*; *The Conservationist*; *A Guest of Honour*; *A Sport of Nature*; *July's People*; "Ah, Woe Is Me"; "The Train from Rhodesia"; "Is There Nowhere Else Where We Can Meet?"; "Something Out There."]

1991. 1042. Temple-Thurston, Barbara. "Nadine Gordimer: The Artist as *A Sport of Nature*." *Studies in Twentieth Century Literature* (15.1): 175-184.

1043. Van Gend, Cecily. "Nadine Gordimer." *The Cape Librarian* (35.10): 12-14.

1992. 1044. Becker, Jillian. "Nadine Gordimer's Politics." *Commentary* (93.2): 51-54.

1045. Beresford, David. "Caught in the Chains of Idealism." *The Guardian* 18 June: 25.

1046. Eckstein, Barbara J. "Nadine Gordimer: Nobel Laureate in Literature, 1991." *World Literature Today* (66.1): 7-10. ["Is There Nowhere Else Where We Can Meet?"; "Town and Country Lovers"; *A Sport of Nature*; *My Son's Story*; "Something for the Time Being"; *Burger's Daughter*; *The Conservationist*; *A Guest of Honour*; "A Soldier's Embrace"; "A City of the Dead, A City of the Living."]

1047. *King, Bruce Alvin. *The Later Fiction of Nadine Gordimer*. New York: St. Martin's.

1048. Lazar, Karen. "*Jump and Other Stories*: Gordimer's Leap into the 1990s: Gender and Politics in Her Latest Fiction." *Journal of Southern African Studies* (18.4): 783-802. ["Jump"; "Safe Houses"; "Amnesty"; "My Father Leaves Home"; "A Journey"; "Spoils"; "What Were You Dreaming?"; "Teraloyna"; "The Ultimate Safari"; "A Find"; "Once upon a Time"; "Keeping Fit"; "Comrades"; "Some Are Born to Sweet Delight"; "The Moment before the Gun Went Off"; Also mentions "A Chip of Glass Ruby"; "The Termitary"; "Good Climate, Friendly Inhabitants"; "The Intruder"; *A Guest of Honour*; *My Son's Story*; *July's People*; "Some Monday for Sure"; "The Gentle Art"; "Something Out There"; "Open House"; *The Conservationist*; "The Train from Rhodesia"; "Out of Season"; "Enemies"; *Burger's Daughter*; *A Sport of Nature*.]

1049. Lazar, Karen Ruth. "'Something Out There' /Something in There: Gender and Politics in Gordimer's Novella." *English in Africa* (19.1): 53-65. [Also mentions *Burger's Daughter*; *A Sport of Nature*.] [Orig. paper presented at a conference on "Women and Gender in Southern Africa", U of Natal, Durban, 30 Jan.-2 Feb. 1991.]

1992. 1050. Louvel, Liliane. "Nadine Gordimer's *My Son's Story* or the Experience of Fragmentation." *Commonwealth Essays and Studies* (14.2): 28-33.

1051. *Petterssen, Rose. "Towards a Decentralised Collective Identity: *The Late Bourgeois World* (1966), *The Conservationist* (1974)." [Paper presented at The Africa Seminar Programme, Centre for African Studies, U of Cape Town.]

1052. Smyer, Richard. "*A Sport of Nature*: Gordimer's Work in Progress." *Journal of Commonwealth Literature* (27.1): 71-86. [Also discusses *Burger's Daughter*; *July's People*; briefly mentions "The Smell of Death and Flowers"; "Something Out There"; *The Lying Days*.]

L. THESES

1956. 1053. Mphahlele, Ezekiel. "The Non-European Character in South African English Fiction." MA diss. UNISA.

1959. 1054. Van Zyl, John Andrew Fullard. "The Afrikaner Way of Life as Depicted in South African English Fiction." MA diss. U of the Orange Free State. [*The Lying Days*; *Face to Face*; *The Soft Voice of the Serpent*; "The Prisoner"; "The Umbilical Cord"; "The Smell of Death and Flowers."]

1960. 1055. Rossouw, Daniël Gerhardus. "The Poetic Image: A Critical Study of Its Functions, Varieties and Values in the Work of Representative Contemporary South African Writers in English." MA diss. U of the Orange Free State. [*The Lying Days*; *Six Feet of the Country*; *Face to Face*; "The Kindest Thing to Do"; "The Umbilical Cord"; "The Soft Voice of the Serpent"; "The Battlefield at No. 29"; "My First Two Women"; "A Present for a Good Girl"; "Happy Event"; "The Amateurs"; "Six Feet of the Country."]

1962. 1056. De Koker, Benjamin. "The Short Stories and Novels of Nadine Gordimer: A Critical Study." MA diss. Potchefstroom U for CHE. ["Which New Era Would That Be?"; "In the Beginning"; "Enemies"; "The Last of the Old-Fashioned Girls"; "A Bit of Young Life"; "Happy Event"; "The Umbilical Cord"; "Ah, Woe Is Me"; "The Amateurs"; "Monday Is Better than Sunday"; "No Luck To-Night"; "The Smell of Death and Flowers"; "Six Feet of the Country"; "The Defeated"; "Is There Nowhere Else Where We Can Meet?"; "An Image of Success"; "The Hour and the Years"; "The Last Kiss"; "A Present for a Good Girl"; "The Battlefield at No. 29"; *The Lying Days*; *A World of Strangers*.]

1962. 1057. Millar, Clive John. "The Contemporary South African Short Story in English (with Special Reference to the Work of Nadine Gordimer, Doris Lessing, Alan Paton, Jack Cope, Uys Krige, Dan Jacobson)." MA diss. U of Cape Town. ["Treasures of the Sea"; "The Talisman"; "A Present for a Good Girl"; "Another Part of the Sky"; "The Soft Voice of the Serpent"; "Happy Event"; "Enemies"; "The Night the Favourite Came Home"; "The Cicatrice"; "Out of Season"; "Friday's Footprint"; "Our Bovary"; "The Gentle Art"; "The End of the Tunnel"; "A Wand'ring Minstrel, I"; "The Hour and the Years"; "An Image of Success"; "Something for the Time Being"; "Ah, Woe Is Me"; "Is There Nowhere Else Where We Can Meet?"; "Which New Era Would That Be?"; "Face from Atlantis"; "The Path of the Moon's Dark Fortnight"; "A Bit of Young Life"; "Six Feet of the Country"; "Harry's Presence"; "Check Yes or No"; "Horn of Plenty"; "A Watcher of the Dead."]

1058. Roloff, Barbra Jean. "Nadine Gordimer: South African Novelist and Short Story Writer." MA diss. U of Texas. ["The Kindest Thing to Do"; "The Soft Voice of the Serpent"; "La Vie Bohème"; "Clowns in Clover"; "A Bit of Young Life"; "Out of Season"; "The Path of the Moon's Dark Fortnight"; "Little Willie"; "Check Yes or No"; *The Lying Days*; *A World of Strangers*; "Monday Is Better than Sunday"; "Ah, Woe Is Me"; "Six Feet of the Country"; "The Happy Event"; "Horn of Plenty"; "The Amateurs"; "The Smell of Death and Flowers"; "The Defeated"; "Which New Era Would That Be?"; "Another Part of the Sky"; "The Bridegroom"; "The Train from Rhodesia."]

1963. 1059. Rossouw, Daniël Gerhardus. "The Poetic Image in South African English Literature." D Litt diss. U of the Orange Free State. [Repr. of chapter in MA diss. with an additional section discussing *A World of Strangers*.]

1967.   1060.   *David, R. "South African Prose Fiction of the Past Two Decades (with Special Reference to Nadine Gordimer, Dan Jacobson and Alan Paton)." MA diss. U of Liverpool.

1969.   1061.   De Koker, Benjamin. "English Playwriting in South Africa 1900 - 1950: A Survey." PhD diss. U of Pretoria. ["The First Circle."]

    1062.   Essa, Ahmed. "Postwar South African Fiction in English: Abrahams, Paton, and Gordimer." PhD diss. U of Southern California. DAI 30(5): 2020A. ["The Soft Voice of the Serpent"; "Treasures of the Sea"; "Horn of Plenty"; "The Kindest Thing to Do"; "A Commonplace Story"; "Ah, Woe Is Me"; "The Defeated"; "The Train from Rhodesia"; "A Present for a Good Girl"; "Is There Nowhere Else Where We Can Meet?"; "La Vie Bohème"; "The Talisman"; "The Catch"; "The Pet"; "The Prisoner"; "Monday Is Better than Sunday"; *The Lying Days*; "Charmed Lives"; "Face from Atlantis"; "Our Bovary"; "Happy Event"; "A Company of Laughing Faces"; "Harry's Presence"; "Through Time and Distance"; "Clowns in Clover"; "Enemies"; "A Bit of Young Life"; "Out of Season"; "My First Two Women"; "The Path of the Moon's Dark Fortnight"; "Six Feet of the Country"; "Which New Era Would That Be?"; "The Bridegroom"; "The Gentle Art"; "The African Magician"; "One Whole Year, and Even More."]

    1063.   Ledbetter, Dorothy E. "The Theme of Isolation in the Short Stories of Nadine Gordimer." MA diss. San Diego State College. ["The Pet"; "My First Two Women"; "Horn of Plenty"; "The Path of the Moon's Dark Fortnight"; "Tenants of the Last Tree-House"; "A Company of Laughing Faces"; "The Bridegroom"; "The Train from Rhodesia"; "A Watcher of the Dead"; "Enemies"; "Through Time and Distance"; "Happy Event"; "The Catch"; "A Present for a Good Girl"; "The African Magician"; "Check Yes or No"; "Friday's Footprint."]

1973.   1064.   Wade, Michael. "The Liberal Tradition in South African Fiction in English." PhD diss. U of Sussex. [*The Lying Days*; "Which New Era Would That Be?"; *A World of Strangers*; "The Smell of Death and Flowers"; *Occasion for*

Loving; "Some Monday for Sure"; "The Train from Rhodesia"; "Is There Nowhere Else Where We Can Meet?"; *The Late Bourgeois World*; *A Guest of Honour*.]

1974. 1065. Wessels, Johannes Hermanus. "From Olive Schreiner to Nadine Gordimer: A Study of the Development of the South African Short Story in English." MA diss. U of the Orange Free State. ["The Train from Rhodesia"; "No Luck Tonight"; "The Last of the Old-Fashioned Girls"; "Is There Nowhere Else Where We Can Meet?"; "The Amateurs"; "The Battlefield at No. 29"; "The Catch"; "Ah, Woe Is Me"; "The Prisoner"; "A Present for a Good Girl"; "Which New Era Would That Be?"; "Horn of Plenty"; "A Wand'ring Minstrel, I"; "The Last Kiss"; "Friday's Footprint"; "Check Yes or No"; "A Company of Laughing Faces."]

1976. 1066. Cooke, John Wharton. "The Novels of Nadine Gordimer." PhD diss. Northwestern U. DAI 37(7) 1977: 4346A. [*The Lying Days*; *A World of Strangers*; *Occasion for Loving*; *The Late Bourgeois World*; *A Guest of Honour*; *The Conservationist*.]

1978. 1067. *Holland, R. W. H. "The Edge of Possibility: A Study of the Inter-Relations of Political, Religious and Existential Beliefs in the Writings of Alan Paton and Nadine Gordimer." M Phil diss. U of Sussex.

1068. Van Rooyen, Danielle Joan. "English-Language Fiction in South Africa from 1945 to 1960: A Survey of Trends, Influences and Cross-Relationships." MA diss. Rand Afrikaans U. [*The Soft Voice of the Serpent*; *Six Feet of the Country*; *The Lying Days*; *A World of Strangers*; "A Present for a Good Girl"; "Enemies"; "Happy Event"; "The Catch."]

1979. 1069. Sarvan, C. P. "Aspects of Freedom in Southern African Fiction: A Study of the Works of Olive Schreiner, Sarah Gertrude Millin, Doris Lessing and Nadine Gordimer." PhD diss. U of London (External). [*The Lying Days*; *A World of Strangers*; *Occasion for Loving*; *The Late Bourgeois World*; *A Guest of Honour*; *The Conservationist*; "The Defeated"; "The Prisoner"; "A Present for a Good Girl"; "A Style of Her Own"; "A Wand'ring Minstrel, I"; "A Company of Laughing Faces"; "A Train from Rhodesia"; "An Intruder"; "The Soft Voice of the Serpent"; "The Amateurs"; "Which New Era

Would That Be?"; "Abroad"; "The Pet"; "Horn of Plenty"; "Happy Event"; "Ah, Woe Is Me"; "Six Feet of the Country"; "The Smell of Death and Flowers"; "Something for the Time Being"; "A Chip of Glass Ruby"; "The African Magician"; "Inkalamu's Place"; "Is There Nowhere Else Where We Can Meet?"; "Good Climate, Friendly Inhabitants"; "The Bridegroom"; "The Catch."]

1980. 1070. Watson, Stephen. "The Liberal Ideology and Some English South African Novelists." MA diss. U of Cape Town. [*The Late Bourgeois World.*]

1982. 1071. Haarhoff, R. Dorian. "Aspects of the South African Novel in Independent Africa: The Background and Context of Key Works by Nadine Gordimer and Ezekiel Mphahlele." MA diss. Rand Afrikaans U. [*A Guest of Honour.*]

1983. 1072. Boyle, JoAnne Woodyard. "The International Novel: Aspects of Its Development in the Twentieth Century with Emphasis on the Work of Nadine Gordimer and V. S. Naipaul." PhD diss. U of Pittsburgh. DAI 45(2): 524A. [*A Guest of Honour; The Conservationist; Burger's Daughter.*]

1073. *Clingman, Stephen. "The Consciousness of History in the Novels of Nadine Gordimer." D Phil diss. Oxford U.

1074. *Lee, Michael Joseph. "The Theme of Despair in a Selection of English South African Fiction: A Study of Mood and Form in Olive Schreiner's *The Story of an African Farm*, William Plomer's *Turbott Wolfe*, Pauline Smith's *The Beadle*, Alan Paton's *Cry, the Beloved Country*, Doris Lessing's *The Grass Is Singing*, Dan Jacobson's *The Trap* and *A Dance in the Sun* (and Stories from *Through the Wilderness* and 'The Stranger' from *A Long Way from London* [and Other Stories]), Nadine Gordimer's *The Conservationist* and J. M. Coetzee's *In the Heart of the Country*." MA diss. U of Cape Town.

1075. Otero, Rosalie C. "The Novels of Nadine Gordimer (South Africa)." PhD diss. U of New Mexico. DAI 45(7) 1985: 2098A. [*A Guest of Honour; Burger's Daughter; Face to Face; July's People; Some Monday for Sure; The Conservationist.*]

1984. 1076. Gray, Rosemary Alice. "The Theme of Dissonance in the Post-War South African Novel in English." MA diss. UNISA. [*The Conservationist*; *July's People*.]

1077. King, Michael. "A Study of the Development of the Structures and Themes in the Short Stories of Nadine Gordimer." MA diss. U of Cape Town. [*Face to Face*; *The Soft Voice of the Serpent*; *Six Feet of the Country*; *Friday's Footprint*; *Not for Publication*; *Livingstone's Companions*; *A Soldier's Embrace*; *Something Out There*; "The Soft Voice of the Serpent"; "The Kindest Thing to Do"; "A Watcher of the Dead"; "La Vie Bohème"; "The Umbilical Cord"; "The Defeated"; *The Lying Days*; "The Prisoner"; "In the Beginning"; "Is There Nowhere Else Where We Can Meet?"; "The Amateurs"; "The Catch"; "Ah, Woe Is Me"; "Monday Is Better than Sunday"; "Another Part of the Sky"; "The Train from Rhodesia"; "The End of the Tunnel"; "The Hour and the Years"; "Treasures of the Sea"; "A Present for a Good Girl"; "The Talisman"; "A Commonplace Story"; "The Battlefield at No. 29"; "The Last of the Old-Fashioned Girls"; "No Luck Tonight"; "Come Again Tomorrow"; "No Place Like Home"; "Poet and Peasant"; "A Sunday Outing"; "Six Feet of the Country"; "Happy Event"; "Which New Era Would That Be?"; "The Smell of Death and Flowers"; *A World of Strangers*; "Horn of Plenty"; "Clowns in Clover"; "My First Two Women"; "Enemies"; "Face from Atlantis"; "The Cicatrice"; "Out of Season"; "A Wand'ring Minstrel, I"; "A Bit of Young Life"; "Charmed Lives"; "The Bridegroom"; "Something for the Time Being"; "Little Willie"; "Harry's Presence"; "The Last Kiss"; "Friday's Footprint"; "Check Yes or No"; *A Guest of Honour*; "Our Bovary"; "A Style of Her Own"; "A Thing of the Past"; "The Gentle Art"; "The Night the Favourite Came Home"; "The Path of the Moon's Dark Fortnight"; "An Image of Success"; "Message in a Bottle"; "Good Climate, Friendly Inhabitants"; "One Whole Year, and Even More"; *The Late Bourgeois World*; "Not for Publication"; "The African Magician"; "Through Time and Distance"; "Some Monday for Sure"; "The Pet"; "Son-in-Law"; "Native Country"; "A Company of Laughing Faces"; "Tenants of the Last Tree-House"; "The Worst Thing of All"; "Vital Statistics"; "Livingstone's Companions"; "Inkalamu's Place"; "No Place Like"; "Rain Queen"; "Abroad"; "The Life of the Imagination"; "An Intruder"; "Open House"; "Africa Emergent"; "A Satisfactory Settlement"; "The Credibility Gap"; "A Third Presence"; "Other Birds Fly In"; "The Bride of Christ"; "A Meeting in Space"; "Why Haven't You Written?"; "A Soldier's Embrace"; "A Hunting Accident"; "Town and Country Lovers *One*"; "Town and Country Lovers *Two*"; "Oral History"; "A Lion on the Freeway"; "The Termitary"; "You Name It"; "The Need for Something Sweet"; "Siblings"; "A Mad One"; "Time Did"; "For Dear Life"; "Something Out There"; "A City of the Dead, A City of the Living"; "Crimes of Conscience"; "A Correspondence Course"; "Terminal"; "Sins of the Third Age"; "Tourism."]

1984. 1078. *Uledi-Kamanga, Brighton James. "The Female Character and the Theme of Identity: A Study in the Fiction of Nadine Gordimer and Bessie Head." PhD diss. Dalhousie U, Halifax.

1985. 1079. *Trump, Martin. "South African Short Fiction in English and Afrikaans since 1948." PhD diss. U of London. IT 35(4) 1987: 1493.

1080. Viljoen, Hendrik Marthinus. "Die Suid-Afrikaanse roman-sisteem *anno* 1981: 'n Vergelykende studie." D Litt diss. Potchefstroom U for CHE. [*July's People*.]

1986. 1081. *Paasche, K. I. "Changing Social Consciousness in the South African Novel after World War Two, with Special Reference to Alan Paton, Peter Abrahams, Nadine Gordimer and Ezekiel Mphahlele." MA diss. UNISA.

1082. *Price, H. G. K. "Didacticism in the Fiction of Nadine Gordimer." M Phil diss. U of Sheffield. IT 37(3) 1988: 921.

1083. Ruth, Damian William. "Psychodynamic Perspectives on the Master-Servant Relationship and Its Representation in the Work of Doris Lessing, Es'kia Mphahlele and Nadine Gordimer. M Phil diss. U of Cape Town. ["Is There Nowhere Else Where We Can Meet?"; "Ah, Woe Is Me"; "Monday Is Better than Sunday"; "Six Feet of the Country"; "Happy Event"; "Horn of Plenty"; "Enemies"; "The Bridegroom"; "The Pet"; *The Lying Days*; *A World of Strangers*; *Occasion for Loving*; *The Late Bourgeois World*; *The Conservationist*; *Burger's Daughter*; *July's People*.]

1987. 1084. Liscio, Lorraine. "Female Definitions of Self and Community (Robinson, Drabble, Gordimer, Morrison)." PhD diss. Boston College. DAI 49(2) 1988: 254A. [*Burger's Daughter*.]

1085. *Read, Daphne Frances. "Rereading *Burger's Daughter*: A Feminist Deconstruction." PhD diss. York U, Canada. DAI 48(10) 1988: 2637A.

1988. 1086. Colleran, Jeanne Marie. "The Dissenting Writer in South Africa: A Rhetorical Analysis of the Drama of Athol Fugard and the Short Fiction of Nadine Gordimer." PhD diss. Ohio State U. DAI 49(9) 1989: 2655A. ["The Train from Rhodesia"; "Is There Nowhere Else Where We Can Meet?"; "A Chip of Glass Ruby"; "A Correspondence Course"; "A Lion on the Freeway"; "Six Feet of the Country"; "Town and Country Lovers *One*"; "Town and Country Lovers *Two*"; "Blinder"; "Open House."]

1087. Fontenot, Deborah B. "A Vision of Anarchy: Correlate Structures of Exile and Madness in Selected Works of Doris Lessing and Her South African Contemporaries." PhD diss. U of Illinois at Urbana-Champaign. DAI 50(2) 1989: 449A. [*July's People*; *The Late Bourgeois World*.]

1088. *Hewson, Kelly Leigh. "Writers and Responsibility: George Orwell, Nadine Gordimer, John Coetzee and Salman Rushdie." PhD diss. U of Alberta, Canada. DAI 49(10) 1989: 3033A. [*The Conservationist*; *Burger's Daughter*.]

1089. Lazar, Karen Ruth. "The Personal and the Political in Some of Nadine Gordimer's Short Stories." MA diss. U of the Witwatersrand. ["Another Part of the Sky"; "Monday Is Better than Sunday"; "The Pet"; "The Catch"; "A Smell of Death and Flowers"; "Happy Event"; "Six Feet of the Country"; "Friday's Footprint"; "The Gentle Art"; "Not for Publication"; "Some Monday for Sure"; "A Satisfactory Settlement"; "The Credibility Gap"; "The Bridegroom"; "Abroad"; "Open House"; "No Place Like"; "Livingstone's Companions"; "A Soldier's Embrace"; "A City of the Dead, A City of the Living"; "A Lion on the Freeway"; "At the Rendezvous of Victory"; "Something Out There"; "The Battlefield at No. 29"; "The Last of the Old-Fashioned Girls"; "A Commonplace Story"; "The Hour and the Years"; "The

Prisoner"; "Is There Nowhere Else Where We Can Meet?"; "The Train from Rhodesia"; "Ah, Woe Is Me"; "Horn of Plenty"; "A Bit of Young Life"; "Out of Season"; "Enemies"; "Which New Era Would That Be?"; "The Night the Favourite Came Home"; "Our Bovary"; "An Image of Success"; "Something for the Time Being"; "Good Climate, Friendly Inhabitants"; "A Chip of Glass Ruby"; "Native Country"; "An Intruder"; "The Bride of Christ"; "A Third Presence"; "Otherwise Birds Fly In"; "The Termitary"; "You Name It"; "The Need for Something Sweet"; "Time Did"; "A Correspondence Course"; "Crimes of Conscience"; "Blinder."]

1988. 1090. O'Connell, Joanna. "Prospero's Daughters: Language and Allegiance in the Novels of Rosario Castellanos and Nadine Gordimer (Mexico, South Africa)." PhD diss. U of California. DAI 50(4) 1989: 944A. [*Burger's Daughter.*]

1091. *Rasebotsa, Nobantu Nkwane Lorato. "The Language of Possibilities: Domination and Demythicization in Gordimer's Art." PhD diss. State U of New York. DAI 50(5) 1989: 1303A-1304A.

1092. Visel, Robin Ellen. "White Eve in the 'Petrified Garden': The Colonial African Heroine in the Writing of Olive Schreiner, Isak Dinesen, Doris Lessing and Nadine Gordimer." PhD diss. U of British Columbia. DAI 49(12.1) 1989: 3721A. [*The Lying Days*; *The Conservationist*; *Burger's Daughter*; "Is There Nowhere Else Where We Can Meet?"; *July's People*; *A Sport of Nature*; briefly mentions "Six Feet of the Country"; "The Smell of Death and Flowers"; *Occasion for Loving*; *A Guest of Honour.*]

1989. 1093. Dubbeld, Catherine Elizabeth. "A Bibliography of South African Short Stories in English with Socio-Political Themes Between 1960 and June 1987." M Library and Information Science diss. U of Natal, Pietermaritzburg.

1094. Lewis, Desirée Anne. "Post-Liberal Vision in Three South African Novels: Serote's *To Every Birth Its Blood*, Gordimer's *The Conservationist* and Coetzee's *Waiting for the Barbarians*." MA diss. U of the Witwatersrand.

1989. 1095. *Loflin, Christine Adams. "Race, Nationalism and Colonialism in the African Landscape." PhD diss. U of Wisconsin, Madison. DAI 50(11) 1990: 3583A. [Chapters 4-5 deal with landscape in Gordimer's novels.]

1990. 1096. Postel, Gitte. "The Present Is a Dangerous Place to Live: Een onderzoek naar vervreemding in de moderne Zuidafrikaanse letterkunde." D Litt diss. Katholieke Universiteit, Nijmegen. [*The Conservationist*.]

1097. *Wong, Cynthia Frances Fung-Ming. "Postmortem Narrative: Nadine Gordimer, John Hawkes, Maurice Blanchot." PhD diss. U of Wisconsin, Milwaukee. DAI 52(2) 1991: 532A-533A.

1991. 1098. Douglas, Eunice W. "Three Novels of the Interregnum: Karel Schoeman's *Promised Land*, Nadine Gordimer's *July's People* and Mongane Serote's *To Every Birth Its Blood*: Some Difficulties of Form and Ideology." MA diss. U of Natal, Durban.

1099. Venter, Delina Charlotte. "The Interaction of Race, Gender and Class in a Selection of Short Stories by Nadine Gordimer." MA diss. Rand Afrikaans U. ["The Umbilical Cord"; "The Defeated"; "Poet and Peasant"; "Sweet Dreams Selection"; "The Peace of Respectability"; "The Hour and the Years"; "The Train from Rhodesia"; "The Amateurs"; "No Luck Tonight"; "Ah, Woe Is Me"; "Monday Is Better than Sunday"; "Six Feet of the Country"; "Happy Event"; "The Catch"; "The Smell of Death and Flowers"; "Something for the Time Being"; "Which New Era Would That Be?"; "Horn of Plenty"; "The Bridegroom"; "A Chip of Glass Ruby"; "The African Magician"; "The Pet"; "Good Climate, Friendly Inhabitants"; "Not for Publication"; "Some Monday for Sure"; "A Satisfactory Settlement"; "Inkalamu's Place"; "Open House"; "Africa Emergent"; "Town and Country Lovers"; "A Soldier's Embrace"; "Blinder"; "Oral History"; "A City of the Dead, A City of the Living"; "At the Rendezvous of Victory"; "A Lion on the Freeway"; "Teraloyna."]

1100. Wagner, Kathrin Margarete. "Rereading Gordimer: Text and Subtext in the Novels 1953-1987." PhD diss. U of the Witwatersrand. [*The Lying Days*; *A World of Strangers*;

Occasion for Loving; The Late Bourgeois World; A Guest of Honour; The Conservationist; Burger's Daughter; July's People; A Sport of Nature; My Son's Story.]

M. REVIEWS OF INDIVIDUAL WORKS

Face to Face

1948. 1101. Rev. of *Face to Face*. *Daily Dispatch* 22 Oct.

1949. 1102. A. R. D. "Young South African's Promising Stories." *Sunday Post* 12 Nov.

1103. "Atomic Cocktail by South African Writer." *The Star* 3 Oct.: 2.

1104. Bernstein, Edgar. "The Uncritical Critic and Some Talented Work." *Democrat Monthly* Oct.: 39-40.

1105. "Bookshelf." *Milady: The Journal for Smart Women* Dec.

1106. C. E. "A New South African Writer." *Common Sense* Oct.: 468-469.

1107. E. W. "*Face to Face* with Life." *Rand Daily Mail* 10 Sept.: 8.

1108. H. "Gifted South African Short Story Writer." *The Friend* 26 Oct.

1109. Heidenfeld, W. "First Works by Two Jewish Story-Tellers: Nadine Gordimer's Short Stories." *Jewish Affairs* (4.10): 48-50.

1110. "A Journal: Young Writer's First Book of Short Stories: *Face to Face.*" *The Star* 30 Aug.: 4.

1111. L. R. "South African Writer." *The Forum* (12.24): 28-29.

1112. M. M. W. "Short Stories by Nadine Gordimer: New South African Writer." *Sunday Times* 16 Oct.

1113. Rev. of *Face to Face*. *Cape Times* 22 Oct.

1114. Rev. of *Face to Face*. *Daily Dispatch* 22 Oct.

1115. Sachs, Joseph. "Books of the Month." *Trek* (13.10): 26.

1949. 1116. "Short Stories by South African." *Diamond Fields Advertiser* 6 Oct.

1117. "Springs Author Acclaimed." *Springs Advertiser* 16 Sept.

1118. W. "Roem te swaar vir jong bene." *Die Vaderland* 8 Oct.

1950. 1119. I. R. "Gordimer, Nadine: *Face to Face.*" *Ons Eie Boek* (16.2): 88.

The Soft Voice of the Serpent

N.D. 1120. Lane, Margaret. Rev. of *The Soft Voice of the Serpent. The Observer.*

1952. 1121. Barkham, John. "African Smiles." *Saturday Review* 24 May: 22. Extr. in *Contemporary Literary Criticism, Vol 33.* Ed. Daniel G. Marowski and Jean C. Stine. Detroit: Gale, 1985: 176-177.

1122. "Briefly Noted: Fiction." *The New Yorker* 7 June: 118, 119.

1123. *Hayes, Richard. "The Moment of Illumination." *Commonweal 56* 30 May: 204.

1124. Peden, William. "Stories from Africa." *New York Times Book Review* 15 June: 17.

1125. *Rev. of *The Soft Voice of the Serpent. San Francisco Chronicle* 26 May.

1126. Rosenfeld, Isaac. "To Win by Default." *The New Republic* 7 July: 19-20. Extr. in *Contemporary Literary Criticism, Vol 33:* 177.

1127. *Stallings, Sylvia. "New Talent Out of Africa." *New York Times Book Review* 25 May: 7.

1953. 1128. "Awkward Moments." *Times Literary Supplement* 27 Feb.: 133.

1129. Delius, Anthony. "Danger from the Digit." *Standpunte* (7.3): 80-92.

1130. L. R. "Nadine Gordimer: *The Soft Voice of the Serpent.*" *The Forum* (2.1): 60-61.

1953. 1131. Rev. of *The Soft Voice of the Serpent. Book Review Digest: Forty-Eighth Annual Cumulation.* New York: Wilson: 357-358.

1132. Rev. of *The Soft Voice of the Serpent. Times Literary Supplement* 27 Feb.: 133.

1133. "S.A. Writer's Short Stories." *Sunday Times* 29 Mar.

1134. "Short Stories." *Rand Daily Mail* 18 Apr.

1135. Tracy, Honor. Rev. of *The Soft Voice of the Serpent. New Statesman and Nation* 11 Apr.: 433-434.

1136. Worrall, John. "S.A. Writer's Short Stories." *Cape Times* 1 Apr.

1954. 1137. Ravenscroft, A. "Gordimer, Nadine: *The Soft Voice of the Serpent.*" *Ons Eie Boek* (20.3): 137-138.

The Lying Days

N.D. 1138. O'Faolain, Sean. Rev. of *The Lying Days. The Observer.*

1953. 1139. Allen, Walter. "New Novels." *New Statesman and Nation* 24 Oct.: 496, 498.

1140. "Coming of Age." *Time* 12 Oct.: 119-120.

1141. "Defying Convention." *Times Literary Supplement* 30 Oct.: 689.

1142. Gill, Brendan. "New Old World." *The New Yorker* 21 Nov.: 194, 197-198.

1143. Hayes, Richard. "A Coming of Age in South Africa." *Commonweal* 23 Oct.: 66. Extr. in *Contemporary Literary Criticism, Vol 33*: 178 and in *Modern Commonwealth Literature.* Ed. John H. Ferres and Martin Tucker. New York: Ungar, 1977: 46-47.

1144. Rev. of *The Lying Days. San Francisco Chronicle* 9 Nov.

1145. Rothman, Nathan. "When Africa Sighs." *Saturday Review* 3 Oct.: 27-28. Extr. in *Contemporary Literary Criticism, Vol 33*: 177.

1953. 1146. *Stallings, Sylvia. Rev. of *The Lying Days*. *New York Herald Tribune Book Review* 4 Oct.

1147. Stern, James. "Out of Rags and Hovels." *New York Times Book Review* 4 Oct.: 4-5. Extr. in *Contemporary Literary Criticism, Vol 33*: 177-178.

1954. 1148. A. O. D. Rev. of *The Lying Days*. *Fighting Talk* (10.3): 13.

1149. Blair, Alison. Rev. of *The Lying Days*. *Encounter* (2.1): 76-77.

1150. Harvey, C. J. D. "Gordimer, Nadine: *The Lying Days*." *Ons Eie Boek* (20.1): 24-25.

1151. Rev. of *The Lying Days*. *Book Review Digest: Forty-Ninth Annual Cumulation*. New York: Wilson: 371-372.

1152. *Rev. of *The Lying Days*. *Sarie Marais* 4 Aug.: 41.

1978. 1153. Rev. of *The Lying Days*. *Sunday Tribune* 20 Aug.: 2.

1984. 1154. Smith, Ellen. "Gordimer's First Reprinted." *The Argus* 16 Feb.: 19.

1985. 1155. *Rev. of *The Lying Days*. *Woman's Value* July: 120.

Six Feet of the Country (1956)

N.D. 1156. "Short Stories by Nadine Gordimer."

1956. 1157. Allen, Walter. "New Short Stories." *New Statesman and Nation* 18 Aug.: 191-192. Extr. in *Contemporary Literary Criticism, Vol 33*: 179.

1158. "Faces in Africa." *Times Literary Supplement* 13 July: 421. Extr. in *Contemporary Literary Criticism, Vol 33*: 178-179.

1159. Harris, Peter. "Nadine Gordimer's Subtle Stories." *Cape Times* 18 July.

1160. L. R. "Front-Rank Stories." *The Forum* (5.9): 52-53.

1161. "Mixed Fiction." *Time* 15 Oct.: 126.

1162. *Nordell, Rod. Rev. of *Six Feet of the Country*. *Christian Science Monitor* 11 Oct.: 6.

1956. 1163. Peden, William. "Eternal Foreigners." *Saturday Review* 27 Oct.: 16-17, 25.

1164. *Rev. of *Six Feet of the Country*. *Milady: The Journal for Smart Women* (11.7): 79.

1165. *Stallings, Sylvia. "Stories of Love and Irony." *New York Herald Tribune Book Review* 21 Oct.: 3.

1166. Stern, James. "Troubled Souls." *New York Times Book Review* 7 Oct.: 5, 34. Extr. in *Contemporary Literary Criticism, Vol 33*: 179.

1167. Van Ghent, Dorothy. "Recent Fiction: The Race, the Moment and the Milieu." *The Yale Review* (46.2): 274-288.

1168. Wyndham, Francis. Rev. of *Six Feet of the Country*. *The London Magazine* (3.8): 67, 69, 71.

1957. 1169. Rev. of *Six Feet of the Country*. *Book Review Digest: Fifty-Second Annual Cumulation*. New York: Wilson: 373.

Six Feet of the Country (1982)

N.D. 1170. Fuller, Roy. Rev. of *Six Feet of the Country*. *Sunday Times*.

1171. Green, Peter. Rev. of *Six Feet of the Country*. *Daily Telegraph*.

1172. Hopkins, Gerard. Rev. of *Six Feet of the Country*. *Time and Tide*.

1982. 1173. *Green, Molly. Rev. of *Six Feet of the Country*. *Cape Times* 21 Sept.

1983. 1174. Garden, Greg. "Gordimer: Flawed Films." *Rand Daily Mail* 23 Mar.: 8.

1175. Slack, Doug. "The South African Way of Life— As Seen by Nadine Gordimer." *The Star* 27 July: 16M.

1985. 1176. Rev. of *Six Feet of the Country*. *SA Literature/Literatuur 1982: Annual Literary Survey Series 3*. Comp. Francis Galloway. Johannesburg: Donker: 28-29.

A World of Strangers

1958. 1177. Anderson, Polly G. Rev. of *A World of Strangers*. *Library Journal* 1 Sept.: 2321.

1178. Balliet, Whitney. "Books: Post-Colonial." *The New Yorker* 29 Nov.: 222, 224.

1179. "Double Life in Africa." *Time* 22 Sept.: 62.

1180. "Escapism under Apartheid." *Times Literary Supplement* 27 June: 357.

1181. *Fuller, Edmund. Rev. of *A World of Strangers*. *Chicago Sunday Tribune* 21 Sept.

1182. Howe, Irving. Rev. of *A World of Strangers*. *The New Republic* 10 Nov.: 17-18.

1183. Johnson, Pamela Hansford. "New Novels." *New Statesman* 24 May: 674-675.

1184. Laski, Marghanita. "Community of the Uncommitted." *Saturday Review* 13 Sept.: 41.

1185. M. F. "A New South African Novel." *Jewish Affairs* (13.7): 39.

1186. Peden, William. "Bonds of Loneliness." *New York Times Book Review* 21 Sept.: 5.

1187. *Peterson, Virginia. Rev. of *A World of Strangers*. *New York Herald Tribune Book Review* 21 Sept.

1188. Rev. of *A World of Strangers*. *The Booklist* 1 Oct.: 74.

1189. Rev. of *A World of Strangers*. *The Forum* (7.3): 46-47.

1190. Rev. of *A World of Strangers*. *Personality* 17 July: 64.

1191. Walker, Oliver. "Miss Gordimer Has a Little Quiet Fun." *The Star*.

1192. Williams, Owen. "A Fine S.A. Writer's Novel Misfires." *Contact* 31 May: 17.

1193. Wyndham, Francis. Rev. of *A World of Strangers*. *The London Magazine* (5.7): 71-73.

1959. 1194. Rev. of *A World of Strangers*. *Book Review Digest: Fifty-fourth Annual Cumulation*. New York: Wilson: 445-446.

1960. 1195. Hendriks, David. Rev. of *A World of Strangers*. *Purple Renoster* (4): 83-85.

1196. W. D. T. "Short Stories by Miss Gordimer." *Jewish Affairs* June: 41-43.

1976. 1197. Bailey, Paul. "Unquiet Graves." *Times Literary Supplement* 9 July: 841. Extr. in *Contemporary Literary Criticism, Vol 10*. Ed. Dedria Bryfonski. Detroit: Gale, 1979: 239-240.

1198. Bentley, Phyllis. Rev. of *A World of Strangers*. *The Yorkshire Post* 10 June.

1199. D. C. C. "Brilliance Still Shines Through." *The Natal Witness* 3 Sept.: 7.

1200. Ingoldby, G. D. "Nadine Gordimer: *A World of Strangers*." *Fortnight* 24 Sept.: 15.

1201. J. C. T. "Banned Gordimer Novel Slots into Place at Last." *Pretoria News* 30 Sept.: 2.

1202. McNay, M. G. "Second Time Round for Two Winners: Other New Fiction." *Oxford Mail* 3 June.

1203. Nicol, Mike. "Books: *A World of Strangers* by Nadine Gordimer." *To the Point* 27 Aug.: 38.

1204. Wilhelm, Peter. "Superseded." *The Star* 23 June.

1205. Wilhelm, Peter. "Testimony to Our Lost Worlds." *The Argus* 14 July: 18.

1977. 1206. Bryer, Lynne. "New Fiction." *Eastern Province Herald* 5 Jan.: 4.

1207. Nemo. Rev. of *A World of Strangers*. *The Times* 22 Jan.

Friday's Footprint

1960. 1208. *Chase, Mary Ellen. "Miss Gordimer's Fine, True Art in Another Brilliant Collection." *New York Herald Tribune Book Review* 10 Jan.: 1. Extr. in *Contemporary Literary Criticism, Vol 33*: 179-180.

1209. Coleman, John. "The Best of Good Manners." *The Spectator* 12 Feb.: 228.

1960. 1210. Curran, Mary Doyle. "Many Views from the Veld." *Saturday Review* 16 Jan.: 64. Extr. in *Contemporary Literary Criticism, Vol 33*: 180.

1211. Hendriks, David. Rev. of *Friday's Footprint*. *Purple Renoster* (4): 85-87.

1212. Lewis, Naomi. "Short Stories." *New Statesman* 20 Feb.: 263.

1213. *Meidner, Olga McDonald. "Semblance of Life." *Contact* 7 May: 8.

1214. Rev. of *Friday's Footprint*. *The Booklist* 1 Jan.: 257.

1215. "The Past Catching Up." *Times Literary Supplement* 12 Feb.: 93.

1216. "Under the Cold Stars." *Time* 11 Jan.: 60.

1217. W. D. T. "Short Stories by Miss Gordimer." *Jewish Affairs* (15.6): 41-43.

1218. Wakeman, John. "Below the Surface of Life." *New York Times Book Review* 10 Jan.: 4.

1219. Webster, Mary Morison. "New Robustness in Nadine Gordimer's Latest Book." *Sunday Times*.

1220. Weeks, Edward. "The Peripatetic Reviewer: Accept with Pleasure." *The Atlantic* Jan.: 94-96. Extr. from *Contemporary Literary Criticism, Vol 33*: 179.

1221. Wyndham, Francis. Rev. of *Friday's Footprint*. *The London Magazine* (7.6): 72-74.

1961. 1222. Rev. of *Friday's Footprint*. *Book Review Digest: Fifty-Seventh Annual Cumulation*. Ed. Dorothy P. Davison. New York: Wilson: 547-548.

Occasion for Loving

1963. 1223. Adams, Phoebe. "Potpourri." *The Atlantic* Feb.: 134-135.

1224. C. E. "The New Gordimer Novel." *Jewish Affairs* (18.6): 39-40.

1963. 1225. Calisher, Hortense. "Fiction: Some Forms Offshore." *The Nation* 16 Mar.: 229-232.

1226. "For Your Bookshelf: Rev. of *Occasion for Loving.*" *Femina & Woman's Life* 23 May: 35.

1227. *Hughes, John. "New Gordimer Novel." *Christian Science Monitor* 10 Jan.: 11.

1228. *Hynes, Samuel. "The Power of Hatred." *Commonweal* 77 22 Mar.: 667-668.

1229. Jackson, Katherine Gauss. "Books in Brief: Fiction." *Harper's Magazine* Feb.: 106.

1230. Malin, Irving. "Occasions for Loving." *The Kenyon Review* (25.2): 348-352.

1231. Norris, Hoke. "South Africa: Perplexities, Brutalities, Absurdities." *Saturday Review* 12 Jan.: 63-64.

1232. *Rev. of *Occasion for Loving. New York Herald Tribune Book Review* 7 Apr.

1233. Ricks, Christopher. "Silver Spoon." *New Statesman* 15 Mar.: 392.

1234. Ross, Alan. Rev. of *Occasion for Loving. The London Magazine* (3.4): 89-90.

1235. "Too Strong a Bar." *Times Literary Supplement* 1 Mar.: 149.

1236. Webster, Mary Morison. "Gordimer's New Novel a Perceptive Study." *Sunday Times* 7 Apr.

1964. 1237. Rev. of *Occasion for Loving. Book Review Digest: Fifty-Ninth Annual Cumulation.* Ed. Dorothy P. Davison. New York: Wilson: 393.

1975. 1238. Leiter, Robert. Rev. of *Occasion for Loving. The New Republic* 13 Sept.: 29-30. Extr. in *Contemporary Literary Criticism, Vol 7.* Ed. Phyllis Carmel Mendelson and Dedria Bryfonski. Detroit: Gale, 1977: 132.

1979. 1239. Sevry, Jean. Rev. of *Occasion for Loving. Mars*: 16-17.

1984. 1240. Norton, Elizabeth. "Gordimer Novel in New Edition." *Eastern Province Herald* 5 June: 11.

Not For Publication

1965. 1241. Brophy, Brigid. "Native Sons." *New Statesman* 4 June: 886-887.

1242. Brown, Edward Hickman. "A Sudden Shaft of Light." *Saturday Review* 8 May: 33. Extr. in *Contemporary Literary Criticism, Vol 33*: 180-181.

1243. *Holzhauer, Jean. "Not for Publication." *Commonweal* 9 July: 511.

1244. Mitchell, Adrian. "Pervaded by the Strangeness of Africa." *New York Times Book Review* 23 May: 5, 47.

1245. *Potter, Nancy-A. J. "Not for Publication." *Studies in Short Fiction* (3): 86-87.

1246. *Rev. of *Not for Publication*. *Newsweek* 10 May.

1247. Rev. of *Not For Publication*. *Times Literary Supplement* 22 July: 609.

1248. Tracy, Honor. "A Bouquet from Nadine Gordimer." *The New Republic* 8 May: 25-26. Extr. in *Contemporary Literary Criticism, Vol 33*: 180.

1249. Webster, Mary Morison. "Miss Gordimer Writes with 'Seeing Eye.'" *Sunday Times*.

1250. Weeks, Edward. "The Peripatetic Reviewer: Short Stories from Africa." *The Atlantic* June: 136, 138, 140.

The Late Bourgeois World

1966. 1251. McCabe, Bernard. "A Code for the Pale." *Saturday Review* 20 Aug.: 32.

1252. Mitchell, Adrian. "Climate of Fear." *New York Times Book Review* 11 Sept.: 54.

1253. "On the Brink." *Times Literary Supplement* 7 July: 589.

1254. Rabkin, Lily. "Book's Theme is S.A. Today." *Sunday Times* 26 June: 5.

1255. *Rev. of *The Late Bourgeois World*. *Commonweal* 4 Nov.

1966.   1256.   *Rev. of *The Late Bourgeois World*. *Newsweek* 4 July.

1257.   Toynbee, Phillip. "Disillusioned Heroine." *The New Republic* 10 Sept.: 24, 26.

1258.   Weeks, Edward. "The Peripatetic Reviewer: Rev. of *The Late Bourgeois World*." *The Atlantic* Aug.: 114-116.

1969.   1259.   *Brutus, Dennis. Rev. of *The Late Bourgeois World*. Ed. Cosmo Pieterse and Donald Munro. *Protest and Conflict in African Literature*. New York: Africana: 97. Extr. in *Modern Commonwealth Literature*: 47.

1975.   1260.   Leiter, Robert. Rev. of *The Late Bourgeois World*. *The New Republic* 13 Sept.: 29-30. Extr. in *Contemporary Literary Criticism, Vol 7*: 132.

1976.   1261.   Bailey, Paul. "Unquiet Graves." *Times Literary Supplement* 9 July: 841. Extr. in *Contemporary Literary Criticism, Vol 10*: 239-240.

1262.   Hatfield, Denis. "Gordimer Novel 10 Years Late." *Cape Times* 14 July: 12.

1263.   J. C. T. "Banned Gordimer Novel Slots into Place at Last." *Pretoria News* 30 Sept.: 2.

1264.   Marquard, Jean. "Samelewing as tronk." *Beeld* 6 Sept.: 7.

1265.   Nicol, Mike. "Nadine Gordimer at Her Best." *To the Point* 27 Feb.: 38.

1266.   Rev. of *The Late Bourgeois World*. *The Natal Mercury* 19 Aug.: 8.

1267.   S. P. "Nadine se verset." *Die Burger* 22 July: 27.

1268.   Wilhelm, Peter. "Superseded." *The Star* 23 June.

1977.   1269.   Bryer, Lynne. "New Fiction." *Eastern Province Herald* 5 Jan.: 4.

1270.   Hillary, Naylor. "Racial Fear and Repression." *The Press* 15 Jan.

1984.   1271.   "Ninety-Nine of the Best." *Sunday Tribune* 29 Apr.: 32.

A Guest of Honour

1970. 1272. Haynes, Muriel. "A Guest of Honour." *Saturday Review* 24 Oct.: 34-36.

1273. *Lask, Thomas. Rev. of *A Guest of Honour*. *New York Times* 30 Oct.

1274. Schott, Webster. "In Search of a New Life in a New State." *New York Times Book Review* 1 Nov.: 4, 48.

1275. Sheppard, R. Z. "Recessional." *Time* 16 Nov.: 72, 74.

1276. Theroux, Paul. "Saviors as Tyrants." *Chicago Tribune Book World* 1 Nov.: 4.

1971. 1277. A. T. "That Novel Feminine Touch." *Huddersfield Daily Examiner* 6 May.

1278. *Beichman, Arnold. Rev. of *A Guest of Honour*. *Christian Science Monitor* 5 Nov.: 12.

1279. *Bell, Pearl K. "Presuming in Africa." *Christian Science Monitor* 4 Nov.: 11.

1280. Berridge, Elizabeth. "Recent Fiction." *Daily Telegraph* 22 Apr.

1281. "Birth of a Nation." *Evening Herald* 17 June.

1282. "Boekenpaspoort." *Litterair Paspoort* May.

1283. *Brown, Andrew. Rev. of *A Guest of Honour*. *South African Outlook* Dec.: 187-188.

1284. Brunner, John. "Whiff of Corruption from Africa." *The Teacher* 28 May.

1285. Byatt, A. S. Rev. of *A Guest of Honour*. *The Times* 29 Apr.

1286. Cami, Ben. "Meesterlijke Afrika-roman." *Het Laatste Nieuws* 30 Sept.

1287. Derwent, Roy. "The Wraiths of War." *Express & Echo* 28 Apr.: 4.

1288. E. J. R. "Books Briefly." *Western Daily Press* 8 May.

1289. F. C. G. "Unrest Is a Newly Independent Land." *Northamptonshire Evening Telegraph* 30 Apr.

1971. 1290. F. E. S. "Gordimer's Fascinating Guest." *Daily Dispatch* 3 July: 8.

1291. "Fiction: The Rumbustious, the Powerful and the Brave." *Halifax Evening Courier* 7 Aug.

1292. Forshaw, Thelma. "A Paler Shade of Realism." *The Australian* 28 Aug.: *18.

1293. G. G. C. "Brilliant Gordimer Novel." *Weekend Magazine* (supp. to the *Evening Post*) 3 July: 10.

1294. Gershon, Karen. "After Liberation - What?" *Jerusalem Post* 28 May.

1295. *Gordon, D. J. Rev. of *A Guest of Honour*. *The Yale Review* (Spring): 437. Extr. in *Modern Commonwealth Literature*: 48.

1296. Graham, Cuthbert. "Pick of 1971 Novels." *The Press and Journal*.

1297. Gray, Stephen. "Nadine se jongste bring agting." *Tydskrif Rapport* (supp. to *Rapport*) 1 Aug.: 18.

1298. "The Great Outdoors." *Bolton Evening News* 8 May.

1299. Grigson, Geoffrey. "Theme and Variation." *Country Life* 29 Apr.

1300. Haxton, Colin. "Siege Story." *Southern Evening Echo* 22 May.

1301. Hewitt, Hope. "An African Brew." *The Canberra Times* 2 Oct.

1302. Holden, Jane. "Torn by Opposing Factions." *Birmingham Evening Mail* 7 May.

1303. Hugo, Leon. "Dilemma of a Guest of Honour." *The Star* 26 June: 5.

1304. Hunter, Alan. "The British Love Affair." *Eastern Daily Press* 30 Apr.

1305. J. McC. "A Return to Africa." *The Oxford Times* 14 May.

1306. J. R. "Powerful Story Is Set in Africa." *Christchurch Star* 26 June.

1971. 1307. J. R. N. Rev. of *A Guest of Honour*. *Sunday Express* 13 June: 3.

1308. Kavanagh, Muriel. "Empathy." *The Argus* 7 July: 8.

1309. Kearney, Mary. "Well-Meant Hypotheses but All a Little Bloodless." *Sunday Tribune* 16 May: M5.

1310. Laski, Audrey. "In Love and Conflict." *Times Educational Supplement* 23 July: 25.

1311. Lister, Richard. "In-Fighting in Africa." *Evening Standard* 27 Apr.: 21.

1312. M. G. H. "Disillusionment through Independence." *South China Morning Post* 31 May.

1313. M. R. "A Wind of Change Parable." *Sunday Mail* 2 May.

1314. MacCormick, Donald. "New Novels: Guests and Exiles." *The Glasgow Herald* 24 Apr.

1315. Marnham, Patrick. "Where the Regime?" *Sunday Telegraph* 25 Apr.

1316. May, Derwent. "Guiding Forces." *Encounter* (37.2): 65-68. Extr. in *Contemporary Literary Criticism, Vol 5*. Ed. Carolyn Riley and Phyllis Carmel Mendelson. Detroit: Gale, 1976: 145.

1317. McGregor, Helen. Rev. of *A Guest of Honour*. *Books & Bookmen* June: 42.

1318. McGuinness, Frank. "Black and White Power." *London Magazine* (11.3): 143-147.

1319. Monk, Wendy. "New Fiction." *Birmingham Post* 24 Apr.

1320. "Nadine's Latest." *The Star Tonight* (supp. to *The Star*) 14 Apr.: 10.

1321. Nesbitt, W. J. Rev. of *A Guest of Honour*. *The Northern Echo* 7 May.

1322. Owen, T. R. "African Corridors of Power." *Church Times* 21 May.

1323. "Personal Drama on Two Levels." *Muster* 4 Aug.

1324. Pugh, John. "Novel That Finds Heart of Africa." *Worcester Evening News* 3 June.

1971.   1325.   R. A. "Africa's Dilemma with Insight and Sympathy." *Rand Daily Mail* 16 July: 11.

1326.   Raban, Jonathan. "Pain and Panic." *New Statesman* 14 May: 677.

1327.   Rev. of *A Guest of Honour. Book Review Digest: Sixty-Sixth Annual Cumulation.* Ed. Josephine Samudio. New York: Wilson: 544.

1328.   Rev. of *A Guest of Honour. British Book News* Aug.: 681-682.

1329.   Rev. of *A Guest of Honour. Guardian Journal* 9 June.

1330.   Rev. of *A Guest of Honour. Manchester Evening News* 22 Apr.

1331.   *Rev. of *A Guest of Honour. New York Times Book Review* 31 Oct.

1332.   *Rev. of *A Guest of Honour. Washington Post Book World* 28 Nov.

1333.   "Scenes from East African Life." *Times Literary Supplement* 14 May: 555. Extr. in *Contemporary Literary Criticism, Vol 3.* Ed. Carolyn Riley. Detroit: Gale, 1975: 201-202.

1334.   Shrapnel, Norman. "Message and Method." *The Guardian* 22 Apr.

1335.   Sly, Christopher. "An Outstanding Major Novel - A True Life Whodunit - and Some History." *Wolverhampton Magazine* May.

1336.   Smith, David. "Another Look at Man by Man." *Evening Express* 4 May.

1337.   Stanley, Dean. "Bringing Life Back to Normal." *Evening Despatch* 16 Apr.

1338.   Strating, J. J. "Bedroevende krantekoppen over Afrika verwerkt tot goede roman." *Het Parool* 11 Sept.

1339.   Symons, Julian. "Fatal Continent." *Sunday Times* 9 May.

1340.   "This One Really Is Different." *Cambridge Evening News* 1 Apr.

1971. 1341. Tomalin, Claire. "Summons from Africa." *The Observer* 25 Apr.

1342. Tucker, John. "Brilliant but Cold Eye on Emergent Africa." *Pretoria News* 11 Aug.: 8.

1343. Urquhart, Fred. "Teething Troubles." *Oxford Mail* 22 Apr.

1344. Van Vactor, Anita. "The Disasters of Conscience." *The Listener* 22 Apr.: 527-528.

1345. Wade, Rosalind. Rev. of *A Guest of Honour*. *Contemporary Review* July: 45-46.

1346. Watkins, Geoffrey. "Powerful Passions of Africa." *Western Mail* 1 May.

1347. Webster, Mary Morison. "Miss Gordimer Takes Mature Look at New Africa." *Sunday Times* 8 Aug.: 4.

1348. Weeks, Edward. Rev. of *A Guest of Honour*. *The Atlantic* Feb.: 126-127.

1349. Wilson, Phillip. "Martyr to the New Africa." *New Zealand Listener* Sept.

1350. Wyndham, Violet. Rev. of *A Guest of Honour*. *Harper's Bazaar* Mar.: 7.

1351. Yglesias, Jose. "Choices and Consequences." *The Nation* 18 Jan.: 87, 89.

1972. 1352. Österling, Anders. "En Världsdels Vånda." *Sydsvenska Dagbladet Snälosten* 13 June.

1353. Rev. of *A Guest of Honour*. *Peace News* 21 Jan.: 8.

1973. 1354. Gray, Stephen. "Landmark in Fiction." *Contrast 30* (8.2): 78-83.

1974. 1355. Sutherland, John. "Love Affair with Africa Today." *Weekend Post* 5 Oct.: B11.

Livingstone's Companions

1971. 1356. *Bell, Pearl K. "Presuming in Africa." *Christian Science Monitor* 4 Nov.: 11.

1971. 1357. Gullason, Thomas A. Rev. of *Livingstone's Companions.* *Saturday Review* 4 Dec.: 50, 52.

1358. *Rev. of *Livingstone's Companions.* *New York Times Book Review* 31 Oct.

1359. *Rev. of *Livingstone's Companions.* *Washington Post Book World* 28 Nov.

1972. 1360. Altman, Dennis. "Writer Writ." *The Bulletin* 7 Oct.: 46-47.

1361. Bailey, Paul. "Well Taylored." *The Observer* 28 May.

1362. Berridge, Elizabeth. "Recent Fiction." *Daily Telegraph* 18 May.

1363. Beynon, Richard. "People in Transit." *To the Point* July: 47.

1364. Blake, Sally. "Gordimer's South Africa." *Jerusalem Post* 1 Sept.

1365. Blumberg, Myrna. "Glorious Guilt." *New Statesman* 18 Aug.: 232.

1366. Brittain, Victoria. "Recent Fiction." *The Illustrated London News* July.

1367. Bryer, Lynne. "Short and Sweet." *Times Educational Supplement* 25 Aug.: 14.

1368. Cunningham, Valentine. "Country Coloureds." *The Listener* 25 May: 693.

1369. D. C. C. "Gordimer Short Stories." *The Natal Witness* 29 July: 4.

1370. Dunn, Douglas. "Tales of Taylor and Gordimer." *The Spectator* 15 July: 97.

1371. E. J. R. Rev. of *Livingstone's Companions.* *Western Daily Press* 19 May.

1372. Edwards, George. "Books." *Gazette* 20 July: 21.

1373. Feinstein, Elaine. "Ghostly Gardens." *London Magazine* (12.3): 159-160. Extr. in *Contemporary Literary Criticism, Vol 3*: 202.

1374. Forshaw, Thelma. "Cool Heads and Hearts in Hot Climates." *The Australian* 7 Oct.

1972. 1375. Freyer, Grattan. "Dark Continent." *The Irish Times* 6 June.

1376. "From Africa, Tales of Today." *Halifax Evening Courier* 23 June.

1377. G. B. B. "A Nation of Substance." *Huddersfield Daily Examiner* 20 July.

1378. G. G. C. Rev. of *Livingstone's Companions*. *Weekend Post* 23 Sept.: 8.

1379. Goodman, Frank. "Books: Not Dr. Livingstone, We Presume." *Northamptonshire Evening Telegraph* 1 Aug.

1380. "Gordimer Short Stories." *Evening Post* 15 July.

1381. "Gordimer Short Stories." *The Daily News* 13 July: 11.

1382. Gray, Stephen. "Gordimer's Territory." *The Star* 1 July: 5.

1383. Grundy, Trevor. "New Books." *Daily Nation* 2 Aug.: 17.

1384. Harvey, Elizabeth. "New Fiction." *Birmingham Post* 20 May.

1385. Haslund, Ebba. "Eventyr og Virkelighet." *Aftenposten* 4 Oct.

1386. Hayden, Norman. "Hope at Last for the Tongue-Tied." *Evening Advertiser* 6 June.

1387. Israel, Noreen. "From Gordimer - an Extra Dimension." *Cape Times* 19 July: 8.

1388. J. C. T. "A Cool Eye, Lively Themes, Mature Style." *Pretoria News* 6 July.

1389. J. McC. "African Stories." *The Oxford Times* 9 June.

1390. Jefferis, Barbara. "Tales of Human Isolation." *Sydney Morning Herald* 30 Sept.: 18.

1391. Jenkins, Valerie. "Cosmo Reads the New Books." *Cosmopolitan* June.

1392. Keesing, Nancy. "Blacks and Whites." *Sunday Telegraph* 1 Oct.

1393. Kepert, L. V. "Shadows with the Sunshine." *Sun-Herald* 10 Sept.

1394. Knight, Susan. "Figures in Landscapes." *Tribune* 7 July.

1972. 1395. L. S. Rev. of *Livingstone's Companions*. *Africa Digest* Dec.: 138.

1396. L. W. "Boredom Easer." *Shropshire Star* 16 May.

1397. Lennox-Short, Alan. Rev. of *Livingstone's Companions*. SABC radio broadcast "Bookshelf". 4 July: 19h17. [Transcript.]

1398. M. K. "Mixed Bag Saved from Censor." Supp. to *Sunday Tribune* 16 July: M3.

1399. M. W. "Africa's Eternal Conflict." *Coventry Evening Telegraph* *24 Aug.

1400. MacManus, Gwen. "A Masterly Collection of Short Stories." *Evening Herald* 18 May.

1401. "A Man Who Understands Women." *Sunday Independent* 2 June.

1402. Manning, Margaret. "Out of a Brooding Mood." *Boston Sunday Globe* 3 Jan.

1403. Marquard, Jean. "Sy tik ons hard op die fingers." *Rapport* 27 Aug.: 6.

1404. McCartney, Maris. "New Novels: Feminine Fantasy." *Glasgow Herald* 20 May.

1405. Millar, D. H. "Short Stories." *The Irish Press* 22 July.

1406. Moody, Roger. Rev. of *Livingstone's Companions*. *Peace News* 18 Aug.

1407. Nesbitt, W. J. "Novels." *The Northern Echo* 2 June.

1408. "A New Gordimer." Supp. to *The Star* 3 *Mar.: B2

1409. O'Donovan, Joan. "An Instinct, above All, for People." *Oxford Mail* 18 May.

1410. "Partitioned Off." *Times Literary Supplement* 26 May: 595. Extr. in *Contemporary Literary Criticism, Vol 3*: 202.

1411. Pugh, John. Rev. of *Livingstone's Companions*. *Worcester Evening News* 1 Aug. Repr. *Hereford Evening News* 1 Aug.

1412. Quigly, Isabel. "Short and Tall." *Financial Times* 1 June.

1972. 1413. R. H. "Modern Africans of All Colours." *The Natal Mercury* 20 July: 10.

1414. Rev. of *Livingstone's Companions*. *Book Review Digest: Sixty-Seventh Annual Cumulation*. Ed. Josephine Samudio. New York: Wilson: 515-516.

1415. Rev. of *Livingstone's Companions*. *Guardian Journal* 12 July.

1416. Rev. of *Livingstone's Companions*. *Manchester Evening News* 21 June.

1417. Rev. of *Livingstone's Companions*. *Neue Züricher Zeitung* 7 Dec.

1418. Rev. of *Livingstone's Companions*. *Nigrizia* Nov.: *34.

1419. Rev. of *Livingstone's Companions*. *Scarborough Evening News* 14 July.

1420. Rev. of *Livingstone's Companions*. *The Star* 10 July.

1421. Rosenbloom, Henry. "Stories from the Sunshine." *Nation Review* 28 Oct.

1422. Shrapnel, Norman. "Real Stories." *The Guardian* 18 May: 8.

1423. Sheldon, Sayre P. "An Explorer of the Human Heart." *Boston Herald Traveler* 1 Sept.

1424. Stanford, Derek. "Gay Fantasy." *The Scotsman* 3 June: 3.

1425. Wade, Rosalind. Rev. of *Livingstone's Companions*. *Contemporary Review* July: 45-49.

1426. Webster, Mary Morison. "Gordimer an Incomparable Teller of Many Tales." *Sunday Times News Magazine* (supp. to *Sunday Times*) 5 June: 18.

1427. West, Rebecca. "When Silent Was the South." *Sunday Telegraph* 18 June.

1428. Wiggin, Maurice. "The Way They Live Now." *Sunday Times* 28 May.

1429. Williams, Owen. "Gordimer at the Height of Her Powers." *The Argus* 2 Aug.

1972.   1430.   Y. J. B. "Brilliantly Developed Stories and Superbly Drawn Characters." *Eastern Province Herald* 20 Sept.: 18.

1973.   1431.   Marquard, Jean. "Cryptic Realism." *Contrast 30* (8.2): 84-85.

1976.   1432.   Bryer, Lynne. "Nadine Stories Out of Embargo." *Eastern Province Herald* 4 Aug.: 11.

1433.   Du Plessis, E. P. "Nadine se eers verbode boek." *Die Burger* 10 June: 17. Repr. as "Afrika van pas gister." *Beeld* 5 July: 10.

The Black Interpreters

1973.   1434.   "Author Has Close Look at African Writing." *Evening Post* 22 Oct.: 6.

1435.   E. D. "Writers 'Shaped by Africa.'" *Eastern Province Herald* 21 Nov.: 23.

1974.   1436.   Brink, André P. "Gordimer skryf Trap-der-jeugd oor S.A. se swart digters." *Rapport* 27 Jan.: 9.

1978.   1437.   Mabogoane, Meshack. Rev. of *The Black Interpreters*. *Staffrider* (1.4): 62.

1438.   St. Clair, Robert N. Rev. of *The Black Interpreters*. *Staffrider* (1.3): 57.

On the Mines (with David Goldblatt)

1973.   1439.   Forsyth, Ian. "Mines in Picture and Prose." *Cape Times* 28 Nov.: 12.

1440.   Godfrey, Denis. "Inspired Look at Our Mines." *The Star* 8 Dec.: 11.

1441.   J. C. T. "Mining - a Joint Effort." *Pretoria News* 16 Nov.: B3.

1442.   Lawrence, Patrick. "Men in Search of Gold." *The Star* 20 Nov.: 41.

1443.   Mence, Lin. "The Reef's Ugly Beauty." *Rand Daily Mail* 16 Nov.: 9.

1973. 1444. "*On the Mines.*" *Rapport* 18 Nov.: 21.

1445. Webster, Mary Morison. "On the Mines - a Lode of Reef History." *Sunday Times* 2 Dec.: 12.

The Conservationist

1974. 1446. A. J. H. "Question Mark on a Prize Novel." *Bulawayo Chronicle* 24 Dec.

1447. Ackroyd, Peter. "Peter Ackroyd on the Booker Prize Boobies." *The Spectator* 9 Nov.: 599.

1448. Ahnlund, Knut. "Under strecket: det Afrikanska dilemmat under mikroskop." *Svenska Dagbladet* 30 Dec.

1449. ". . . and a New Gordimer." *The Star* 13 Sept.

1450. Bailey, Paul. "Ghosts on the Veld." *The Observer* 3 Nov.

1451. Berridge, Elizabeth. "Recent Fiction." *Daily Telegraph* 31 Oct.

1452. "The Best from Women Writers." *Woman's Journal with Flair* Nov.

1453. Bourke, Barbara. "African Vignettes." *The Irish Times* 2 Nov.

1454. Brittain, Victoria. "Recent Fiction." *The Illustrated London News* Dec.

1455. "Burning Stabs in New Novel." *The Star* 9 Nov.

1456. Butler, Guy. "Provocative Parable." *Eastern Province Herald* 23 Nov.

1457. Cavaliero, Glen. "Self-Tormented Jewish Hero." *Eastern Daily Press* 8 Nov.

1458. Chettle, Judith. "Puppets on a Racial String." *To the Point* 20 Dec.

1459. Clayton, Cherry. "A Secret Life." *New Nation* Dec.: 19.

1460. Conway, Arthur. Rev. of *The Conservationist*. BBC radio broadcast "Book Talk". 19 Nov. [Transcript.]

1974. 1461. Cunningham, Valentine. "Kinds of Colonialism." *Times Literary Supplement* 1 Nov.: 1217.

1462. F. W. L. "No, No, Nadine." *Sunday News* 9 Dec.

1463. Ferguson, Ian. "Wit, ryk eensaamheid in wye Afrika." *Beeld* 4 Dec.

1464. Firth, Brian. "Life-Styles." *The Tablet* 23 Nov.: 1139.

1465. G. B. "A Disturbing S. African Novel." *The Natal Mercury* 28 Nov.

1466. Gilliatt, Penelope. "Books of the Year." *The Observer* 15 Dec.

1467. Gillott, Jacky. "*The Conservationist*: by Nadine Gordimer." *The Times* 31 Oct.

1468. Gray, Stephen. "She Sees SA Better than Other Authors . . . ." *The Star* 13 Nov.: 21.

1469. Harris, Noreen. "Gordimer's Living Ghost." *Cape Times* 13 Nov.: 14.

1470. Hatfield, Denis. Rev. of *The Conservationist*. SABC radio broadcast "Talking of Books." 13 Dec. [Transcript.]

1471. J. L. "Books: Along Corridors of Power." *Huddersfield Daily Examiner* 29 Nov.

1472. Jordan, Mary. "Gordimer Gives Unslanted View." *Sunday Express* 22 Dec.: 19.

1473. Kiewiet, Keith. "Gordimer Story: Man Who Could Not Bend Africa." *Weekend Argus* 9 Nov.: 12.

1474. Levin, Doreen, and Pamela Diamond. "Gordimer's New Book Is Barred." *Sunday Times* 10 Nov.: 16.

1475. Mellors, John. "Day of Accomplishment." *The Listener* 21 Nov.: 684-686.

1476. Morgan, Patricia. "Ray of Hope at Last." *Melbourne Herald* 10 Dec.

1477. "Nadine May Get the Booker Prize." *The Daily News* 8 Nov.

1478. "Nadine's Best Novel Shares Top Award." *Pretoria News* 28 Nov.

1974. 1479. Naudé, Charles. "Gebrek aan diepte." *Die Burger* 19 Dec.: 16

1480. "New Novels: Dark Africa." *Glasgow Herald* 21 Dec.

1481. "Persecution That is Approved by the Establishment." *Evening Star* 10 Dec.

1482. Powley, Neville. Rev. of *The Conservationist*. BBC radio broadcast "Bookcase." 30 Nov.: 21h00; rept. 2 Dec.: 13h15; 4 Dec.: 23h15. [Transcript.]

1483. "The £5,000 Prize . . . for Two Ways of Life." *Daily Mail* 28 Nov.

1484. Quigly, Isabel. "Done with Mirrors." *Financial Times* 31 Oct.: 34.

1485. Randall, Peter. "Kaleidoscopic View on SA Society." *Rand Daily Mail* 18 Nov.: 15.

1486. Rev. of *The Conservationist*. *Liverpool Daily Post* 16 Nov.

1487. Rev. of *The Conservationist*. *New Fiction Society* Oct.: 11.

1488. Rev. of *The Conservationist*. *Sunday Telegraph* 3 Nov.

1489. Richardson, Jean. "New Fiction." *Birmingham Post* 18 Nov.

1490. Share, Bernard. "New Fiction." *Hibernia* 8 Nov.

1491. Shrapnel, Norman. Rev. of *The Conservationist*. *The Guardian* 31 Oct.

1492. Smith, Godfrey. "Cold Comfort Farm." *Sunday Times* 3 Nov. Repr. as "Review: Books." *Weekend Argus* 9 Nov.: 2.

1493. 't Hoen-Croll, R. D. H. Rev. of *The Conservationist*. *Prisma - Lectuurinformatie* (1837).

1494. Taylor, Jackie. Rev. of *The Conservationist*. *Hard Times* Dec.

1495. Theroux, Paul. "In Retreat." *New Statesman* 8 Nov.: 656-658.

1496. Toebosch, Wim. "Twee blanken vertellen zwart Afrika." *Het Laatste Nieuws* 5 Dec.

1974. 1497. Tucker, John. "How the Black Stranger Came Home to Mehring's Place." *Pretoria News* 4 Dec.

1498. Urquhart, Fred. "Prize from the Veldt." *Oxford Mail* 31 Oct.

1499. Usher, Dick. "Flaws amid the Ironies of *The Conservationist.*" *Sunday Tribune* 22 Dec.: 10.

1500. W. J. C. "Description Out of Place in Novel." *Umtali Post* 6 Dec.

1501. "Winning Author on Plight of Blacks." *The Argus* 28 Nov.: 27.

1502. Woods, Eddie. Rev. of *The Conservationist. Morning Star* 12 Dec.

1975. 1503. Abrahams, Lionel. "Books: Ecology of the Bourgeois World." *Snarl* May: 10-11.

1504. *Archer, W. H. Rev. of *The Conservationist. Bestsellers* 15 Mar.

1505. Bell, Pearl K. "Writers & Writing: Confronting Hateful Legacies." *The New Leader* 31 Mar.: 17-18. Extr. in *Contemporary Literary Criticism, Vol 5*: 146-147.

1506. Bellette, A. F. Rev. of *The Conservationist. Ariel* (6.3): 106-108.

1507. Berner, Robert L. Rev. of *The Conservationist. Books Abroad* (49.3): 597.

1508. "Book Reviews: Life in South Africa." *Sunday Gleaner* 5 Jan.

1509. "Briefly Noted: Fiction." *The New Yorker* 12 May: 141-142. Extr. in *Contemporary Literary Criticism, Vol 5*: 148.

1510. Dahl, Tor Edvin. "Hvem eier Afrika?" *Aftenposten* 16 Jan.

1511. Even-Paz, Aviva. "African Symbol." *Jerusalem Post Magazine* 17 Jan.: 15.

1512. Geismar, Maxwell. "Black Man's Burden." *Saturday Review* 8 Mar.: 24-25. Extr. in *Contemporary Literary Criticism, Vol 5*: 146.

1513. *Geng, Veronica. "Disputed Territory." *Ms.* July: 39-41. Extr. in *Contemporary Literary Criticism, Vol 5*: 148.

1975. 1514. *Glover, Elaine. Rev. of *The Conservationist*. *Stand* (16.3): 68-*70. Extr. in *Contemporary Literary Criticism, Vol 7*: 131-132.

1515. Gray, Stephen. "Review of Gordimer Book Inept." *Sunday Times* 16 Feb.: 7. [Response to "*Conservationist* Hard Going, but Rewarding" by A. B. Hughes. *Sunday Times* 26 Jan.: 7.]

1516. Halligan, Marion. "An Africa of the Mind." *The Canberra Times* 10 Oct.

1517. Hughes, A. B. "*Conservationist* Hard Going, but Rewarding." *Sunday Times* 26 Jan.: 7. [See response "Review of Gordimer Book Inept" by Stephen Gray. *Sunday Times* 16 Feb.: 7]

1518. J. M. "Booktalk." *Fair Lady* 19 Feb.: 33.

1519. *Johnson, Diane. "Out of Africa." *Washington Post Book World* 6 Apr.: 3. Extr. in *Contemporary Literary Criticism, Vol 5*: 147.

1520. Leiter, Robert. Rev. of *The Conservationist*. *The New Republic* 13 Sept.: 29-30. Extr. in *Contemporary Literary Criticism, Vol 7*: 132.

1521. Lester, Margot. "White and Black." *Jewish Quarterly* (Winter): 44-45.

1522. Mackintosh, Peter. "Cultural Isolation." *The African Communist* (3rd Quarter): 108-110.

1523. N. S. "Brooding Theme." *Auckland Star* 5 July.

1524. "Nadine bloedloos intellektueel?" *Rapport* 5 Jan.: 7.

1525. *Nordell, Roderick. "South African Tightrope Act." *Christian Science Monitor* 19 May: 23.

1526. P. R. G. "The Pig-Iron Curtain." *To the Point* 25 Jan.: 53.

1527. "Popular New Books to Read." *The Friend* 18 Sept.: 2.

1528. Prescott, Peter S. "Down in the Dirt." *Newsweek* 10 Mar.: 43-44. Extr. in *Contemporary Literary Criticism, Vol 5*: 146.

1529. "Prizewinning Novel." *The Citizen* 17 Jan.

1530. R. T. Rev. of *The Conservationist*. *The Universe* 3 Jan.

1975. 1531. Raban, Jonathan. "Taking Possession." *Encounter* (44.2): 80-82. Extr. in *Contemporary Literary Criticism, Vol 5*: 145-146.

1532. Ravenscroft, Arthur. "Nadine Gordimer's New Assurance." *Journal of Commonwealth Literature* (10.1): 80-81.

1533. Rev. of *The Conservationist*. *British Book News* Jan.: 69.

1534. Rev. of *The Conservationist*. *Choice* May: 392.

1535. Rev. of *The Conservationist*. *Manchester Evening News* 4 Jan.

1536. Rev. of *The Conservationist*. *Time* 7 July: 60. Extr. in *Contemporary Literary Criticism, Vol 7*: 132.

1537. Ricks, Christopher. "Fathers and Children." *The New York Review of Books* 26 June: 13-15. Extr. in *Contemporary Literary Criticism, Vol 7*: 131.

1538. Smith, Rowland. Rev. of *The Conservationist*. *Journal of Southern African Studies* (1.2): 259-260.

1539. Swift, Mark. "Large Tapestry." *Contrast 36* (9.4): 79-81.

1540. *Taliaferro, Frances. Rev. of *The Conservationist*. *Book-letter* 28 Apr.: 12. Extr. in *Contemporary Literary Criticism, Vol 5*: 147.

1541. Theroux, Paul. "*The Conservationist*: Nadine Gordimer's Mehring Would Leave the World Alone." *New York Times Book Review* 13 Apr.: 4-5. Extr. in *Modern Commonwealth Literature*: 48-49.

1542. Toulson, Shirley. "Strength or Style from South Africa." *Tribune* 10 Jan.

1543. Voss, A. E. Rev. of *The Conservationist*. *Reality* (7.2): 15-17.

1544. W. N. C. W. "Fiction." *Methodist Recorder* 24 Apr.

1545. Wästberg, Per. "En Konservator." *Dagens Nyheter* 26 May: 4.

1546. Wauthier, Claude. "D'hier á demain: folie au pays de l'apartheid." *Jeune Afrique* 13 June: 8.

1976. 1547. "Yarn Is Worth Award." *Northamptonshire Evening Telegraph* 2 Jan.

1548. Rev. of *The Conservationist*. *Book Review Digest: Seventy-First Annual Cumulation*. Ed. Josephine Samudio. New York: Wilson: 493-494.

1977. 1549. King, Bruce. "Recent Commonwealth Fiction." *The Sewanee Review* (Spring): 126-134. Extr. in *Contemporary Literary Review, Vol 10*: 126-127.

Selected Stories

1975. 1550. A. L. W. "Thirty Years of Change." *Rhodesia Herald* 29 Dec.

1551. Ackroyd, Peter. Rev. of *Selected Stories*. *The Spectator* 29 Nov.: 704.

1552. Barras, Leonard. "Short Stories." *Sunday Times* 7 Dec.

1553. Berridge, Elizabeth. "Recent Fiction." *Daily Telegraph* 27 Nov.

1554. "Best of Nadine Gordimer." *The Natal Mercury* 18 Dec.: 16.

1555. Biddulph, Michael. "The Gordimer Definition." *Oxford Mail* 4 Dec.

1556. Case, Frederick Ivor. "Nadine Gordimer: *Selected Stories*." *World Literature Written in English* (17.1): 54-55.

1557. Cunninghan [sic], Valentine. "Native Daughter." *New Statesman* 28 Nov.: 686.

1558. Ford, James Allan. "The Life-Giving Drop." *The Scotsman* 6 Dec.

1559. Hill, Susan. "Masterly Sprints." *The Times* 4 Dec.

1560. Nesbitt, W. J. "Short and Long." *The Northern Echo* 28 Nov.

1561. Pryce-Jones, David. "With Eyes Wide Open." *Jewish Chronicle* 19 Dec.: 11.

1562. *Rev. of *Selected Stories*. *Daily Mail* 27 Nov.

1563. Rev. of *Selected Stories*. *Express & Echo* 10 Dec.

1975. 1564. Spurling, John. Rev. of *Selected Stories*. BBC radio broadcast "Kaleidoscope". 26 Nov.: 21h30. [Transcript.]

1565. "Tales Old and New." *Southern Evening Echo* 31 Dec.

1566. "Telling It in Brief." *Glasgow Herald* 18 Dec.

1567. Thwaite, Anthony. "Where No Birds Sing." *The Observer* 7 Dec.: 32.

1568. Vale, Adrian. "Story Times." *The Irish Times* 11 Dec.

1569. W. H. "Selected Stories by Gordimer." *Cape Times* 17 Dec.: 12.

1570. Woods, Eddie. "Victorian Look at the East End." *Morning Star* 18 Dec.: 4.

1571. Wordsworth, Christopher. "Caliban's Inheritance." *The Guardian* 27 Nov.

1976. 1572. Banville, John. "A Sense of Proportion." *Hibernia* 30 Jan.: 26.

1573. Breytenbach, Kerneels. "Goeie beeld van 'n ontwikkeling." *Beeld* 9 Feb.: 11.

1574. Brink, André P. "'n Sfeer draai stadig voor jou verby." *Rapport* 1 Aug.: 7.

1575. Bryer, Lynne. "A Penetrating Talent." *Eastern Province Herald* 11 Feb.: 18.

1576. Chesnick, Eugene. "A Writer's Space." *The Nation* 28 Aug.: 149-151. Extr. in *Contemporary Literary Criticism, Vol* 7: 133-134.

1577. Dahl, Tor Edvin. "Bøker verden snakker om: Afrikas ansikt under forandring." *Aftenposten* 3 Jan.

1578. Godwin, Gail. "Out of Africa and India." *Harper's Magazine* Apr.: 101-102.

1579. Greig, Robert. "Aiming for That Essence." *The Star* 8 Apr.: 21.

1580. Harvey, Elizabeth. "Living Images of Africa." *Birmingham Post* 3 Jan.

1581. J. "Gordimer, vat haar of los haar." *Die Burger* 18 Mar.: 10.

1976. 1582. J. L. "Selected Ghosts." *Huddersfield Daily Examiner* 15 Jan.

1583. Jones, D. A. N. "Limited by the Law." *Times Literary Supplement* 9 Jan.: 25.

1584. Kermode, Frank. "Coming Up for Air." *New York Review of Books* 15 July: 43-44. Extr. in *Contemporary Literary Criticism, Vol 10*: 240.

1585. Lavin, Deborah. Rev. of *Selected Stories*. BBC Radio Ulster broadcast 4 Jan. [Transcript.]

1586. Maitland, Sara. "Fiction." *Time Out* 20 Feb.

1587. Mortimer, Penelope. "Selected Stories." *New York Times Book Review* 18 Apr.: 7. Extr. in *Contemporary Literary Review, Vol 7*: 132-133.

1588. Naylor, Derek. "Now You Can Catch Up with 'Clayhanger' in a Fine Paperback Trilogy." *Yorkshire Evening Post* 10 Jan.: 8.

1589. Omond, Mary. "Nadine's Moments under Microscope." *Daily Dispatch* 19 Mar.: 4.

1590. Nicol, Mike. "Nadine Gordimer at Her Best." *To the Point* 27 Feb.: 38.

1591. *Nye, Robert. "Something True about Humans in Any Environment." *Christian Science Monitor* 5 July: 24.

1592. Pogrund, Anne. "Fruits of a Restless Mind." *Rand Daily Mail* 3 May: 9.

1593. Quigly, Isabel. "Tribal and Formal." *Financial Times* 22 Jan.: 31.

1594. *Rev. of *Selected Stories*. *America* 17 Apr.

1595. Rev. of *Selected Stories*. *Contemporary Review* Jan.: 47-48.

1596. Stander, Siegfried. "Marvellous - a Joy to Dig Down Into." *Pretoria News* 10 Mar.: 18.

1597. Stern, James. "Collective Guilt." *London Magazine* (16.1): 109-112.

1977.   1598. Thwaite, Anthony. Rev. of *Selected Stories*. BBC radio broadcast 3 Jan. [Transcript.]

1599. "Vivid Tales of Southern Africa." *Sunday Gleaner* 29 Feb.

1600. Berner, Robert. Rev. of *Selected Stories*. *World Literature Today* (51.2): 322.

1601. King, Bruce. "Recent Commonwealth Fiction." *The Sewanee Review* (Spring): 126-124. Extr. in *Contemporary Literary Criticism, Vol 10*: 240-241.

1602. Rev. of *Selected Stories*. *Book Review Digest: Seventy-Second Annual Cumulation*. Ed. Josephine Samudio. New York: Wilson: 454.

1978.   1603. Case, Frederick Ivor. "Nadine Gordimer, *Selected Stories*." *World Literature Written in English* (17.1): 54-55.

1604. Paulin, Tom. "Evidence of Neglect." *Encounter* (50.6): 67-70.

1984.   1605. *Hill, Mervyn. "The Politics of Good Intentions." Supp. to *Voice* Sept.: 1, 6-8.

Some Monday for Sure

1976.   1606. Bailey, Paul. "Unquiet Graves." *Times Literary Supplement* 9 July: 841. Extr. in *Contemporary Literary Criticism, Vol 10*: 239-240.

1607. Bevan, David. "Gordimer on Race Problem." *Weekend Post* 30 Oct.: 6.

1608. M. H. F. "The Flaws of a Famous Writer." *The Friend* 28 Oct.: 6A.

1609. Marquard, Jean. "'n Ontoegeeflike konfrontasie." *Beeld* 1 Nov.: 9.

1610. P. S. "One for the Exiles." *Sunday Tribune* 5 Dec.: 4.

1977.   1611. Gardner, Colin. "Nadine's World of Strangers." *Reality* (8.6): 13-15.

Burger's Daughter

N.D. 1612. Stewart, Ian. "Recent Fiction." *The Illustrated London News.*

1613. M. M. "Powerful Fiction and Baker's Dozen." *Newsagent & Bookshop* 24 May: 26.

1979. 1614. Abrahams, Lionel. "Gordimer Breaks Up the Smooth Assumptions." *Oggendblad* 31 Aug.: 1. Extr. in "What the Literary Press Thought of the Novel." *What Happened to Burger's Daughter or How South African Censorship Works.* Johannesburg: Taurus, 1980: 63.

1615. Ackroyd, Peter. "A Matter of Size." *Sunday Times* 9 Dec.

1616. *Barclay, Dolores. Rev. of *Burger's Daughter. Chicago Tribune.*

1617. Bean, Lucy. "It's Not Her Best." *The Argus* 21 Nov.: 18.

1618. *Begemann, Niente. Rev. of *Burger's Daughter. Vrij Nederland Kleurkatern* (supp. to *Vrij Nederland*) 28 Apr.

1619. Biddulph, Michael. "Golden Days to Horror." *Oxford Mail* 14 June.

1620. Blakeston, Oswell. "Critics' Choice '79." *Gay News* 13 Dec.-9 Jan.

1621. Blakeston, Oswell. "Search, Commitment and Suffering." *Tribune* 22 June.

1622. Bowers, Frances. "Unbanned, Overweight - Gordimer's Novel." *Cape Times* 17 Oct.: 12.

1623. "Briefly Noted: Fiction." *The New Yorker* 3 Sept.: 105-106. Extr. in "What the Literary Press Thought of the Novel." *What Happened to Burger's Daughter or How South African Censorship Works*: 64.

1624. Brode, Tony. Rev. of *Burger's Daughter. Southern Evening Echo* 26 July.

1625. Broyard, Anatole. "Books of the Times." *New York Times* 19 Sept.: C22. Extr. in "What the Literary Press Thought of the Novel." *What Happened to Burger's Daughter or How South African Censorship Works*: 62.

1979. 1626. C. P. "Separate Identities." *Eastern Daily Press* 27 Aug.

1627. Caute, David. "What Next?" *New Statesman* 15 June: 876-877. [Incomplete - typesetting error.]

1628. Clayton, Cherry. "In the Political Bloodstream." *Financial Mail* 26 Oct.: 403.

1629. *Cohen, George. Rev. of *Burger's Daughter*. *Chicago Tribune Book World* 9 Sept. Extr. in "What the Literary Press Thought of the Novel." *What Happened to Burger's Daughter* or *How South African Censorship Works*: 65.

1630. Curry, Joan. "An Awesome Talent." *The Press*.

1631. Dale, Celia. "Remembrance of Things Past." *Homes & Gardens* Sept.

1632. De la Ruelle, Marc. "Zuid-Afrika: Zonder de vooroordelen." 29-30 Sept.: 11.

1633. "The Deeds of the Father. . . ." *Post* 10 June: 3.

1634. "Destiny of a Small Girl in a Gymslip." *Express & Echo* 18 Aug.

1635. Firth, Brian. "Particular Drama." *The Tablet* 18 Aug.: 803.

1636. Goff, Martyn. "Recent Fiction." *Daily Telegraph* 7 June. Extr. in "What the Literary Press Thought of the Novel." *What Happened to Burger's Daughter* or *How South African Censorship Works*: 61.

1637. Goodman, Frank. "The Action is Packed." *Northamptonshire Evening Telegraph* 10 Sept.

1638. "Gordimer Novel Wins Critical Acclaim." *Rand Daily Mail* 8 June: 4.

1639. "Gordimer Panned." *Cape Times* 29 June: 10.

1640. "Gordimer-roman kry oorsee lof." *Die Burger* 13 July: 10.

1641. Gray, Stephen. "Gordimer's Boldest Bid for Greatness." *The Star* 29 Nov.: 22. Extr. in "What the Literary Press Thought of the Novel." *What Happened to Burger's Daughter* or *How South African Censorship Works*: 65-66.

1979. 1642. *Grumbach, Doris. "Heritage and Its Burdens." *Books & Arts* (1.2): 8-9. Extr. in *Contemporary Literary Criticism, Vol 18*. Ed. Sharon R. Gunton. Detroit: Gale, 1981: 188.

1643. Harvey, Elizabeth. "Making Sense of South Africa?" *Birmingham Post* 14 June.

1644. *Hauptman, Robert. Rev. of *Burger's Daughter*. *Best-sellers* (39): 278.

1645. Hepburn, Neil. "Everything in Its Place." *The Listener* 5 July: 30.

1646. Herbert, Hugh. "Left Turn on the Freedom Road." *The Guardian* 5 June: 9. [Interview.]

1647. Herbert, Hugh. "Living to be Judged." *The Guardian* 7 June.

1648. Hinde, Thomas. "Cat-and-Mouse Game." *Sunday Telegraph* 10 June.

1649. Hope, Christopher. "Endangered Species." *London Magazine* (19.5&6): 137-140. Extr. in *Contemporary Literary Criticism, Vol 18*: 187-188.

1650. Hope, Mary. "My Book of the Year." *Financial Times* 29 Dec.: 13.

1651. Jacobs, Gerald. "A Most Gifted Novelist." *Jewish Chronicle* 22 June: 19.

1652. Jansen, Ena. "Gordimer-boek in Nederland." *Beeld* 28 July: 8. [Report on reception of *Burger's Daughter* by the Dutch press.]

1653. Jillett, Neil. "Craggy Bleakness and Psychological Truth." *The Age* 3 Nov.

1654. Johnson, R. W. "Growing Up to Martyrdom." *New Society* 14 June: 657-658. Extr. in "What the Literary Press Thought of the Novel." *What Happened to Burger's Daughter or How South African Censorship Works*: 63-64.

1655. K. M. "Imprisoned by Prejudice." *West Africa* 16 July: 1270.

1656. Kennedy, Randall. Rev. of *Burger's Daughter*. *The New Republic* 29 Sept.: 37-39.

1979. 1657. Kennedy, Susan. "Striking Out." *Times Literary Supplement* 7 Dec.: 103.

1658. King, Francis. "Sub Rosa." *The Spectator* 9 June.

1659. L. C. "A Masterpiece from S Africa." *Evening Standard* 30 Nov.

1660. Langley, Andrew. "A Novel Response to the Threat of Tv." *Bath & West Evening Chronicle* 23 July.

1661. Laurence, Patrick. "Communism Novel Touches a Raw Nerve in South Africa." *The Guardian* 5 July [also on censorship in South Africa].

1662. Lavinia. "Gordimer's South Africa." *Esquire* Oct.: 19. Extr. in "What the Literary Press Thought of the Novel." *What Happened to Burger's Daughter* or *How South African Censorship Works*: 64.

1663. Lennox-Short, Alan. Rev. of *Burger's Daughter*. SABC radio broadcast "Talking of Books". 11 Oct.; rept. 12 Oct. [Transcript.]

1664. *Lescaze, Lee. Rev. of *Burger's Daughter*. *Washington Post* 4 Dec.

1665. "Literary Supplement: Quarterly Fiction Review." *Contemporary Review* Oct.: 213-216.

1666. Lundkvist, Artur. "En stridens dotter." *Svenska Dagbladet* 17 July: 6.

1667. Minervini, Rina. "Panorama of Possibilities." *Rand Daily Mail* 28 May: 8.

1668. "Nadine's Book Pronounced 'Unreadable.'" *The Daily News* 22 June: 7.

1669. *Neier, Aryeh. Rev. of *Burger's Daughter*. *Los Angeles Times* 23 Sept. Extr. in "What the Literary Press Thought of the Novel." *What Happened to Burger's Daughter* or *How South African Censorship Works*: 62.

1670. Neller, Shelly. "She Will Overcome." *The Australian* 10 Nov.

1671. Nesbitt, W. J. "In the Land of Apartheid." *The Northern Echo* 8 June.

1979. 1672. Neville, Jill. "The Red-Eyed Radical in a Force 8 Political Gale." *The National Times* 4 Aug.: 41.

1673. "New Books". *Middlesborough Evening Gazette* 16 June.

1674. "New Gordimer Novel Praised." *Daily Dispatch* 9 June: 4.

1675. O'Brien, Conor Cruise. "Waiting for Revolution." *New York Review of Books* 25 Oct.: 27-31. Extr. in "What the Literary Press Thought of the Novel." *What Happened to Burger's Daughter* or *How South African Censorship Works*: 61-62.

1676. P. D. D. "Political." *Evening Post & Chronicle* 18 Aug. Repr. in *Leisurepost* 18 Aug.: 5; *Lancashire Evening Post* 18 Aug.

1677. Paulin, Tom. "Operatic Surface, Deep Politics." *Encounter* (53.2): 51-52. Extr. in "What the Literary Press Thought of the Novel." *What Happened to Burger's Daughter* or *How South African Censorship Works*: 62.

1678. Prescott, Peter S. "The Reluctant Revolutionary." *Newsweek* 27 Aug.: 53.

1679. Pugh, John. "Somewhat Disappointing." *Worcester Evening News* 4 Sept. Repr. in *Hereford Evening News* 4 Sept.

1680. *Redman, Eric. Rev. of *Burger's Daughter*. *Washington Post Book World* 26 Aug. Extr. in "What the Literary Press Thought of the Novel." *What Happened to Burger's Daughter* or *How South African Censorship Works*: 63.

1681. Reinders, P. M. "Een dochter op zoek naar haar vader." *Cultureel* (supp. to *NRC Handelsblad*)15 June.

1682. Rev. of *Burger's Daughter*. *Bedfordshire on Sunday* 24 June.

1683. Rev. of *Burger's Daughter*. *Daily Mail* 14 June.

1684. *Rev. of *Burger's Daughter*. *Detroit News* 2 Sept.

1685. *Rev. of *Burger's Daughter*. *Evening Gazette* 16 June.

1686. Rev. of *Burger's Daughter*. *The Observer* 15 July.

1687. "S.A. Author's Book Criticised." *Pretoria News* 21 June: 19.

1979. 1688. Sampson, Anthony. "Books of the Year." *The Observer* 9 Dec.: 35.

1689. Sampson, Anthony. "Heroism in South Africa." *New York Times Book Review* 19 Aug.: 1, 29. Extr. in "What the Literary Press Thought of the Novel." *What Happened to Burger's Daughter or How South African Censorship Works*: 64.

1690. Servotte, Herman. "Dochter van haar vader." *De Standaard* 15 June.

1691. Snow, C. P. "Malamud and Gordimer." *Financial Times* 9 June: 14. Extr. in "What the Literary Press Thought of the Novel." *What Happened to Burger's Daughter or How South African Censorship Works*: 65.

1692. Somerville-Large, Gillian. "Novels." *The Irish Times* 16 June.

1693. Spray, Campbell. "Lust for Words and Passion." *Yorkshire Post* 7 June.

1694. Sterner, Zara. "My Book of the Year." *Financial Times* 29 Dec.: 13.

1695. "Family Troubles." *The Oxford Times* 29 June.

1696. Taaning, Tage. "En piges liv, strøget af censuren." *Berlingske Tidende* 13 Aug.

1697. Thwaite, Anthony. "Voyages of Discovery." *The Observer* 10 June: 37. Extr. in "What the Literary Press Thought of the Novel." *What Happened to Burger's Daughter or How South African Censorship Works*: 62.

1698. Tomalin, Claire. "African Exodus." *Punch* 27 June: 1133.

1699. Tucker, Eva. "The Dominating Daughter." *Hampstead & Highgate Express* 6 July.

1700. Tucker, John. "Gordimer - Captive Progeny." *Pretoria News* 1 June: 18.

1701. Tyler, Anne. Rev. of *Burger's Daughter*. *Saturday Review* 29 Sept.: 44, 46. Extr. in "What the Literary Press Thought of the Novel." *What Happened to Burger's Daughter or How South African Censorship Works*: 65.

1979. 1702. "U.K. Praise for Nadine Gordimer Novel." *Eastern Province Herald* 8 June: 11.

1703. Veltkamp, Patricia. Rev. of *Burger's Daughter. The Southland Times* 22 Dec.

1704. "Verbod op roman word opgehef." *Oggendblad* 4 Oct.: 3.

1705. Wade, Michael. "Soweto Aftermath." *Jerusalem Post* 14 Sept.

1706. Wade, Rosalind. Rev. of *Burger's Daughter. Contemporary Review* Oct.: 213-216.

1707. "Waiting for the Censors." *Rand Daily Mail* 5 July: 5.

1708. Waugh, Auberon. "I Give Up!" *Evening Standard* 19 June: 23.

1709. "Waugh Pans Gordimer Book." *Daily Dispatch* 11 Aug.: 4. [Response to Waugh's review "I Give Up!" *Evening Standard* 19 June: 23.]

1710. "Waugh Slams Gordimer Book." *The Natal Mercury* 20 June: 3. [Response to Waugh's review "I Give Up!" *Evening Standard* 19 June: 23.]

1711. Weir, Alison. "The Narrow Path." *Glasgow Herald* 7 June. Extr. in "What the Literary Press Thought of the Novel." What *Happened to Burger's Daughter* or *How South African Censorship Works*: 63.

1712. *Winder, David. Rev. of *Burger's Daughter. Christian Science Monitor* 10 Sept. Extr. in "What the Literary Press Thought of the Novel." *What Happened to Burger's Daughter* or *How South African Censorship Works*: 63.

1713. Woods, Eddie. "Tommy's Enemies and False Friends." *Morning Star* 12 July: 4.

1980. 1714. Brock, George. "The Banning of *Burger's Daughter.*" *The Observer* 23 Mar.: 36. Adapt. as "African Censorship Victory over South." *Daily National* 28 Mar.

1715. Dunlevy, Maurice. "Dull Refractions." *The Canberra Times* 21 June.

1716. Edwards, Bob. Rev. of *Burger's Daughter. Liberation* (23.1).

1980. 1717. Epstein, Joseph. "Too Much Even of Kreplach." *The Hudson Review* (33.1): 97-110. Extr. in *Contemporary Literary Criticism, Vol 18*: 188.

1718. Gilmour, Peter. Rev. of *Burger's Daughter*. *British Book News* Jan.: 57.

1719. "Gordimer skryf oor verbod op haar boek." *Beeld* 24 Mar.: 4.

1720. Le May, Jean. "The Strange Story of *Burger's Daughter*." *Sunday Express* 30 Mar.: 20.

1721. Levin, Doreen. "Nadine Tells What Happened to Her Daughter." *Sunday Times* 30 Mar.: 8.

1722. Lindfors, Bernth. "Pungent Acuity." *CRNLE Reviews Journal* (1): 63-64.

1723. Rev. of *Burger's Daughter*. *Book Review Digest: Seventy-Fifth Annual Cumulation*. Ed. Martha T. Mooney. New York: Wilson: 486.

1724. Z. N. "The Politics of Commitment." *African Communist* (80): 100-101. [Nadine Gordimer corrects factual discrepancy in "Facts and Interpretation." *African Communist* (82): 109.]

1981. 1725. Barry, Jo-Anne. "Gordimer's South Africa: An Undercurrent of Hope." *Daily Dispatch* 9 May: 4.

1983. 1726. H. V. "*Burger's Daughter*." *The Citizen* 21 Nov.: 6.

1992. 1727. Gorra, Michael. "An Afrikaner Underground." *New York Times Book Review* 12 Jan.: 6. [Rev. of *An Act of Terror* by André Brink; mentions *Burger's Daughter*.]

A Soldier's Embrace

N.D. 1728. Bailey, Hilary. "March Choice: *A Soldier's Embrace*: Nadine Gordimer." *New Fiction* (23).

1729. "Nadine Gordimer's Short Stories."

1980. 1730. Aitken, Helen. "Compelling South African Stories without Sentiment." *Hawkesbay Herald Tribune* 27 Sept.

1980. 1731. Askeland, Elsa. "Omfanvnelsens dag - og etterpå." *Recorder* 25 Nov.: 20.

1732. Auchincloss, Eve. "Out of Africa." *Time* 11 Aug.: 63-64.

1733. Bailey, Paul. "Telling Tales." *The Observer* 4 May.

1734. *Barclay, Dolores. Rev. of *A Soldier's Embrace*. *Chicago Tribune* 18 May.

1735. Birkby, Carel. "Gordimer - Deep Wells of Lonely Sadness." *To the Point* 3 Oct.: 54.

1736. Bowers, Frances. "The Range and Gifts of Nadine Gordimer." *Cape Times* 9 July: 8.

1737. Breslin, J. B. Rev. of *A Soldier's Embrace*. *America* 11 Oct.: 214.

1738. Bryer, Lynne. "High on Detail." *Eastern Province Herald* 16 Sept.: 11.

1739. Clayton, Cherry. "Gordimer's New Collection Shows Up Her Strengths." *Rand Daily Mail* 8 Dec.: 10.

1740. D. A. M. B. "Stories of Detail and Detachment." *The Natal Witness* 10 Dec.: 1.

1741. Davis, Peter. "A Slice of Life from One of Africa's Finest." *Sunday Tribune* 12 Dec.

1742. Elliott, Janice. "Elegy in Black and White." *Sunday Telegraph* 27 Apr.

1743. Evans, Stuart. "Fiction." *The Times* 24 Apr.: 10.

1744. Firth, Brian. "Tragic Narratives." *The Tablet* 17 May: 481-482.

1745. Fyvel, T. R. Rev. of *A Soldier's Embrace*. *Jewish Chronicle* 4 July.

1746. Galaun, Jackie. "The Sum of Six Senses." *Jerusalem Post Magazine* 26 Sept.: 12.

1747. Garner, Lesley. Rev. of *A Soldier's Embrace*. *Good Housekeeping* 1 Aug.: 133.

1748. Glover, Stephen. "Recent Fiction." *Daily Telegraph* 24 Apr.

1980. 1749. *Gornick, Vivian. "Gordimer Confined." *The Village Voice* 17-23 Sept.: 40. Extr. in *Contemporary Literary Criticism, Vol 18*: 190-191.

1750. Gray, Paul. "Something of a Jamesian Quality." *The Star* 24 Sept.: 22.

1751. Green, Michael. "Nadine Sets a Sombre Tone." *Tonight!* (supp. to *The Daily News*) 25 Sept.: 7.

1752. Greyvensteyn, Zanné. "Thought Provoking Short Stories." *The Citizen* 15 Sept.: 6.

1753. Hagerty, Sylvia. "Gordimer Shows Skill as Story-Teller." *Daily Dispatch* 25 Oct.: 4.

1754. Heald, Tim. "Short, but Not Too Sweet." *Now!* 2 May: 72.

1755. Hodgins, Robert. "Nadine's Newest Has Few Faults." *Sunday Times* 19 Oct.

1756. "Holiday Reading." *The Observer* 13 July.

1757. "Intrigues with Diamonds." *Halifax Evening Courier* 19 May.

1758. J. C-W. "Soldiers' Stories." *The Natal Mercury* 18 Sept.: 10.

1759. J. P. Rev. of *A Soldier's Embrace*. *Fair Lady* 5 Nov.: 22.

1760. Jefferis, Barbara. "Gordimer's Exiles." *Morning Herald* 6 Sept.

1761. Jillett, Neil. "A Pain Too Intense for Frivolity." *The Age* 4 Oct.

1762. Jones, D. A. N. "Tyrant-Prisoners." *The Listener* 24 Apr.: 547-549.

1763. Lavender, John. Rev. of *A Soldier's Embrace*. *Huddersfield Daily Examiner* 15 May.

1764. Lee, Hermione. "Bending the Bars." *New Statesman* 16 May: 751. Extr. in *Contemporary Literary Criticism, Vol 18*: 189.

1765. *Milton, Edith. "Books: *A Soldier's Embrace*." *New York Magazine* 25 Aug.: 54-55. Extr. in *Contemporary Literary Criticism, Vol 18*: 190.

1980. 1766. Motjabai, A. G. "Her Region Is Ours." *New York Times Book Review* 24 Aug.: 7, 18.

1767. Nesbitt, W. J. "57 Stories." *The Northern Echo* 23 May.

1768. Nye, Robert. "Tailtips, Watercolours, Ivory Towers." *The Guardian* 1 May.

1769. Owen, Lyn. Rev. of *A Soldier's Embrace. Cosmopolitan* May: 7.

1770. *Paulin, Tom. "Issi." *Quarto* (7): 15.

1771. "Recording of Eye and Heart." *Tribune* 2 May.

1772. Rev. of *A Soldier's Embrace. Evening Press* 24 May.

1773. *Rev. of *A Soldier's Embrace. The Scotsman* 24 May.

1774. *Rev. of *A Soldier's Embrace. Washington Post Book World* 7 Sept.

1775. Robertson, Janet. "Battles and Embraces." *The Advertiser* 13 Sept.: 27.

1776. Rudman, Frank. Rev. of *A Soldier's Embrace. The Spectator* 26 Apr.: 22-23.

1777. S. P. R. "Apartheid Problem." *Grimsby Evening Telegraph* 25 July: 9.

1778. Servotte, Herman. "Het leven is toch sterker." *De Standaard* 23 May: *7.

1779. "Short Stories." *Coventry Evening Telegraph* 22 May: 12.

1780. Stewart, Ian. "Recent Fiction." *The Illustrated London News* July: 69.

1781. Stuart, Francis. "Shallow Roots." *Hibernia* 15 May.

1782. Thody, Philip. "Two Ways of Looking at Life." *Yorkshire Post* 5 June.

1783. Thompson, John. "Perilous Relations." *New York Review of Books* 23 Oct.: 46. Extr. in *Contemporary Literary Criticism, Vol 18*: 191.

1784. Tuohy, Frank. "Breaths of Change." *Times Literary Supplement* 25 Apr.: 462. Extr. in *Contemporary Literary Criticism, Vol 18*: 188-189.

1980.   1785.   Wastell, Frank. Rev. of *A Soldier's Embrace*. SABC radio broadcast "Talking of Books". 7 Aug.; rept. 10 Aug. [Transcript.]

1786.   Woods, Eddie. "Look Back on MacInnes' World." *Morning Star* 8 May.

1980/1.   1787.   Perez, Gilberto. "These Days in the Holocene." *The Hudson Review* (33.4): 575-588.

1981.   1788.   E. C. I. "A Selection of Recent Fiction: The Apache Story Vividly Told from the Indian Viewpoint." *Otago Daily Times* 15 Apr.

1789.   Halligan, Marion. "Elegant Prose." *The Canberra Times* 14 Mar.

1790.   Hill, Barry. "Listening to the Lions Roar at Night." *The National Times* 22 Feb.: 51, 52.

1791.   Le Roux, André. "Gordimer maak groot indruk." *Die Burger* 8 Jan.: 7.

1792.   Rev. of *A Soldier's Embrace*. *Book Review Digest: Seventy-Sixth Annual Cumulation*. Ed. Martha T. Mooney. New York: Wilson: 473.

1793.   Wästberg, Per. "Nadine Gordimer noveller: Engagerad hetta, ironisk överblick." *Dagens Nyheter* 12 Jan.: 4.

1982.   1794.   Louw, Josandra. "Gordimer se aansien neem steeds toe." *Die Transvaler* 15 Mar.: 7.

1795.   Rev. of *A Soldier's Embrace*. *SA Literature/Literatuur 1980: Annual Literary Survey Series 1*. Comp. Francis Galloway. Johannesburg: Donker: 46-47.

1984.   1796.   *La Salle, Peter. "More Moving Fiction from Nadine Gordimer." *Africa Today* April-June: 69-70.

1797.   Roberts, Beryl. "Naught for Our Comfort Here." *Sunday Times* 22 July: 7.

1985.   1798.   *Beard, L. S. Rev. of *A Soldier's Embrace*. *Ba Shiru* (12.2): 97-98.

July's People

1981. 1799. Ableman, Paul. "Unknown Quantities." *The Spectator* 5 Sept.: 23.

1800. "An About-Turn in a Land of Tragedy." *Express & Echo* 12 Sept.

1801. Bailey, Paul. "A Lesson in Humanity." *The Observer* 6 Sept.: 28.

1802. Bailey, Paul. "My Quartet of the Year's Best." *The Standard* 30 Dec.: 12.

1803. *Begemann, Niente. Rev. of *July's People*. *Vrij Nederland* 19 Sept.: 70-71.

1804. Binding, Paul. "Unrealised." *New Statesman* 11 Sept.: 18-19.

1805. Bowers, Frances. "South African Fugitives; Gordimer's New Novel." *Cape Times* 22 July: 12.

1806. Bowker, V. J. "Not Always Convincing." *Eastern Province Herald* 22 Dec.: 14.

1807. Boyd, William. "After the Explosion." *Sunday Times* 6 Sept.

1808. Boyers, Robert. "The Testing Out of Tomorrow." *Times Literary Supplement* 4 Sept.: 1001.

1809. Brewer, John. Rev. of *July's People*. *South Wales Argus* 16 Nov.

1810. Brodie, Cynthia. "Brutal, Chilling — but Stunning Masterpiece." *Daily Dispatch* 25 July: 4.

1811. *Broyard, Anatole. Rev. of *July's People*. *New York Times* June.

1812. *Brusse, Peter. Rev. of *July's People*. *De Volkskrant*.

1813. Cherry, Lance. "A Way of Life Disintegrates. . ." *Sowetan* 6 Aug.: 7.

1814. *Chettle, Judith. Rev. of *July's People*. *National Review* 25 Dec.: 1561. Extr. in *Contemporary Literary Criticism, Vol* 33: 181.

1981.   1815. Cilliers, Helen. "Nadine se talent weer bewys." *Die Volksblad* 22 Sept.: 2.

1816. Clayton, Cherry. "Whites Flee into the Void." *Rand Daily Mail* 27 July: 10.

1817. "Critics Hail New Gordimer Novel." *The Argus* 16 June: 2.

1818. D. T. W. K. "Prophetic Look at South Africa." *Bop Times* 22 May.

1819. Davidson, Robyn. "Revolution Turns the Racial Tables." *Sydney Morning Herald* 12 Dec.

1820. Davies, David Twiston. "Recent Fiction." *Daily Telegraph* 3 Sept.

1821. Davis, Clive. "On the Shelf." *Westindian World* 6 Nov.: 7.

1822. Dax, Henrietta. "July Book of the Month." *The Argus* 17 July: 6.

1823. E. H. "After the Revolution." *The Natal Mercury* 27 Aug.: 36.

1824. Ellis, Gill. Rev. of *July's People*. *Huddersfield Daily Examiner* 10 Sept.

1825. F. G. "Grey Areas of Black and White." *Northamptonshire Evening Telegraph* 16 Oct.

1826. Firth, Brian. "Into the Valley." *The Tablet* 3 Oct.: 972.

1827. Fyvel, T. R. "Adjusting." *Jewish Chronicle* 18 Sept.

1828. Glendinning, Victoria. "Morbid Symptoms." *The Listener* 10 Sept.: 281.

1829. "Gordimer's Latest Book May Be Banned: I Don't Know What to Expect." *Sunday Tribune* 19 July: 5.

1830. "Gordimer Novel Acclaimed." *The Star* 16 June: 9.

1831. "Gordimer se jongste." *Beeld* 17 July: 12.

1832. Gould, Tony. "Morbid Symptoms." *New Society* 3 Sept.: 402.

1833. Gray, Paul. "Future Tense." *Time* 8 June: 79.

1834. Greig, Robert. "Strengths Blend into Achievement." *Weekend Post* 12 Sept.: 4.

1981. 1835. Grenfell-Williams, Dorothy. Rev. of *July's People*. BBC African Service radio broadcast "Book Talks: When South Africa Boils Over." 6 Sept. [Transcript.]

1836. Greyling, Aletta. "Nadine gee krasse kyk na rasseprobleme." *Die Vaderland* 23 June: 15.

1837. Harvey, Elizabeth. "Powerful Voice from Africa." *Birmingham Post* 10 Sept.

1838. Hinde, Thomas. "On Shifting Sands." *Sunday Telegraph* 6 Sept.

1839. Hope, Mary. "Gordimer's Guess." *Financial Times* 12 Sept.

1840. Hough, Barrie. "Dit wat oud is, sterf . . . ." *Beeld* 28 Sept.: 18. Repr. as "Helderheid en krag van Gordimer." *Die Oosterlig* 11 Jan., 1982: 6.

1841. Isacowitz, Roy. "A Bleak and Powerful Vision." *Financial Mail* 7 Aug.: 716.

1842. J. M. E. Rev. of *July's People*. *Booklist* 15 Feb.: 774.

1843. Jacoby, Tamar. "A Harsh and Unforgiving Vision." *The Nation* 6 June: 705-706.

1844. Jansen, Ena. "*July's People* goed in Nederland ontvang." *Beeld* 21 Nov.: 4.

1845. Jillett, Neil. "Gordimer's Village of the Damned." *The Age* 14 Nov.

1846. Kenney, Henry. "Complex, Tortured, Angry, Agonised - and Very, Very Heavy!" *Sunday Times* 29 Nov.: 8.

1847. Klaaste, Aggrey. "When the Giant Rises, Something Will Give." *Sowetan* 3 Aug.: 6.

1848. Kros, Cynthia. "Truth and Terror in the Revolution." *The Star* 15 July: *16.

1849. Lindenberg, Anita. "Weinig in Suid-Afrika kan skryf soos Gordimer." *Die Vaderland* 29 Oct.: 39, 44.

1850. "A Long Look at the Summer Fiction." *Southern Evening Echo* 10 Sept.: 36.

1851. M. R. "Speller's World." *Evening Express* 7 Sept.

1981.   1852. Macleod, Sheila. "Black and White." *Evening Standard* 15 Sept.

1853. Mariën, Wim. "Meester en knecht in Zuid-Afrika." *De Morgen* 19 Dec.: 22.

1854. Massie, Allan. "Dangerous Truths of Nadine Gordimer." *Weekend Scotsman* 23 May.

1855. Massie, Allan. "A Fine, Nervous Disturbing Work." *Weekend Scotsman* 5 Sept.: 3.

1856. Meades, Jonathan. "*July's People*." *Books & Bookmen* Oct.: 29-30.

1857. Molefe, Z. B. "Revolution Is Given an Airing." *Sowetan* 19 June.

1858. Nesbitt, W. J. "Power Victims." *The Northern Echo* 11 Sept.

1859. Nicholson, John. "Fiction." *The Times* 10 Sept.: 13.

1860. Nkosi, Lewis. Rev. of *July's People*. **Worldview* Sept. Repr. in *Home and Exile and Other Selections*. Nkosi. Harlow: Longman, 1983: 157-159.

1861. Paton, Alan. "Alan Paton Reviews *July's People*, the Latest Novel by Nadine Gordimer." *Sunday Tribune* 19 July: 26.

1862. Paton, Alan. "Gordimer's South Africa." *Saturday Review* May: 67.

1863. Phillips, Carla. "In the Bleakness of God's Silence. . . ." *Eastern Daily Press* 25 Sept.

1864. Pownall, David. "Putting People before Politics." *The Guardian* 3 Sept.: 16.

1865. *Pritchard, David. Rev. of *July's People*. *Library Journal* 15 Mar.

1866. Pugh, John. "Brilliant Example of Modern Fiction." *Worcester Evening News* 19 Sept.

1867. Rev. of *July's People*. *Aberdeen Evening Examiner Record* 13 Sept.

1868. *Rev. of *July's People*. *Daily Express* 10 Sept.

1869. Rev. of *July's People*. *Harpers & Queen* Sept.

1981. 1870. *Rev. of *July's People*. *Sunday Express* 6 Dec.

1871. Riddell, Elizabeth. "Dark Insights into South Africa's Future." *The Bulletin* 15 Dec.: 79-80.

1872. Royle, Trevor. "Prophecy on Peril Facing Humanity." *Glasgow Herald* 8 Sept.: 6.

1873. Seddon, Joan. "Black Future." *Manchester Evening News* 10 Sept.

1874. *Seton, Cynthia Propper. Rev. of *July's People*. *The Daily News* June.

1875. Silber, Joan. Rev. of *July's People*. *Ms.* June.

1876. "South African Fable That's Too Cold for Comfort." *Bath & West Evening Chronicle* 26 Sept.

1877. Stein, Jackie. "Instinct for Survival." *Jerusalem Post Magazine* 16 Oct.: 14.

1878. *Strouse, Jean. Rev. of *July's People*. *Newsweek* 26 June.

1879. Taubman, Robert. "Test Case." *London Review of Books* 3-16 Sept.: *19-20.

1880. Thema, Derrick. "Nadine Gordimer on *July's People*: Chilling Prophecy." *The Star* 18 July: 7.

1881. Thody, Philip. "Not Tonight, Bonaparte." *Yorkshire Post* 10 Sept.

1882. Tucker, Eva. "Struggle of the Benighted to Survive." *Hampstead & Highgate Express* 4 Sept.

1883. Tyler, Anne. "South Africa after Revolution." *New York Times Book Review* 7 June: 1, 26. Extr. in *Contemporary Literary Criticism, Vol 33*: 181.

1884. *Van Montfrans, Manet. Rev. of *July's People*. *NRC Handelsblad*.

1885. W. S. "Meester en knecht." *Het Parool* 21 Nov.: 20.

1886. Wästberg, Per. "Vad händer sedan de svarta gjort revolt i Sydafrika?" *Dagens Nyheter* 14 Nov.

1887. Winder, David. "*July's People*: Nadine Gordimer's Warning to South Africa." *Christian Science Monitor* 23 June: 27.

1981.   1888. Woodley, Ray. "Gordimer A-Bomb in Small Package." *Sunday Express* 26 July: 28.

1889. Woods, Donald. Rev. of *July's People*. BBC radio broadcast "Kaleidoscope". 3 Sept.: 9h30. [Transcript.]

1890. Woods, Eddie. "Blowin' in the Wind across South Africa." *Morning Star* 5 Nov.

1891. Woods, Eddie. "Surviving on Dreams of How It All Could Be." *Morning Star* 10 Dec.

1892. X. "Fall of a House." *New York Review of Books* 13 Aug.: 14-18. *Repr. in *The Age* 2 Nov.: 3-4.

1981/2. 1893. Bernstein, Hilda. Rev. of *July's People*. *Liberation* Dec./ Jan.

1894. Perez, Gilberto. "The First and Other Persons." *The Hudson Review* (34.4): 606-620.

1895. Winegarten, Renee. "The World of Nadine Gordimer." *Jewish Quarterly* (Winter): 49-50.

1982.   1896. Agnew, Trevor. "Novel of S. African Survival." *The Southland Times* 30 Jan.

1897. Aitken, Helen. "S. African Novel a Little Too Tense." *Hawkesbay Herald Tribune* 2 Oct.

1898. Cronin, John. Rev. of *July's People*. *Studies* (Summer): 207-208.

1899. Dunn, Douglas. "In the Vale of Tears." *Encounter* (58.1): 49-53.

1900. Elstob, Peter. "Not Just Black and White." *P.E.N* (Spring): 21-22.

1901. Hill, Barry. "South Africa after the Revolution." *The National Times* 4-10 Apr.: 40.

1902. Louw, Josandra. "Roman beeld swart oorname uit." *Die Transvaler* 15 Mar.: 7.

1903. *Milton, Edith. Rev. of *July's People*. *The Yale Review* (71): 254.

1904. Moss, Rose. Rev. of *July's People*. *World Literature Today* (56.2): 394.

1982. 1905. "Nadine Gordimer: *July's People.*" *Kroniek* 22 Nov.: 10-11.

1906. Niven, Alastair. Rev. of *July's People*. *British Book News* Feb.

1907. Omer-Cooper, John. "Beyond a Liberal Ideal." *Otago Daily Times* 4 Apr.

1908. Parker, Mushtak. "Naive View of African Revolution." *Arabia: The Islamic World Review* Feb.: 77-78.

1909. *Rev. of *July's People*. *Afram Newsletter* (14): 30-31.

1910. *Rev. of *July's People*. *Publishers Weekly* 14 May: 214.

1911. Rev. of *July's People*. *Book Review Digest: Seventy-Seventh Annual Cumulation*. Ed. Martha T. Mooney. New York: Wilson: 559.

1912. Richards, Sally. "Bookshelf." *Toorak Times* 26 Jan.

1913. *Thompson, Betty. Rev. of *July's People*. *The Christian Century* 26 May: 642-643. Extr. in *Contemporary Literary Criticism, Vol 33*: 181-182.

1914. Valentine, Nina. "A Disturbing, Telling Novel: Trouble in South Africa." *The Courier* 2 Jan.: 16.

1915. Walsh, Jill Paton. Rev. of *July's People*. *South* Jan.: 85.

1983. 1916. Géniès, Bernard. "Sous le couvert de la fiction." *La Quinzaine Littéraire* 16-31 July: 11.

1917. Rev. of *July's People*. *SA Literature/Literatuur 1981: Annual Literary Survey Series 2*. Comp. Francis Galloway. Johannesburg: Donker: 38-39.

1918. *Vivan, Itala. "Ritornano Robinson e Venerdi." *Nigrizia* Dec.: 48-50.

1987. 1919. Jay, Salim. "*Ceux de July.*" *L'Afrique Littéraire* (80/81/82): 135-136. [Special issue L'Afrique de l'occident 1887-1987.]

1920. *Scholtz, M. "Die Suid-Afrikaanse romansisteem anno 1981 - 'n Vergelykende studie, H. Viljoen: Boekresensie." *Journal of Literary Studies* (3.2): 97-99.

Something Out There

1984. 1921. Atwood, Margaret. "Van maand tot maand: proza." *Kultuurleven* June: 399-401.

1922. Aucamp, Hennie. "Gordimer se *Something Out There*: Net Afrikaners skuldig?" *Die Burger* 6 Sept.: 15.

1923. Bailey, Paul. "Heart of the Matter." *The Observer Review* 25 Mar.: 23.

1924. Barnett, Ursula A. "Review Didn't Serve Readers." *Cape Times* 29 Aug.: 14. [Response to Frances Bowers's review "Familiar Themes of Nadine Gordimer." *Cape Times* 4 July: 10.]

1925. Bernstein, Hilda. Rev. of *Something Out There*. *Liberation* July/Aug.: 15.

1926. Bowers, Frances. "Familiar Themes of Nadine Gordimer." *Cape Times* 4 July: 10. [See Ursula Barnett's response, "Review Didn't Serve Readers." *Cape Times* 29 Aug.: 14.]

1927. Brownfield, Alan. "Nuwe Gordimer-verhale verras." *Die Volksblad* 9 May: 20.

1928. Bryer, Lynne. "Echoes in the Mind." *Eastern Province Herald* 11 Sept.: 11.

1929. Byatt, A. S., and Stuart Evans. Rev. of *Something Out There*. *The Times* 22 Mar.: 11.

1930. Clayton, Cherry. Rev. of *Something Out There*. *Leadership SA* (3.2): 141.

1931. Clayton, Sylvia. "Saboteurs." *London Review of Books* 5-18 Apr.: 23.

1932. Conyngham, John. "Acute Observations of Present South African Society." *The Natal Witness* 28 Aug.: 10.

1933. Creagh, Ursula. "Unsettled Calm." *The Literary Review* Apr.: 40-41.

1934. Dasenbrock, Reed Way. Rev. of *Something Out There*. *World Literature Today* (58.4): 653-654.

1935. Davies, Clive. "Monkey Business." *Yorkshire Post* 5 Apr.

1984. 1936. De Groot, Frances. "Gordimer: Finely Ironic." *The Star* 11 July.

1937. Edwardes, Pamela. Rev. of *Something Out There*. *Time Out* 5-11 July: 36.

1938. Enright, D. J. "Which New Era?" *Times Literary Supplement* 30 Mar.: 328.

1939. Evans, Stuart. "Tensions of Suburban South Africa." *The Daily News* 31 Mar.: 8.

1940. Girdwood, Alison. "Gordimer's South Africa." *Cencrastus* (Autumn): 50.

1941. "Gordimer Collection Praised." *Pretoria News* 16 July: 3. Repr. as "Gordimer's New Book Praised by New York Critic." *The Star* 12 July.

1942. "Gordimer tref met verhale." *Beeld* 25 Apr.: 3. Repr. as "Nuwe bundel binnekort: Gordimer is nou 'op haar beste.'" *Die Burger* 27 Apr.: 13. "Gordimer is nou op haar beste." *Oosterlig* 7 May: 11.

1943. "Gordimer's New Book Acclaimed." *The Argus* 2 Aug.: 5.

1944. Gray, Paul. "Tales of Privacy and Politics." *Time* 23 July: 72.

1945. Halligan, Marion. "Gordimer: Universal Themes." *The Canberra Times* 26 Sept.: 18.

1946. Hambidge, Joan. "Gordimer se bundel imponeer." *Beeld* 5 Nov.: 8. Repr. as "Gordimer se bundel briljante werk." *Oosterlig* 17 Dec.: 8.

1947. Hammond, David. Rev. of *Something Out There*. *Huddersfield Daily Examiner* 12 Apr.

1948. Hardwick, Elizabeth. "Somebody Out There." *New York Review of Books* 16 Aug.: 3-6.

1949. Hastings, Selina. "Recent Fiction." *Daily Telegraph* 23 Mar.

1950. Hattingh, Marion. "Finale waarheid bly ontwyk in bundel." *Die Volksblad* 15 Sept.: 6.

1951. *Hill, Mervyn. "The Politics of Good Intentions." Literary supp. to *Voice* Sept.: 1, 6-8.

1984. 1952. Hinde, Thomas. "Playing the Kafka Game." *Sunday Telegraph* 25 Mar.

1953. "In Nederlandse pers: SA boek trek aandag." *Die Burger* 6 Sept.: 14.

1954. Ingoldby, Grace. "Lessons in Life." *New Statesman* 23 Mar.

1955. J. C. T. "Essence of Gordimer." *Pretoria News* 26 July: 4.

1956. J. G. "The Shades of Grey in a Country's Agony." *Wigan Leader* 4 Apr.

1957. Jillett, Neil. "Nadine Gordimer Explores Universal Themes of Betrayal." *The Age* 4 Aug.

1958. Johnston, Karl. "Recent Fiction." *Evening Press* 11 May.

1959. Jones, Mervyn. "Breaking-Point." *The Listener* 29 Mar.: 29-30. Extr. in *Contemporary Literary Criticism, Vol 33*: 184.

1960. Langley, Andrew. "Hell in the Suburbs." *Bath & West Evening Chronicle* 24 Apr.

1961. *Lehmann-Haupt, Christopher. Rev. of *Something Out There*. *New York Times* 12 July.

1962. Leonard, Christopher. "Baboons and Guerillas in Gordimer's Suburbia." *The National Times* 6-12 July.

1963. Macleod, Sheila. "Lady Lying in Wait." *Evening Standard* 25 Apr.

1964. Marquard, Jean. "Homegrown Fiction: Confining the Beast." *Frontline* (5.2): 59.

1965. Marx, Paul. "A South African Literary Conscience." *The New Leader* 25 June: 18-20. Extr. in *Contemporary Literary Criticism, Vol 33*: 185.

1966. Massie, Allan. "Gordimer: Literary Art Succumbs to Advocacy." *The Scotsman* 31 Mar.

1967. Mellors, John. "Moral Surrender." *London Magazine* (24.3): 101-103.

1968. Minervini, Rina. "Society Made Them . . . ." *Rand Daily Mail* 4 June: 9.

1969. Moggach, Deborah. "Art Beat: Books." *Cosmopolitan* Mar.

1984. 1970. "Nadine ,oordryf oor SA toestande."' *Die Vaderland* 26 Mar.: 3.

1971. "Nadine stel stelsel self aan die woord." *Beeld* 10 Sept.: 8.

1972. O'Brien, Martin. "Books: Short and Sweet." *Riverside Magazine* May.: 41.

1973. Parker, Margaret. Rev. of *Something Out There*. *The Daily News* 21 Sept.: 7.

1974. Paul, Anthony. "Laat staan de revolutionair." *Vrij Nederland* 24 Mar.: 33, 36.

1975. Peel, Quentin. "Black and White Betrayals." *Financial Times* 24 Mar.: 16.

1976. Prescott, Peter S. "Gordimer's Tales of Betrayal." *Newsweek* 16 July: 42.

1977. R. M. "Nordimer [sic] Stories Reach the Heart." *The Natal Mercury* 7 June: 8.

1978. Rev. of *Something Out There*. *Church Times* 13 Apr.

1979. Riddell, Elizabeth. "Movement Toward a Black Solution." *The Bulletin* 24 July: 67-68.

1980. Roberts, Beryl. "Naught for Our Comfort Here." *Sunday Times* 22 July: 7.

1981. Rogers, Jane. "Ashamed to Be Human." *Artful Reporter* May.

1982. Ronge, Barry. Rev. of *Something Out There*. *Fair Lady* 3 Oct.: 21.

1983. Rostron, Bryan. Rev. of *Something Out There*. *Books & Bookmen* Mar.: 35.

1984. Rubin, Merle. "Gordimer's Stories: A Stark, Harsh View of South African Life." *Christian Science Monitor* 9 Aug.: 24. Repr. in *Christian Science Monitor* 22-28 Sept.: 17.

1985. Rushdie, Salman. "No One Is Ever Safe." *New York Times Book Review* 29 July: 7-8.

1986. Ruskin, Pamela. Rev. of *Something Out There*. *Toorak Times* 1 Aug.

1984. 1987. Russell, Brandon. "Eavesdropping." *Times Educational Supplement* 17 Aug.

1988. Schwartz, Pat. "Changing Words in the Short Story of South Africa." *Rand Daily Mail* 2 June: 7.

1989. Shapcott, Thomas. "An Eye for the Dividing Detail." *Morning Herald* 4 Aug.

1990. Stuart, Francis. "Heart of Darkness." *Sunday Tribune* 25 Mar.

1991. Symons, Julian. "The Conscience of South Africa." *Sunday Times* 25 Mar. Repr. as "Gordimer - South Africa's Conscience." *The Star* 5 Apr.: 7M.

1992. Tennant, Emma. "Political Economy." *The Guardian* 22 Mar.

1993. Tomin, Zdena. "Beautiful Possibilities of a Life to Be Lived." *Jewish Chronicle* 4 May.

1994. Trump, Martin. "Something Out There?" *Third World Book Review* (1.2): 21-23.

1995. Van Montfrans, Manet. "Verhalen van Nadine Gordimer: Verraad en verval." *Cultureel* (supp. to *NRC Handelsblad*) 4 May.

1996. Watson, Robert. Rev. of *Something Out There*. *The Gadfly* (7.2): 79-81.

1997. Waugh, Harriet. "Recent Fiction." *The Illustrated London News* June.

1998. Wieseltier, Leon. Afterword to *Something Out There*. *Salmagundi* (62): 193-196. Extr. in *Contemporary Literary Criticism, Vol 33*: 183-184.

1999. Woods, Eddie. "Alienation in a Split Society." *Morning Star* 5 Apr.

1984/5. 2000. "Changing Attitudes — Via the Short Story." *Commonwealth* (27.3): 109.

2001. Kearns, George. "Recent Fiction 1." *The Hudson Review* (37.4): 616-621.

1985. 2002. Du Plessis, Menán. "Literary Realism at Its Furthest Limits." *Contrast* (15.3): 84-92.

1985. 2003. Forni, Jacqueline. "Comment en finir avec Soweto?" *La Quinzaine Littéraire* 1-15 Sept.: 9-10.

2004. O'Connor, John. "Gordimer's Stories of South Africa." *New York Times* 1 July, sec. 3: 14.

2005. O'Connor, John. "Mesmerizing Dramas of South Africa." *New York Times* 28 July, sec. 2: 1, 21.

2006. Rev. of Something Out There. Book Review Digest: *Eightieth Annual Cumulation.* Ed. Martha T. Mooney. New York: Wilson: 598.

2007. Waugh, Harriet. "More Books of the Year." *The Spectator* 5 Jan.: 23.

1986. 2008. Gibson, Patrick. "Novella Highlights Society's Dilemmas." *The Daily News* 29 May: 27.

2009. Mackie, Heather. "Poignant Tale of Woman's Search for Identity." *Cape Times* 19 Nov.: 10.

1989. 2010. Rev. of *Something Out There. SA Literature/Literatuur 1984: Annual Literary Survey Series 5.* Comp. Francis Galloway. Pretoria: HAUM: 28-29.

Lifetimes: Under Apartheid

1986. 2011. "Apartheid in Words and Pictures." *The News Line* 21 Nov.: 8.

2012. Brittan, David. Rev. of *Lifetimes: Under Apartheid. Amateur Photographer* 13 Dec.: 75.

2013. Greenblo, Allan. "Guilt Trip." *Finance Week* 4-10 Dec.: 699.

2014. Pearson, Deanne. Rev. of *Lifetimes: Under Apartheid. Time Out* 12 Nov.

2015. Pogrund, Anne. Rev. of *Lifetimes: Under Apartheid. Today Sunday* 9 Nov.

2016. *Rev. of *Lifetimes: Under Apartheid. Tribune* 28 Nov.

2017. "Under Apartheid." *The Scotsman* 13 Dec.: 3.

1987. 2018. Crankshaw, P. "A Potent Blend of Words and Images." *New Nation* 12-18 Feb.: 17.

2019. Dubow, Neville. "Leadership: Books." *Leadership* (6.1): 98-99.

2020. Heron, Liz. "Politics of Colour." *New Statesman* 20 Feb.: 23-24.

2021. Macmillan, Mona. "White Consciousness." *The Tablet* 7 Feb.

2022. *Nixon, Rob. Rev. of *Lifetimes: Under Apartheid*. *The Nation* 2 May.

2023. Rev. of *Lifetimes: Under Apartheid*. *The Literary Review* Jan.: 30.

2024. Rev. of *Lifetimes: Under Apartheid*. *Race & Class* Jan.: 92-93.

2025. Segal, Ronald. "History through a Glass Darkly." *The Guardian* 9 Jan.

2026. *Thomas, Paul H. Rev. of *Lifetimes: Under Apartheid*. *Library Journal* 1 Mar.

2027. "Too Much Left Unsaid. . . ?" *The Citizen* 30 Jan.

2028. Valentine, Nina. "Two Whites Look at a Wrong." *The Courier* 19 Sept.

1988. 2029. Rev. of *Lifetimes: Under Apartheid*. *Book Review Digest: Eighty-Third Annual Cumulation*. Ed. Martha T. Mooney. New York: Wilson: 712.

A Sport of Nature

N.D. 2030. Broeder, Leonoor. "Nadine Gordimer legt haar politieke betrokkenheid uit: In Zuid-Afrika afzijdig blijven kan niet meer." *Het Parool*: 9.

2031. Field, Michele. "Nadine Gordimer: A Balancing Act in South Africa." *Good Weekend*: 33-35.

2032. Hope, Christopher. "Coming to the Point." *The Guardian* Apr.

1987. 2033. Alaya, F. Rev. of *A Sport of Nature*. *Choice* (25.1) Sept.: 123.

2034. Barry, Maggie. "Fighting for the Oppressed." *Evening Express* 2 May.

2035. Berridge, Elizabeth. "Beyond the Killing." *Daily Telegraph* 10 Apr.: 13.

2036. Björkstén, Ingmar. "Gordimer, Coetzee och Sydafrika." *Svenska Dagbladet* 13 July.

2037. Boyd, Betty. "Troubled Tale of a Teenager in South Africa." *Evening Post* 18 Apr.

2038. Brandmark, Wendy. "A Gift for Living in the Present." *The Listener* 16 Apr.: 36-37.

2039. Bronzwaer, W. "De ideale vrouw." *De Volkskrant* 31 July.

2040. Cadogan, Mary. "The Fire That Is Burning S. Africa." *Birmingham Post* 2 Apr.

2041. Chase, Elise. Rev. of *A Sport of Nature*. *Library Journal* 15 Apr.: 98.

2042. Clingman, Stephen." At Last. Gordimer Invents a Character She Loves." *The Weekly Mail* 29 May-4 June: 23.

2043. Craig, Patricia. "The Wayward Girl's New Departure." *Times Literary Supplement* 17 Apr.: 411. Extr. in *Contemporary Literary Criticism, Vol 51*. Ed. Daniel G. Marowski and Roger Matuz. Detroit: Gale, 1989: 156-157.

2044. Creevey, Coralie. "A Different Woman's Racial War." *Newcastle Herald* 15 Aug.

2045. Dinner, Tony. "Three Novels That Evoke Distant Worlds." *Jewish Chronicle* 29 May: 17.

2046. Dobson, Sue. "Novel News." *Woman & Home* July.

2047. Dowrick, Stephanie. "Gordimer Stays with the Action." *Sydney Morning Herald* 20 June: 48.

2048. Dunn, Douglas. "Fiction 1: Vision of Africa." *Glasgow Herald* 28 Mar.

1987. 2049. E. J. H. "Powerful New Gordimer Novel." *The Natal Mercury* 18 June: 6.

2050. Evans, Stuart. "Black and White." *The Times* 2 Apr.: 13.

2051. Gerrard, Nicci and Colin Hughes. "Over the Moon." *Marxism Today* Dec.: 50.

2052. Glendinning, Victoria. "Cool, Courteous and Revolutionary." *The Daily News* 31 Mar.: 7.

2053. Glenn, Ian. "Hodiernal Hillela - Gordimer's Kim." *Contrast 64* (16.4): 75-81.

2054. Godson, Stevie. "Looking at White Angst in Liberal SA." *Sunday Times* 28 June: 23.

2055. Gray, Paul. "Life in the Territory of Exile." *Time* 6 Apr.: 56. Extr. in *Contemporary Literary Criticism, Vol 51*: 156.

2056. Greenstein, Susan. "Laws of Skin and Hair." *The Women's Review of Books* (5.2): 1, 3-4.

2057. Grütter, Wilhelm. "Verrassende legkaart van liefde." *Die Burger* 2 July: 15.

2058. Guptara, Prabhu. "But Always a Woman. . . ." *Evening Standard* 9 Apr.

2059. Harvey, Joanne. Rev. of *A Sport on Nature*. *Fair Lady* 16 Sept.

2060. Hill, M. H. "Gordimer's Credo on Political Impasse." *Daily Dispatch* 25 July: 4.

2061. Howard, Maureen. "The Rise of Hillela, The Fall of South Africa." *New York Times Book Review* 3 May: 1, 20, 22. Extr. in *Contemporary Literary Criticism, Vol 51*: 158-159.

2062. Hughes, Glyn. "Bodies Politic and Private." *New Statesman* 10 Apr.: 27-28.

2063. Jillett, Neil. "Brutal Messenger of Truth." *The Age* 13 June.

2064. Johnson, Diane. "Living Legends." *New York Review of Books* 16 July: 8-9. Extr. in *Contemporary Literary Criticism, Vol 51*: 161-162.

2065. Jones, D. A. N. "Vies de bohème." *London Review of Books* 23 Apr.: 17.

1987. 2066. Jones, Mervyn. "Liberating Woman." *Sunday Telegraph* 5 Apr.

2067. Kemp, Peter. "One Woman's Path in the African Desert." *The Independent* 2 Apr.: 13.

2068. King, Francis. "Heart Lost in Darkness." *The Spectator* 4 Apr.: 37-38.

2069. Krauss, Jennifer. "Activism 101." *The New Republic* 18 May: 33-36. Extr. in *Contemporary Literary Criticism, Vol 51*: 159-161.

2070. Kuper, Adam. "Into Africa." *New Society* 3 Apr.: 32.

2071. Leach, Christopher. "Flesh and Blood — but No Life." *The Daily News* 2 Apr.: 19.

2072. Lee, Patrick. "A Perilous Progress." *Financial Mail* 17 July: 99.

2073. Lesserday, Lynton. "Monkey Business." *Punch* 15 Apr.: 51.

2074. Leverton, Basil. "Gordimer's New Book Ranks Her with the Best." *The Argus* 30 June: 10.

2075. Levin, Bernard. "Art Must Wait until the End of the Struggle." *Sunday Times* 5 Apr.

2076. M. J. "Gordimer Heroine Faces Up to Moral Dilemma." *Daily Dispatch* 30 May: 4.

2077. Madelung, Marianne. "Det befriede Sydafrika." *Politiken* 13 Oct.: 4.

2078. Massie, Allan. "Cause of Diminishing Returns." *The Scotsman* 2 May: 3.

2079. McCue, Jim. "Sport of Kingmakers." *Country Life* 30 Apr.

2080. McMahon, Sean. "Last White South African Optimist." *Irish Independent* 11 Apr.

2081. Mellors, John. "Frontline Women." *London Magazine* (27.1&2): 153-157.

2082. Molefe, Z. B. "White South Africans' Dilemma Is Explored." *City Press* 23 Aug.: 15.

2083. Murphy, Marese. "Winter Fire." *The Irish Times* 18 Apr.

1987. 2084. Newman, Judie. "Future Landscapes." *Third World Quarterly* (9.4): 1395-1399. [The review of *A Sport of Nature* was revised and reworked as "Conclusion" in *Nadine Gordimer.* Newman. London: Routledge, 1988: 93-102.]

2085. *Owen, I. M. Rev. of *A Sport of Nature. Books in Canada* (16.33) June/July.

2086. Pierce, Peter. "Gordimer, a Liberal in the *Laager.*" *The Canberra Times* 12 Sept.

2087. Potterton, Mark. "A New Flag Flies over SA." *New Nation* 2-8 July: 12.

2088. Proske, Rolf. Rev. of *A Sport of Nature. Upstream* (5.3): 34-35.

2089. Quigly, Isabel. "Hillela's Hopes." *Weekend Financial Times* 4 Apr.: XXII.

2090. R. J. "Books in Brief." *Evening Argus* 19 June.

2091. *Rev. of *A Sport of Nature. City Limits* 26 Mar.

2092. Rev. of *A Sport of Nature. The Illustrated London News* July.

2093. *Rev. of *A Sport of Nature. N.S.W. Sun Telegraph* 27 Dec.

2094. *Rev. of *A Sport of Nature. The Guardian* 4 Apr.

2095. *Rev. of *A Sport of Nature. Vrij Nederland* 4 Dec.

2096. Rev. of *A Sport of Nature. The Weekly Mail* 28 Aug.-3 Sept.: 19.

2097. Richards, Sally. "Bookshelf." *Toorak Times* 26 Aug.

2098. Riddell, Elizabeth. "Gordimer's Guide to the Devious and Dissident." *The Bulletin* 16 June.

2099. Rostron, Bryan. "The Priviledge and the Anguish." *Books* May: 7.

2100. *Rubin, Merle. Rev. of *A Sport of Nature. Los Angeles Times Book Review* 19 Apr.: 2, 9. Extr. in *Contemporary Literary Criticism, Vol 51*: 157-158.

2101. Scheltema, Margot. "De ware stemmen uit Zuid-Afrika." *Cultureel* (supp. to *NRC Handelsblad*) 26 June.

1987. 2102. Schwartz, Pat. "The Writer at the Walls of Jericho." *The Weekly Mail* 12-18 June: 22.

2103. *Semsandburg, S. Rev. of *A Sport of Nature*. *Bonniers Litterara Magasin* (56.4): 302-303.

2104. "Skidding into a Beautiful World." *Middlesborough Evening Gazette* 16 June.

2105. Smith, Susann. Rev. of *A Sport of Nature*. *Chronicle & Echo* 6 June.

2106. *Snitow, Ann. "A New Old-Fashioned Girl." *The Nation* 30 May: 731-733.

2107. Straatman, Tineke. "Deze afstand heeft Gordimer niet bedoeld." *Het Vrije Volk* 29 May.

2108. *Stuewe, Paul. Rev. of *A Sport of Nature*. *Quill & Quire* (53.25) May.

2109. Thurman, Judith. "Books: Choosing a Place." *The New Yorker* 29 June: 87-90.

2110. Tomalin, Claire. "An Innocent Totem." *The Observer* 5 Apr.

2111. Trewin, Ion. "A Sport That Defies All Black and White Rules." *Hampstead & Highgate Express* 17 Apr.

2112. V. v. S. "A 'Diaspora's' Fate Shaped by Lovers." *The Star* 10 July: 10.

2113. Van Kuik, Marianne. Rev. of *A Sport of Nature*. *Fair Lady* 16 Sept.: 27.

2114. Vanderhaeghen, Yves. "Hillela Unbound - the Spirit of the New African." *Business Day* 29 June: 12.

2115. Wade, Michael. "Gordimer's Rainbow." *Southern African Review of Books* July: 13-14. Extr. as "Gordimer's Return." *Jerusalem Post Magazine* 27 Nov.

1988. 2116. De Kock, Leon. Rev. of *A Sport of Nature*. *UNISA English Studies* (26.1): 46-47.

2117. Howard, Maureen. "Semi-Samizdat and Other Matters." *The Yale Review* (77.2): 243-258.

2118. Johnston, Alexander. "Nadine Gordimer in Fine Form." *Sunday Tribune* 14 Feb.: 7.

1988.   2119.   Kumar, Girja. "Woman Power and Sexuality." *Sunday Herald* 22 May: 6.

2120.   Rev. of *A Sport of Nature*. *Book Review Digest: Eighty-Third Annual Cumulation*. Ed. Martha T. Mooney. New York: Wilson: 713.

2121.   *Rev. of *A Sport of Nature*. *T.V. Times* 5 Jan.

2122.   Tsajwa, Zodwa. Rev. of *A Sport of Nature*. *Tribute* Mar.: 135.

2123.   Voss, Tony. "Everything Happens for the First Time." *Reality* (20.2&3): 35-36.

2124.   Wilhelmus, Tom. "Nothing Pretentious about Life and Art." *The Hudson Review* (40.4): 669-676.

1989.   2125.   Abrahams, L. "Revolution, Style and Morality." *Sesame* (12): 27-30.

2126.   Segal, Aaron. "A Memorable Character." *Africa Today* (36.2): 26.

The Essential Gesture

1988.   2127.   Appignanesi, Lisa. "Writer of Conscience." *Times Educational Supplement* 30 Sept.: 31.

2128.   Barrett, Graham. "Ice-Axe against Apartheid." *The Age* 16 Oct.

2129.   Boyd, William. "Agitprop Isn't Enough." *New York Times Book Review* 27 Nov.: 8.

2130.   Brown, Robert E. Rev. of *The Essential Gesture*. *Library Journal* 15 Oct.: 91-92.

2131.   Cronin, Jeremy. "Honest Voice from Africa." *Morning Star* 20 Oct.

2132.   Donoghue, Denis. "The Essential Posture." *The New Republic* 28 Nov.: 28-31.

2133.   Dunn, Douglas. "Good Behaviour." *Glasgow Herald* 1 Oct.

2134.   Egan, Anthony. "Gordimer - Profound and Thought-Provoking." *The Argus* 8 Dec.: 28.

1988. 2135. French, Sean. "Writing and Fighting." *New Statesman & Society* 23 Sept.: 35-36.

2136. Gutteridge, William. "Chronicling South African Problems." *Birmingham Post* 10 Nov.

2137. Haines, Janine. "A Black and White Tapestry." *The Herald* 30 Sept.: 17.

2138. Hayman, Ronald. "Birdsong Near Soweto." *The Independent* 28 Sept.

2139. "Holiday Reading." *The Australian Jewish News* 2 Dec.: 28.

2140. Jarrett, Nigel. "Events Analysed." *South Wales Argus* 6 Oct.

2141. Klue, Tony. "One Family Living through It." *Sydney Morning Herald* 22 Oct.

2142. Kuper, Adam. "A Brilliant Realist's New View of Reality." *Jewish Chronicle* 30 Sept.: 10.

2143. Lerner, Laurence. "Black at the End of the Tunnel." *The Spectator* 17 Sept.: 45-46.

2144. Liverani, Mary Rose. "Pertinent to the Impertinent." *Weekend Australian* 15 Oct.

2145. Maja-Pearce, Adewale. Rev. of *The Essential Gesture*. *London Magazine* (28.7&8): 141-142.

2146. *Packer, George. Rev. of *The Essential Gesture*. *The Nation* 26 Dec.

2147. Papineau, David. "Hoping for Hope." *Times Literary Supplement* 23-29 Sept.: 1043.

2148. Phillips, Caryl. "The Necessity of Writing, the Tyranny of Silence." *The Guardian* 16 Sept. Repr. as "Inside an Ever-Probing, Ever-Troubled Mind." *The Weekly Mail* 28 Oct.-3 Nov.: 9.

2149. Raphael, Frederic. "The Sham and Shame of South Africa." *Sunday Times* 25 Sept.: G2. Abbr. as "Worldly Wisdom." *The Sunday Star* 6 Nov.: 44.

2150. Rushdie, Salman. "Falling into South Africa." *The Observer* 4 Sept.

1988.   2151.   Rushdie, Salman. "Gordimer Tells of Her SA Awakening." *The Sunday Star* 16 Oct.: 2.

2152.   Walsh, Stephen. "Reassessing Alan Paton." *The Oxford Times* 16 Sept.

1988/9. 2153.   Kinkead-Weekes, Mark. Rev. of *The Essential Gesture. Wasafiri* (9): 30.

1989.   2154.   Ascherson, Neal. "Inside the Whale." *New York Review of Books* 30 Mar.: 12-14.

2155.   Coetzee, J. M. "Gordimer - Formidable 'Visitor from the Future.'" *Die Suid-Afrikaan* Dec.: 50-51.

2156.   Du Plessis, Menán. "*The Essential Gesture*: Writing, Politics and Places." *Contrast 67* (17.3): 74-78.

2157.   Durbach, Elaine. "Cold and Ponderous." *Cape Times* 14 Jan.: 4.

2158.   Engelbrecht, Theunis. "Literêre profiel: 'Die waarheid is ontwykend.'" *Beeld* 31 Aug.: 4.

2159.   Fritz-Piggott, Jill. "Stranger in a Strange Land." *The Women's Review of Books* (6.5): 1, 3.

2160.   Guy, Bill. "White South African Writer's Expression of Pain and Protest." *The Advertiser* 18 Feb.

2161.   Halldin, Jan. "Nadine Gordimer på svenska: I skuggan av den ökade terrorn." *Göteborgs-Posten* 10 Sept.: *4-5.

2162.   Helgesson, Stefan. "Nadine Gordimer brev från Johannesburg: Att stå mitt i tragedin." *Göteborgs-Posten* 10 Sept.: *4-5.

2163.   Johnson, George. "New and Noteworthy." *New York Times Book Review* 12 Nov.: 62.

2164.   Liebenberg, Wilhelm. "Gordimer is lankal besig met die struggle." *Vrye Weekblad* 7 Apr.: 4.

2165.   Marais, Michael. Rev. of *The Essential Gesture. Upstream* (7.2): 63-64.

2166.   *Nkosi, Lewis. "White Writing." *Third World Quarterly* (11.1): 157-161.

1989. 2167. Rev. of *The Essential Gesture*. *Book Review Digest: Eighty-Fourth Annual Cumulation*. Ed. Martha T. Mooney. New York: Wilson: 668.

2168. *Rubin, Merle. Rev. of *The Essential Gesture*. *Christian Science Monitor* 3 Jan.: 11.

2169. Wade, Michael. "On the Other Side of Gordimer." *Southern African Review of Books* (2.3): 18-19.

2170. "Writers in Depth." *The Natal Mercury* 27 Feb.: 5.

1992. 2171. Coetzee, J. M. "Nadine Gordimer, *The Essential Gesture* (1989)." *Doubling the Point: Essays and Interviews: J. M. Coetzee*. Ed. David Attwell. Cape Town: Philip: 382-388.

My Son's Story

1990. 2172. "All the Reading Matter That Matters for Christmas." *Exclusive Communiqué* (supp. to *The Weekly Mail* 7-13 Dec.) (14): 3.

2173. Annan, Gabriele. "Love and Death in South Africa." *New York Review of Books* 8 Nov.: 8-10.

2174. Bentley, Kin. "Gordimer Novel Warmly Praised." *Eastern Province Herald* 10 Sept.: 7.

2175. Cartwright, Justin. "No Mere Bimbo on the Side." *Cape Times* 29 Sept.: 4.

2176. Clark, Ross. "Sons, Lovers and a Broadcaster." *The Spectator* 13 Oct.: 38-40.

2177. Coles, Robert. "A Different Set of Rules." *New York Times Book Review* 21 Oct.: 1, 20-21.

2178. D. J. S. "Influences of Another Struggle." *Daily Dispatch* 6 Oct.: 4.

2179. Darke, Neill. "Latest Novels by Top SA Authors." *Weekend Argus* 27 Oct.: 5.

2180. Du Toit, Albert. "Vintage Gordimer, but Lacks Fresh Vision." *Eastern Province Herald* 7 Nov.: 8.

2181. "Editor's Choice: Best Books for 1990." *New York Times Book Review* 2 Dec.: 81.

1990.   2182.   Elliott, Martin. "Uncivilized States." *London Magazine* (30.7/8): 132-134.

2183.   French, Sean. "Writing and Action." *New Statesman & Society* 21 Sept.: 40.

2184.   "Gordimer Praised for Novel." *Daily Dispatch* 19 Sept.: 14.

2185.   "Gordimer's New Book Wows London Critics." *Cape Times* 7 Sept.: 3.

2186.   Gray, Paul. "Abstractions." *Time* 29 Oct.: 63.

2187.   Greig, Robert. "Gordimer Produces Another Rewarding Work." *Business Day* 29 Oct.: 10.

2188.   Heller, Zoe. "Cool Hand Stirs the Cauldron." *The Star* 1 Oct.: 14.

2189.   "High Praise for Gordimer." *The Daily News* 5 Dec.: 18.

2190.   Hotz, Paul. "Gordimer's Latest Offering Interesting and Readable." *The Daily News* 1 Nov.: 13.

2191.   Hough, Barrie. "Nadine se storie." *Rapport* 9 Dec.: 9.

2192.   Lazar, Carol [sic] [Karen]. "Feeling of deja vu to *My Son's Story*: Brilliant but at Times Tedious." *The Sunday Star* 28 Oct.: 4.

2193.   MacKenzie, Craig. "Gordimer's Story of Disillusionment: Sachs's Triumph Over Agents of Apartheid." *Grocott's Mail* 2 Nov.: 8.

2194.   Martin, Bridget. "When Hollywood Came to Parkview." *Saturday Star Weekend* 1 Dec.: 3.

2195.   Nel, Jo. "Gordimer se roman stel teleur: Politieke verandering het verhaal ingehaal." *Beeld* 31 Dec.: 8. Repr. as "Politiek het verhaal ingehaal." *Die Volksblad* 5 Jan., 1991: 15.

2196.   Nixon, Rob. "Sons and Lovers: Nadine Gordimer Grows Old Gracefully." Literary supp. to *Voice* Nov.: 23-24.

2197.   P. S. P. *My Son's Story*. *Newsweek* 1 Oct.: 46.

2198.   *Packer, George. Rev. of *My Son's Story*. *The Nation* 17 Dec.

1990. 2199. Papineau, David. "Of Loyalty and Betrayal." *Times Literary Supplement* 28 Sept.-4 Oct.: 1037.

2200. Parrinder, Patrick. "What His Father Gets Up To." *London Review of Books* 13 Sept.: 17-18.

2201. Rev. of *My Son's Story. Booknews 60*: 12.

2202. *Rubin, Merle. Rev. of *My Son's Story. Christian Science Monitor* 15 Nov.: 13.

2203. Streak, Diana, and Yvonne Fontyn. "Metropolis: Books." *Sunday Star Magazine* (supp. to *Sunday Star*) 2 Dec.: 52.

2204. Van Zyl, Charlotte. Rev. of *My Son's Story. Exclusive Communiqué* (supp. to *The Weekly Mail* 26 Oct.-1 Nov.) (13): 3.

2205. Von Klemperer, Margaret. "The Revolutionary Has No Place for a Second Obsession." *The Natal Witness* 1 Nov.: 24.

1990/1. 2206. Green, Michael. "Gordimer neem die gisters saam na môre." *Insig* Dec./Jan.: 50.

1991. 2207. Abrahams, Lionel. "Speak to Me of Limpet Mines." *Sesame* (14): 24-25.

2208. Caradoc-Davies, Gillian. "Local Letters." *Fair Lady* 30 Jan.: 20.

2209. Dunbar, Pamela. "'I' Witness." *Southern African Review of Books* (4.1): 15-16.

2210. Fritz-Piggott, Jill. "Son and Lover." *The Women's Review of Books* (8.4): 8-9.

2211. Fronz, Ralf. "Gewöhnliche Liebe in außergewöhnlicher Zeit." *Sächsisches Tageblatt* (3.5): 7.

2212. G. W. "Rassepolitiek menslik bekyk." *Oosterlig* 19 Apr.: 17.

2213. Greet, Annie. "Raw, Tender and Tough: Head and Gordimer." *CRNLE Reviews Journal* (2): 65-69.

2214. Hotz, Paul. "Theme of Heroism Links Award Books." *The Daily News* 22 Aug.: 30.

2215. King, Bruce. Rev. of *My Son's Story. World Literature Today* (65.2): 351.

1991. 2216. Kossick, S. G. Rev. of *My Son's Story. UNISA English Studies* (29.1): 54.

2217. Liebenberg, Wilhelm. "'n Feniks herrys uit die as." *Vrye Weekblad* 8 Feb.: 20.

2218. MacKenzie, Craig. "Novels for the Nineties." *Language Projects Review* (5.4): 21-23.

2219. Malan, Charles. "Singewing in die gevaarlike land." *De Kat* Apr.: 92-.

2220. Mukherjee, Bharati. "A Tragedy in Black and White." *Guardian Weekly* 3 Feb.: 20.

2221. "New & Noteworthy." *New York Times Book Review* 8 Dec.: 42.

2222. P. A. S. "The Realities of Life behind the Headlines." *Daily Dispatch* 10 Nov.: 4.

2223. Riordan, Rory. "Top Award and a Writer Recognised." *Eastern Province Herald* 4 Nov.: 4.

2224. Sboros, Marika. "A Passionate Tale." *The Star Tonight!* (supp. to *The Star*) 21 Nov.: 6.

2225. Wagner, Kathrin. "Credentials for Interpreting the Struggle." *Die Suid-Afrikaan* Feb./Mar.: 44-45.

2226. Weideman, George. "Boodskap van hoop inspireer: Nadine Gordimer spreek politieke probleme menslik aan." *Die Burger* 16 Apr.: 5.

1992. 2227. La Vita, Murray. "'n Nadine Gordimer-meesterstuk." *Die Transvaler* 16 Apr.: 6.

2228. R. G. "Gordimer Story Cuts to Core of Family Life." *Pretoria News* 6 Jan.: 11.

2229. Rev. of *My Son's Story. Book Review Digest: Eighty-Seventh Annual Cumulation.* Ed. Martha T. Mooney. New York: Wilson: 721.

2230. Smith, Margaret Shepherd. "Gordimer Demonstrates Her Skill Again." *Sunday Tribune* 24 May: 7.

Jump and Other Stories

1991. 2231. Bailey, Paul. "Moving Short Stories Show Gordimer at Her Best." *Business Day* 21 Oct.: 14.

2232. Bayley, John. "Dry Eyes." *London Review of Books* 5 Dec.: 20.

2233. D. J. S. "Saying Exactly What She Means." *Daily Dispatch* 21 Dec.: 4.

2234. Du Toit, Albert. "Peak of Gordimer's Creativity." *Eastern Province Herald* 4 Dec.: 12.

2235. Hough, Barrie. "Gordimer bewys sy verdien die prys." *Insig* Dec.: 5.

2236. Jaggi, Maya. "Interregnum." *New Statesman & Society* 18 Oct.: 38.

2237. Kanga, Firdaus. "A Question of Black and White: Nadine Gordimer's Political Novels and Stories." *Times Literary Supplement* 11 Oct.: 14.

2238. Kaye/Kantrowitz, Melanie. "Leaps of Faith." *The Women's Review of Books* (9.3): 1, 3-4.

2239. Mantel, Hilary. "Irrecoverably Dark, without All Hope of Day." *The Spectator* 19 Oct.: 43-44.

2240. Prescott, Peter with Marc Peyser and Arlene Getz. "Two Sides of Nadine Gordimer: South Africa's Great Fiction Writer Wins the Nobel." *Newsweek* 14 Oct.: 48.

2241. Wideman, John Edgar. "So Much is Always at Stake." *New York Times Book Review* 29 Sept.: 7.

2242. Wood, James. "Just a Little Too Superb." *Review/Books* (supp. to *The Weekly Mail*) 29 Nov.-5 Dec.: 4.

1992. 2243. Blumer, Arnold. "Die onbekende wêreld net buite die vel gewys." *Die Burger* 14 Jan.: 7.

2244. Coleman, David. "An Extraordinary Insight into Human Nature." *The Natal Mercury* 24 Feb.: 6.

2245. De Kock, Shirley. "Stunning Few in Gordimer Stories." *Cape Times* 1 Feb.: 4.

1992. 2246. Dugmore, Harry. Rev. of *Jump and Other Stories*. *Tribute* Feb.: 27.

2247. Gordon, Nancy. Rev. of *Jump and Other Stories*. *Sash* Jan.: 44.

2248. Green, Pippa. "After the Jump." *South African Literary Review* (2.3): 10-11.

2249. Hotz, Paul. "Some Good Stories but Collection Disappointing." *The Daily News* 20 Feb.: 13.

2250. Lovell, Moira. "Stunning Jump by Gordimer." *The Natal Witness* 31 Jan.: 1.

2251. McAinsh, Gillian. "To the Bone of Apartheid SA." *Weekend Post* 29 Feb.: 3.

2252. McGhee, Martin. "Stories from the Formidable Gordimer." *The Citizen* 27 Jan.: 6.

2253. Rev. of *Jump and Other Stories*. *Book Review Digest* (88.1): 40.

2254. Rev. of *Jump and Other Stories*. *Book Review Digest* (88.3): 202.

2255. Southey, Nicholas. "Splendid Collection of Short Stories." *New Nation* 29 May-4June: 26.

2256. Thorpe, Michael. Rev. of *Jump and Other Stories*. *World Literature Today* (66.1): 192-193.

2257. Van Gend, Cecily. Rev. of *Jump and Other Stories*. *The Cape Librarian* (36.7): 46.

2258. Ward, James. "Lyrical Analyst of a Nation." *Guardian Weekly* 9 Feb.: 28.

Crimes of Conscience

1991. 2259. Lenta, Margaret. "Black and White Women Yesterday and Today." *Current Writing* (3.1): 165-166.

2260. Rev. of *Crimes of Conscience*. *Sunday Times* 9 June.

2261. Upchurch, Michael. "Miniatures in Black and White." *New York Times Book Review* 2 June: 21.

1992. 2262. Thorpe, Michael. Rev. of *Crimes of Conscience*. *World Literature Today* (66.2): 390-391.

2263. Van Gend, Cecily. Rev. of *Crimes of Conscience*. *The Cape Librarian* (36.3): 23.

Conversations with Nadine Gordimer

1992. 2264. Kohler, Peter. "Language, Politics & Author(ity)." *South African Literary Review* (2.2): 6-7.

2265. Rev. of *Conversations with Nadine Gordimer*. *Book Review Digest* (88.2): 75.

Why Haven't You Written?

1992. 2266. "Gordimer's Insights." *The Star Tonight!* (supp. to *The Star*) 1 Oct.: 4.

N. REVIEWS OF CRITICISM

1975. 2267. Brink, André. Rev. of *Nadine Gordimer*, by Robert F. Haugh. *Books Abroad* (2): 840.

2268. Rev. of *Nadine Gordimer*, by Robert F. Haugh. *Choice* May: 392.

1977. 2269. Cooke, John. Rev. of *Nadine Gordimer*, by Robert F. Haugh. *Research in African Literatures* (8.1): 147-149.

1978. 2270. Driver, Dorothy. Rev. of *Nadine Gordimer*, by Michael Wade. *English in Africa* (5.1): 77-80.

1980. 2271. Coetzee, J. M. Rev. of *Nadine Gordimer*, by Michael Wade. *Research in African Literatures* (11.2): 253-256.

1981. 2272. Smith, Rowland. Rev. of *Nadine Gordimer*, by Michael Wade. *Canadian Journal of African Studies* (15.2): 395-397.

1984. 2273. Peek, Andrew. "African Studies." Rev. of *Nadine Gordimer*, by Michael Wade. *CRNLE Reviews Journal* (1): 42-44.

1986. 2274. Alaya, F. Rev. of *The Novels of Nadine Gordimer: Private Lives/Public Landscapes*, by John Cooke. *Choice* Sept.: 118.

2275. Bean, Lucy. "In-Depth Look at the Novels of Nadine Gordimer." Rev. of *The Novels of Nadine Gordimer: History from the Inside*, by Stephen Clingman. *The Argus* 4 Dec.: 23.

2276. Berner, Robert L. Rev. of *The Novels of Nadine Gordimer: Private Lives/Public Landscapes*, by John Cooke. *World Literature Today* (60.3): 512.

2277. Hofmeyr, Isabel. "An Inner Pathway through SA History." Rev. of *The Novels of Nadine Gordimer: History from the Inside*, by Stephen Clingman. *The Star* 2 Dec.: 14. Repr. as "A Critical Study of Gordimer's Novels." *The Daily News* 29 Dec.: 12.

2278. J. E. Rev. of *The Novels of Nadine Gordimer: Private Lives/Public Landscapes*, by John Cooke. *Booklist* 1 May: 1276.

2279. "*The Novels of Nadine Gordimer.* By Stephen Clingman (Ravan)." *Fair Lady* 17 Sept.: 26.

2280. Roberts, Sheila. Rev. of "Nadine Gordimer: Politics and the Order of Art" in *Salmagundi* (62) 1984. *Research in African Literatures* (17.3): 408-411.

2281. Stevenson, Robin. "Thorough Study of Nadine's Novels." Rev. of *The Novels of Nadine Gordimer: History from the Inside*, by Stephen Clingman. *Evening Post* 11 Dec.: 16.

1986/7. 2282. Starfield, Jane. "Gordimer Revisited: Fiction as History from the Inside." Rev. of *The Novels of Nadine Gordimer: History from the Inside*, by Stephen Clingman. *The Weekly Mail* 19 Dec.-8 Jan.: 26.

1987. 2283. Alaya, F. Rev. of *The Novels of Nadine Gordimer: History from the Inside*, by Stephen Clingman. *Choice* Jan.: 758, 760.

2284. C. E. F. "Style of a Genius." Rev. of *The Novels of Nadine Gordimer: History from the Inside*, by Stephen Clingman. *Daily Dispatch* 25 July: 4.

1987. 2285. Rowe, Margaret Moan. Rev. of *The Novels of Nadine Gordimer: Private Lives/Public Landscapes*, by John Cooke. *Modern Fiction Studies* (33.2): 363-365.

2286. Smith, Malvern van Wyk. Rev. of *The Novels of Nadine Gordimer: History from the Inside*, by Stephen Clingman. *English in Africa* (14.2): 83-86.

2287. "Superb Study of Gordimer's Work." Rev. of *The Novels of Nadine Gordimer: History from the Inside*, by Stephen Clingman. *Cape Times* 4 Mar.: 6.

2288. Wade, Michael. "Gordimer's Rainbow." Rev. of *The Novels of Nadine Gordimer: History from the Inside*, by Stephen Clingman. *Southern African Review of Books* July: 13-14.

2289. "When Fiction Is the Only Available Fact." Rev. of *The Novels of Nadine Gordimer: History from the Inside*, by Stephen Clingman. *City Press* 11 Jan.: 7.

1988. 2290. Clayton, Cherry. Rev. of *The Novels of Nadine Gordimer: History from the Inside*, by Stephen Clingman. *World Literature Written in English* (28.1): 63-65.

2291. De Kock, Leon. Rev. of *The Novels of Nadine Gordimer: History from the Inside*, by Stephen Clingman. *UNISA English Studies* (26.1): 45-46.

2292. Gugelberger, George M. Rev. of *The Novels of Nadine Gordimer: History from the Inside*, by Stephen Clingman. *Canadian Journal of African Studies* (22.3): 670-672.

2293. Harlow, Barbara. Rev. of *The Novels of Nadine Gordimer: History from the Inside*, by Stephen Clingman. *Research in African Literatures* (19.2): 252-258.

2294. T. B. Rev. of *The Novels of Nadine Gordimer: History from the Inside*, by Stephen Clingman. *Modern Fiction Studies* (34.4): 756-757.

2295. Wade, Michael. Rev. of *The Novels of Nadine Gordimer: Private Lives/Public Landscapes*, by John Cooke. *Research in African Literatures* (19.2): 248-252.

1989. 2296. Alaya, F. Rev. of *Nadine Gordimer*, by Judie Newman. *Choice* May: 1516.

1989. 2297. Ascherson, Neal. "Inside the Whale." Rev. of *The Novels of Nadine Gordimer: History from the Inside*, by Stephen Clingman. *New York Review of Books* 30 Mar.: 12-14.

2298. "Shorter Reviews." Rev. of *Nadine Gordimer*, by Judie Newman. *Contemporary Review* May: 280.

1990. 2299. Morphet, Tony. "Collection an Academic Exchange." Rev. of *Rendering Things Visible*, ed. Martin Trump. *Weekend Mail* (supp. to *The Weekly Mail*) 24-26 Aug.: 17.

1991. 2300. Choonoo, R. Neville. Rev. of *Rendering Things Visible*, ed. Martin Trump. *Research in African Literatures* (22.4): 191-194.

2301. Lenta, Margaret. Rev. of *Critical Essays on Nadine Gordimer*, ed. Rowland Smith. *Current Writing* (3.1): 161-166.

2302. McDowell, John N. Rev. of *Critical Essays on Nadine Gordimer*, ed. Rowland Smith. *Ariel* (22.4): 147-150.

2303. Visel, Robin. Rev. of *Critical Essays on Nadine Gordimer*, ed. Rowland Smith. *Research in African Literatures* (22.4): 189-191.

1992. 2304. Abrahams, Lionel. "Gordimer, Clingman and the Mystique of History." Rev. of *The Novels of Nadine Gordimer: History from the Inside*, by Stephen Clingman. *South African Literary Review* (2.1): 7-9.

O. FILMS

1982. *Six Feet of the Country.* Released in USA as *The Nadine Gordimer Stories: Films from South Africa.*
A Series of Six Films and an Interview with Nadine Gordimer.
Producer: Chris Davies.
Profile Film Productions [South Africa] and Telepool [Germany].
Adapted for Television by Bavaria TV and Teleculture Inc.
First screened in South Africa at Cape Town Film Festival in 1982.
Subsequently screened in 21 countries around the world and banned in South Africa.
Screened on BBC TV Channel Four, Jan., 1983.

1. *Six Feet of the Country*.
Screenplay: Barney Simon.
Director: Lynton Stephenson.
Cast: Sandra Prinsloo, Wilson Dunster and Fats Bookholane.

2. *Country Lovers*.
Screenplay: Nadine Gordimer.
Director: Manie van Rensburg.
Cast: Ryno Hattingh, Nomsa Nene, Brian O'Shaunnessey and Isabel Pienaar.

3. *City Lovers*.
Screenplay: Barney Simon.
Director: Barney Simon.
Cast: Joe Stewardson, Denise Newman and Bill Flynn.

4. *Chip of Glass Ruby*.
Screenplay: Nadine Gordimer.
Director: Ross Devenish.
Cast: Muthal Naidoo, Kessie Govender, Shaida Shaik and Chris Pillay.

5. *Good Climate, Friendly Inhabitants*.
Screenplay: Barney Simon.
Director: Lynton Stephenson.
Cast: Trix Pienaar, Danny Keogh and Sam Williams.

6. *Praise*.
Screenplay: Nadine Gordimer.
Director: Richard Green.
Cast: Janet Suzman, Richard Haines and Dale Cutts.

7. *Interview with Nadine Gordimer*.
Interviewer: Dr Joachim Braun.
Filmed by Peter Frense.

General

1981.   2305. Berdal, Garth. "Profile - on South African Writers." *The Daily News* 17 June: 5.

1982.   2306. "Gordimer on Role as Script-Writer." *Cape Times* 14 Sept.: 6.

2307. "Gordimer's Films for Festival." *Daily Dispatch* 29 Sept.: 26.

2308. Harber, Anton. "For TV - Six Nadine Gordimer Short Stories." *Rand Daily Mail* 17 May: 9.

2309. Levin, Doreen. "Censors Give Gordimer Films Limited Go-Ahead Here." *Sunday Times* 12 Sept.

2310. "Writer Backs Black Struggle for Liberation." *Eastern Province Herald* 8 Nov.: 3. Extr. as "Gordimer Committed to Liberation Struggle." *Daily Dispatch* 9 Nov.: 11.

1983.   2311. "Board Told of Colour Bar Sex in SA Films." *The Star* 30 July: 3. Different version as "Board to Decide on 'Sex across Colour Line' Films." *Pretoria News* 30 July: 5.

2312. "Censorship 'Is Strict as Ever.'" *Rand Daily Mail* 31 Aug.: 4.

2313. Christie, Roy. "New Hope for SA Movie Industry . . . ." *The Argus Tonight* (supp. to *The Argus*) 13 Sept.: 1. Orig. pub. in *The Daily News* 9 Sept.: 7.

2314. "Colour Bar Sex Films Unbanned." *The Star* 27 Aug.

2315. Daniel, Raeford. "Chance to See Gordimer Films." *Rand Daily Mail* 9 Mar.

2316. De Lange, Ilse. "Dié 2 prente 'n Appèlraad-turksvy." *Die Transvaler* 1 Aug.: 7.

2317. "Films: Gordimer Replies." *The Star Tonight* (supp. to *The Star*) 9 Sept.: 1.

2318. "Gordimer TV Series Rumpus." *Sowetan* 22 Feb.: 7.

2319. "Gordimer's *Six* Voted among the Top Ten on UK's Channel Four." *The Star* 15 Dec.

2320. "Landmark Ruling for Film Industry." *The Star* 10 Sept.

2321. Raine, Sheryl. "Appeal over 'Morals' Films Could Herald a New Era." *The Star* 3 Aug.: 8.

1983. 2322. "Realistic." Editorial. *The Friend* 5 Sept.: 8.

2323. "Steyn Takes 'Right to Reply' to Channel Four." *The Star* 21 Mar.: 3.

2324. "Verdict on Films Reserved." *Weekend Post* 30 July: 3.

2325. Vollenhoven, Sylvia. "Unbanning of *Lovers* Hailed as Milestone." *Sunday Times* 18 Sept.: 5.

1985. 2326. "Gordimer-prente." *Beeld* 9 Jan.: 2.

2327. Kramer, Pam. "Banned Gordimer Film to Be Resubmitted for Approval." *Sunday Express* 13 Jan.: 5.

2328. "Now SA Can See Gordimer's 'Glass Ruby.'" *The Star Tonight* (supp. to *The Star*) 17 Oct.: 1. Repr. as "'Glass Ruby' Gets Past Last." *Pretoria News* 21 Oct.: 1. Extr. as "'Glass Ruby' Cleared." *The Argus Tonight* (supp. to *The Argus*) 23 Oct.: 1.

2329. O'Connor, John J. "Gordimer's Stories of South Africa." *New York Times* 1 July: C14.

2330. "Return Season of Gordimer's *Six Feet of the Country*." *The Star Tonight* (supp. to *The Star*) 10 Jan.: 16.

1989. 2331. "Gordimer se TV-storie." *Die Volksblad* 1 Dec.: 6.

2332. Rautenbach, Elmari. "Gordimer-verhaal op M-Net." *Beeld* 4 Dec.: 10.

1991. 2333. "Boost for Gordimer Series." *The Star Tonight* (supp. to *The Star*) 25 Oct.: 1.

Reviews

1982. 2334. Green, Molly. "SA Films - the Highest Standard." *Cape Times* 21 Sept.: 6.

1983. 2335. Canby, Vincent. "Film: 7 Stories by Nadine Gordimer." *New York Times* 18 May: C26.

2336. Daniel, Raeford. "Missing the Texture of the Originals." *Rand Daily Mail* 23 Mar.

2337. Garden, Greg. "Gordimer: Flawed Films." *Rand Daily Mail* 23 Mar.: 8.

1983.   2338.   Jackman, Tony. "*Six Feet* Holds Promise." *The Star* 15 Mar.

2339.   Lelyveld, Joseph. "South Africa on Film, as Seen by Nadine Gordimer." *New York Times* 15 May: H1, H13.

2340.   Smith, Margaret. "Gordimer - Laying Bare SA Thinking." *Daily Dispatch* 27 Jan.: 22.

1985.   2341.   "*City Lovers* handel oor ontugwet se hartseer." *Die Transvaler* 11 July: 7.

2342.   "Gordimer's 'Glass Ruby' Wins High Praise from US TV Critics." *The Star Tonight* (supp. to *The Star*) 11 July. Extr. as "Gordimer TV Story Acclaimed." *Diamond Fields Advertiser* 20 July: 7.

2343.   Haysom, Cheetah. "Gordimer TV Series 'Depressingly Familiar Horror.'" *The Star Tonight* (supp. to *The Star*) 3 July: 11.

2344.   O'Connor, John J. "Mesmerizing Dramas of South Africa." *New York Times* 28 July, sec. 2: 1, 21.

2345.   Roland, Nic. "Rolprent propvol rassekonflik." *Die Transvaler* 11 July: 7.

1986.   2346.   Tomaselli, Keyan. "Le cinéma anti-apartheid à l'extérieur." *L'Afrique Littéraire* (78): 90-98.

P. BIOGRAPHY (and miscellaneous material)

1949.   2347.   "Author of Short Stories." *Zionist Record* 2 Sept.

2348.   "A Journal: Author Gives Reading of Her Own Work." *The Star* 3 Nov.: 4.

2349.   "A Journal: Publishers' Party for Short Story Writer." *The Star* 5 Sept.: 4.

2350.   "A Journal: Young Writer's First Book of Short Stories." *The Star* 30 Aug.: 4.

2351.   Pienaar, W. J. B. "Engelse drama deur Suid-Afrikaners." Rev. of *Six One-Act Plays by South African Authors*. *Ons Eie Boek* (15.2): 98-101.

1951. 2352. "Authoress Was Told: You Don't Write English Properly." *Sunday Times* 12 Aug.

2353. "Book of Short Stories by Rand Woman Will Be Published in U.S." *The Star* 2 Aug.: 3.

2354. "Nadine Gordimer's Book Accepted in U.S." *Rand Daily Mail* 3 Aug.: 7.

2355. "Nadine Gordimer's Success: Book to Be Published in America." *South African Jewish Times* 17 Aug.

2356. The Pilgrim. "Stoep Talk: Writer's Success." *The Star* 26 June: 11.

2357. "S.A. Novelist." *The Star* 9 Aug.: 7.

1952. 2358. "City Noises Distract Author." *The Star* 7 Jan.: 3.

1953. 2359. "Our Women Novelists." Editorial. *The Forum* (2.8): 3.

1954. 2360. Macdonald, Tom. "Miss Gordimer Was Excited: Spotlight on a New Best Seller." *Spotlight* Jan.: 24-25.

1960. 2361. "Nadine Gordimer Novel for TV." *The Star* 17 Sept.: 5.

1961. 2362. "Stranger in Her Own Country." *Topic: The British News Weekly* [London] 4 Nov.: 50-51.

2363. "Women of the Year: Nadine Gordimer: Literary Award Winner." *Femina & Woman's Life* 23 Nov.: 18-19, 21, 23, 101 [Gordimer: 19, 21].

1962. 2364. "Ban Angers Writers." *Rand Daily Mail* 3 Mar.: 7.

2365. "Error in Gordimer Book Ban." *Rand Daily Mail* 6 Mar.: 1.

2366. Nkosi, Lewis. "*A World of Strangers* Secretly Filmed." *South Africa: Information and Analysis* Aug.: 7-8.

2367. Nkosi, Lewis. "Novelist Slates Millionaire Oppenheimer." *South Africa: Information and Analysis* Nov.: 5.

1963. 2368. Nkosi, Lewis. "The Writers." *South Africa: Information and Analysis* Apr.: 4-6.

1965. 2369. "Author Stops Story Being Read to 'Whites Only.'" *Sunday Express* 1 Aug.: 15.

2370. "Nadine Gordimer in Protest over Passport Withdrawal." *South Africa: Information and Analysis* Oct.: 3-4.

1966.   2371.   Attwell, Lionel. "Ban's 'Tragic,' Says Gordimer: Nadine: 'I Have No Intention of Leaving South Africa': Writers Urged to Take a Definite Stand." *Sunday Times* 26 June: 5.

2372.   "Gordimer's New Race Novel Is Banned." *Rand Daily Mail* 22 June.: 1.

2373.   Levin, M. M. "Book Trade to Discuss Gordimer Banning." *Sunday Times* 26 June: 5.

1969.   2374.   *De Beer, Mona.   "Nadine Writes from a Position of Involvement." *The Times* 9 Apr.: 7.

2375.   "Novelist Defends Free Expression." *Eastern Province Herald* 9 July.

2376.   "Praise for Two S.A. Authors." *Eastern Province Herald* 10 July: 5.

2377.   "S.A. Writing Seen as 'Precious Jewel.'" *Eastern Province Herald* 10 July: 5.

1970.   2378.   Beichman, Arnold. "Nadine Gordimer: Eloquent Elegance." *Christian Science Monitor* 9 Dec.: 23.

2379.   *Casey, Phil. "South African Author on Liberation." *Style* (supp. to *Washington Post*) 3 Nov.: B1, B4.

2380.   "Gordimer, Nadine." *Two Thousand Women of Achievement*. 2nd ed. Ed. Ernest Kay. London: Melrose: 476.

2381.   "Petition on Fugard." *Weekend Post* 15 Aug.: 7.

1971.   2382.   "Academy Row Amazes Nadine." *Sunday Times* 18 July: 7.

2383.   "Censorship Linked to Apartheid Design: Publications Board under Fire." *The Argus* 26 Mar.: 2.

2384.   "Gordimer, Nadine (1923-)." *The Penguin Companion to Literature I: Britain and the Commonwealth*. Ed. David Daiches. Harmondsworth: Penguin: 218.

2385.   "Gordimer Novel Held by Customs." *The Argus* 30 Apr.: 1.

2386.   "Gordimer on 'Sham Respect for the Law.'" *The Daily News* 12 Aug.: 5.

1971. 2387. Levin, Doreen. "Censorship: Writers, Artists Speak Up: They Reject Publications Control Board: The Arts Have Withered, Says Nadine Gordimer." *Sunday Times News Magazine* (supp. to *Sunday Times*) 25 Apr.: 1.

2388. "Name in the News." *Natal Mercury* 12 Aug.: 14.

2389. "New Novel on Africa Embargoed." *The Star* 30 Apr.: 20.

2390. "Novelist to Give Freedom Lecture." *Evening Post* 10 Aug.: 7. Repr. in *The Natal Witness* 11 Aug.: 9.

2391. "Protests Frustrating, but Important, Students Told." *Daily Dispatch* 12 Aug.: 9. Extr. as "Protest Futile, Says Writer." *Pretoria News* 12 Aug.: 15.

2392. "Religious Prejudice." *Natal Mercury* 11 Aug.: 2.

2393. "S.A. Writer's Novel Embargoed." *Evening Post* 3 Mar.: 8.

2394. Schwartz, Pat. "Critics Slash Censors at Wits Talks." *Rand Daily Mail* 26 Mar.: 4.

2395. Smith, Margaret. "Pleas for Political Prisoners: Aid Group Formed." *Sunday Times* 7 Feb.: 14.

2396. "We're Afraid to Protest, Says Author." *The Star* 12 Aug.: 5.

2397. "Writer on the Power of Protest." *The Natal Witness* 12 Aug.: 9.

1972. 2398. "Author on African Writing." *The Argus* 8 Feb.: 3.

2399. *Billson, J. "Best Sellers." *Modern Woman* Aug.

2400. "Black Literature 'Stunted.'" *Rand Daily Mail* 13 Dec.: 11.

2401. Coy, Elizabeth. "I Write What I Like . . . ." *Cape Times* 12 Feb.: 7.

2402. "Cramped Writers." Editorial. *Rand Daily Mail* 11 Feb.: 14.

2403. "Gordimer, Nadine." *Contemporary Novelists*. Ed. James Vinson. London: St. James: 500-501.

2404. "Miss Gordimer." *Rand Daily Mail* 26 Aug.: 13.

2405. "Nadine Gordimer Awarded Prize." *Natal Mercury* 14 Apr.: 13.

1972. 2406. Roberts, Brian. "Drag on S.A. Writing: Nadine Gordimer Supported." Letter. *Cape Times* 29 Feb.: 10.

2407. "SA Writers Persecuted, P.E.N. Told." *Cape Times* 10 Feb.: 2. Different version as "We Are a Persecuted Group— Writer." *Rand Daily Mail* 10 Feb.: 5.

2408. *"A Writer Is Always Writing the Same Story." *Rand Daily Mail* 27 July.

2409. "Writers' Freedom." Editorial. *Cape Times* 12 Feb.: 6.

1973. 2410. "Ban on Book Lifted." *Cape Times* 12 May: 17. [*A World of Strangers*.]

2411. Laurence, Patrick. "When Poetry Is a Hiding Place." *The Star* 13 Oct.: 5.

2412. Seymour-Smith, Martin. *Guide to Modern World Literature*. London: Wolfe: 1042.

1974. 2413. "Authors Read Their Own Work." *Rand Daily Mail* 27 Nov.: 26.

2414. "Award for S.A. Woman Writer." *The Natal Mercury* 5 Nov.: 2. Adapt. as "Award for Nadine Gordimer." *Eastern Province Herald* 5 Nov.: 3. Adapt. as "Top UK Prize for SA Woman Author." *Cape Times* 5 Nov.: 1.

2415. "Booby Prize." Editorial. *Pretoria News* 11 Nov.: 3.

2416. "Censors 'Closing World of Ideas' - Author." *The Argus* 26 Mar.: 11.

2417. Clark, Caroline. "Gordimer vs Paton: Top SA Writers Clash: Nadine Hits Back at Alan over 'Liberal' Label." *Sunday Times* 22 Dec.: 2.

2418. Collins, Frank. "Nadine: Censored and Embarrassed - but a Winner All the Way . . . ." *Weekend Argus* 9 Nov.: 5.

2419. "Danger." Editorial. *The Natal Witness* 21 Nov.: 14.

2420. "Don't Read This!" *The Star* 15 Nov.: 28.

2421. "Embargo on Book to Be Lifted." *The Star* 22 Nov.: 15.

2422. "Embargo Placed on New Gordimer Novel." *Cape Times* 13 Nov.: 15.

2423. "Gordimer Book Award Mystery." *The Star* 7 Nov.: 6.

1974. 2424. "Gordimer Book Embargo." *The Star* 19 Nov.: 3.

2425. "Gordimer Book Embargoed." *Evening Post* 12 Nov.: 2. Extr. as "Embargoed." *The Friend* 13 Nov.: 9. "Gordimer's Novel under Embargo." *The Natal Witness* 13 Nov.: 15. "Gordimer Book Ban Confirmed." *Daily Dispatch* 13 Nov.: 13.

2426. "Gordimer Novel Gets the Nod." *Rand Daily Mail* 22 Nov.: 17. Extr. as "Censor Passes Novel." *The Natal Mercury* 22 Nov.: 11. "Censors Pass Nadine's Novel." *The Natal Witness* 23 Nov.: 3.

2427. "Gordimer's Novel: Publishers Had No Copy for the PCB." *Weekend Argus* 16 Nov.: 9.

2428. "Green Light for Gordimer Novel." *Cape Times* 22 Nov.: 1.

2429. Lee, Marshall. "The Grey Ones . . . ." *Rand Daily Mail* 30 Mar.: 11.

2430. Levin, Doreen, and Pamela Diamond. "Gordimer's New Book Is Barred." *Sunday Times* 10 Nov.: 16.

2431. "Miss Gordimer Tipped for Nobel Literature Prize." *Pretoria News* 31 July: 1. Also as "Nadine Tipped for the Nobel Prize." *The Daily News* 31 July: 1.

2432. "Nadine Booked for Big Night." *The Daily News* 26 Nov.: 10.

2433. "Nadine Gordimer." Editorial. *Cape Times* 25 Nov.: 14.

2434. "Nadine Gordimer Honoured." Editorial. *The Argus* 28 Nov.: 26.

2435. "Nadine Gordimer kan Nobelprys kry." *Oggendblad* 7 Aug.: 2.

2436. "Nadine Gordimer on List." *The Daily News* 31 Oct.: 17.

2437. "Nadine Gordimer Wins British Book Award." *Daily Dispatch* 28 Nov.: 17. Also as "Nadine Shares Richest Prize." *Cape Times* 28 Nov.: 19. "SA Novelist Wins Top Fiction Prize." *Rand Daily Mail* 28 Nov.: 10. Abbr. and trans. as "Britte bekroon Nadine Gordimer." *Oggendblad* 28 Nov.: 5.

1974. 2438. "Nadine - Nobel Laureate?" *The Star Literary Review* (supp. to *The Star*) 13 Sept.: 2.

2439. "Nadine's Attack Sparked a Running Battle." *Sunday Times* 29 Dec.: 7.

2440. "Nadine's Best Novel Shares Top Award." *Pretoria News* 28 Nov.: 7.

2441. "Novel Put on Ice." *The Star* 13 Nov.: 11.

2442. Paton, Alan. "Back to Basics." *Sunday Times* 29 Dec.: 4. [Gordimer replies in "Rose Is a Rose." *Sunday Times* 29 Dec.: 4.]

2443. "Plight of SA Black Writers Acute - Gordimer." *Daily Dispatch* 3 Dec.: 14.

2444. "Prize for Gordimer?" *The Star* 6 Nov.: 9.

2445. "Rasseboek toegelaat na 2 weke." *Oggendblad* 26 Nov.

2446. *Ratcliffe, M. "A South African Radical Exulting in Life's Chaotic Variety." *The Times* 29 Nov.: 21.

2447. "Roman deur Gordimer goedgekeur." *Die Suidwester* 26 Nov.: 2.

2448. "Sale of Book Is Stopped." *The Star* 12 Nov.: 11.

2449. Smuts, Ray. "Paton to Gordimer: Express Regret: New Blow in 'Liberal' Row." *Sunday Times* 29 Dec.: 7.

2450. "Thanks, but We'd Rather You Didn't." *The Star* 22 Nov.: 28.

2451. "Winning Author on Plight of Blacks." *The Argus* 28 Nov.: 27.

2452. "Writers Back Gordimer on Definition of a Liberal." *Daily Dispatch* 24 Dec.: 3.

1975. 2453. "Bannings Terrible Hazard—Gordimer." *Eastern Province Herald* 8 Sept.: 2.

2454. "CNA Award for Miss Gordimer." *The Daily News* 17 Mar.: 7.

2455. "CNA Award for Nadine Gordimer." *Pretoria News* 17 Mar.: 5.

1975. 2456. Clayton, Cherry. "Midde-in die kruisvuur tussen links en regs." *Beeld* 18 Mar.: 9.

2457. "Dark Ages Loom for South Africa." Editorial. *Rand Daily Mail* 9 Sept.: 12.

2458. Dendy-Young, Louise. "These Censors Aren't Special." *The Star* 6 June: 6.

2459. "Gordimer, Nadine (November 20, 1923-)." *World Authors, 1950-1970: A Companion Volume to Twentieth Century Authors.* Ed. John Wakeman. New York: Wilson: 577-579.

2460. "Gordimer, Rousseau Win CNA Awards." *Cape Times* 18 Mar.: 3.

2461. Hirschson, Niel. "Gordimer Letter Made Startling Reading." *Sunday Times* 26 Jan.: 4.

2462. Holloway, David. "Nadine Gordimer Just Keeps on Winning." *Daily Dispatch* 30 Apr.: 9.

2463. "Literary Award for Nadine Gordimer." *The Friend* 17 Mar.: 9.

2464. "Nadine Gordimer to Address Teachers in Durban." *The Daily News* 16 July: 5.

2465. "Nadine Gordimer Wins CNA Writing Award." *Rand Daily Mail* 18 Mar.: 9. Abbr. as "Nadine Gordimer Wins CNA Award." *Eastern Province Herald* 18 Mar.: 17.

2466. "Nadine Gordimer's Wry Smile at Censor." *The Daily News* 2 July: 12.

2467. "New Chapter in Clash of Top Authors." *The Daily News* 9 Jan.: 2. Abbr. as "Paton, Gordimer Bury Hatchet." *The Argus* 10 Jan.: 5.

2468. "Novelist for Library Talk." *Daily Dispatch* 18 July: 6.

2469. Paton, Alan. "From Dr Alan Paton to Nadine Gordimer." Letter. *The Natal Witness* 12 Feb.: 6.

2470. "Pryse vir boeke: Gordimer, Rousseau wen." *Die Burger* 18 Mar.: 14.

2471. Smith, Margaret. "Nadine Refused Award." *Sunday Times* 20 July: 9.

1975.   2472. "Top Writers." Editorial. *The Argus* 17 Mar.: 16.

2473. Wauthier, C. "Nadine Gordimer ou le refus de l'exil." *L'Afrique Littéraire et Artistique* (36): 12-14.

2474. "Why S.A. Writers Cannot Tell the Whole Story." *The Daily News* 7 Apr.: 6. Adapt. as "SA Colour Bar Fetters Writers." *The Friend* 7 Apr.: 2. "Gordimer on Writers' Problems." *The Argus* 8 Apr.: 2. "Writers in SA Subverted, Says Gordimer." *The Star* 7 Apr.: 5.

2475. "Writers' Awards." Editorial. *Cape Times* 18 Mar.: 12.

1976.   2476. "Apolitical in a Political World: Focus on Nadine Gordimer." *The Natal Mercury* 1 Nov.: 5.

2477. "Attack Injustice - Writer." *The Star* 18 Oct.: 9. Exp. as "Nadine Tells SA Writers: 'Fight Injustice.'" *The Daily News* 19 Oct.: 13.

2478. "Author Tells of Her Dilemma." *Eastern Province Herald* 19 Oct.: 8. Extr. as "Politics Forced on Us, Says Nadine Gordimer." *Rand Daily Mail* 19 Oct.: 8. "Top Writer Will 'Never Leave S.A.'" *The Natal Mercury* 19 Oct.: 3.

2479. "Censorship in South Africa." *Sechaba* (10.4): 59-62.

2480. "A Common Duty." Editorial. *Pretoria News* 20 Oct.: 18.

2481. "Embargo Puzzles Novelist." *Daily Dispatch* 19 Oct.: 1.

2482. "Gordimer Blames Apartheid for Riots." *Rand Daily Mail* 28 June: 5. Also pub. as "Riots: Racism Blamed." *Daily Dispatch* 28 June: 3. Trans. as "Apartheid is die oorsaak, sê Nadine." *Beeld* 28 June: 4.

2483. "Gordimer Book Ban Lifted." *The Argus* 15 Apr.: 3.

2484. "Gordimer Book Embargoed." *Cape Times* 19 Oct.: 1.

2485. "Gordimer on Censorship." *The Argus* 28 Jan.: 3.

2486. "Gordimer-boek se verbod opgehef." *Die Oosterlig* 15 Apr.: 2.

2487. Griffin, Margaret. "Nadine's Nadir." *The Argus* 6 Feb.: 12.

2488. Levin, Doreen. "I'm for a Boycott!: But Nadine Is Almost Alone." *Sunday Times* 22 Feb.: 9.

1976. 2489. Levin, Doreen. "Lift the Ban, Says Nadine." *Sunday Times* 25 July: 39.

2490. Levin, Doreen. "Second Bid to Unban Gordimer Novel." *Sunday Times* 29 Feb.: 13.

2491. "Literatuur, sensuur." *Die Burger* 27 Jan.: 8.

2492. "Nadine Bares Her Soul." *Sunday Times* 24 Oct.: 21.

2493. "Nadine's Nadir." Letters. *The Argus* 19 Feb.: 2. [Letters in response to Margaret Griffin's article in *The Argus* 6 Feb.: 12.]

1977. 2494. "Author Backs Young." *Evening Post* 5 May: 3. Repr. as "Nadine Backs Young." *The Natal Witness* 6 May: 16.

2495. "Gordimer Book Cleared from Banned List." *The Citizen* 3 June: 13. Abbr. as "Ban Lifted on Books." *Pretoria News* 3 June: 6.

2496. "Gordimer, Nadine." *The International Authors and Writers Who's Who*. 8th ed. Ed. Adrian Gaster. International Biographical Centre, Cambridge: Melrose: 377.

2497. "Nadine Will Be There." *The Star* 15 Mar.: 21.

2498. Van Oudtshoorn, Nic. "Professor Profits from Setwork Book." *Sunday Times* 16 Oct.: 3.

2499. Van Oudtshoorn, Nic. "Professor's Amazing Outburst: He Accuses Authors of Urging Revolution." *Sunday Times* 9 Oct.: 3.

2500. Van Oudtshoorn, Nic. "Prof's Book Sparks Varsity Row." *Sunday Times* 6 Nov.: 7.

2501. "White's Root Culture Not of Africa - Writer." *The Natal Witness* 18 May: 15.

1978. 2502. "André Brink to Write Gordimer Film." *Pretoria News* 17 May: 3.

2503. "Author Censors Booklet." *Eastern Province Herald* 1 May: 13.

2504. "Author Gordimer Honoured." *Post* 4 Sept.: 3. Extr. as "Honour for SA Writer." *Rand Daily Mail* 5 Sept.: 13.

1978. 2505. "Brink Finishes Gordimer Screenplay." *Pretoria News* 10 July: 1.

2506. "Ek is jammer: Prof.: Openbare apologie teenoor Nadine Gordimer." *Die Transvaler* 1 May: 2.

2507. "Lektor sê 2e keer ekskuus." *Oggendblad* 1 May: 3.

2508. Raphaely, Rosemarie. "No Nadine on Our TV?" *The Star Tonight* (supp. to *The Star*) 25 Sept.: 1.

2509. Robbertse, Elmarie. "Nadine lag nou die laaste: Beweringe, 'heeltemal onwaar.'" *Beeld* 1 May: 4. Also pub. as "Prof. Du Randt se apologie in pers." *Die Oosterlig* 1 May: 2.

2510. Rosenthal, Eric. "Gordimer, Nadine." *Encyclopaedia of Southern Africa.* 7th ed. Ed. Rosenthal. Cape Town: Juta: 190.

2511. Van Oudtshoorn, Nic. "Du Randt Admits Statements Were 'Untrue.'" *Sunday Times* 30 Apr.: 9.

2512. Wilson, Derek. "Local Actors, Crew for R2-m Film of Gordimer Novel." *The Argus Tonight* (supp. to *The Argus*) 18 Apr.: 1.

1979. 2513. Allen, Geoffrey. "Gordimer Book Held Back." *Sunday Times* 1 July: 1.

2514. "Another Banning." Editorial. *The Daily News* 6 July: 16.

2515. Ashton, Len. "Nadine Brings the Censors 'to Book.'" *Sunday Times* 8 July: 16.

2516. "'Author Smeared' Says Report." *The Friend* 1 Dec.: 3. Exp. as "Experts Accuse Censors of Bias, Prejudice, Literary Incompetence." *Cape Times* 4 Dec.: 7.

2517. "Authors Wade into Censors." *Rand Daily Mail* 1 Dec.: 2.

2518. Ball, Tony. "On-the-Shelf, Off-the-Shelf - Costly Saga." *Weekend Argus* 6 Oct.: 6.

2519. "Ban Lifting Beat Nadine." *The Star* 12 Oct.: 5.

2520. "Ban on *Burger's Daughter* Is Lifted." *Rand Daily Mail* 13 Oct.: 3. Also pub. as "Banned Book List." *Cape Times* 13 Oct.: 9.

1979. 2521. "Ban on Gordimer Book Lifted." *The Natal Witness* 4 Oct.: 1. Also pub. as "Gordimer Novel Off Banned List." *Cape Times* 4 Oct.: 3. "Ban on Novel Lifted." *The Friend* 4 Oct.: 12. "Gordimer Book Ban Lifted." *Evening Post* 4 Oct.: 2. Exp. as "Nadine Gordimer's Book Unbanned." *Rand Daily Mail* 4 Oct.: 1.

2522. "Banned Again." Editorial. *Rand Daily Mail* 9 July: 6.

2523. "Banning: PEN Protest." *The Argus* 10 July: 2. Trans. as "PEN geskok oor verbod." *Die Burger* 11 July: 7.

2524. "Brink, Gordimer en Mphahlele saam." *Die Oosterlig* 17 Apr.: 8.

2525. Brownfield, Allan C. "Verhale weerspieël verandering." *Beeld* 27 Dec.: 6. Repr. as "Gordimer en verandering: Verhale weerspieël ommeswaai." *Die Burger* 29 Dec.: 4.

2526. "*Burger's Daughter*." Editorial. *The Argus* 6 July: 10.

2527. "*Burger's Daughter* Is 'Undesirable.'" *The Argus* 5 July: 2.

2528. "*Burgher's* [sic] *Daughter* Banned." *The Natal Witness* 6 July: 1.

2529. "Censors Accused of Prejudice." *The Argus* 30 Nov.: 2.

2530. "Censors Lift Ban on *Daughter*." *The Citizen* 13 Oct.: 10.

2531. "Censorship." Editorial. *The Natal Witness* 9 July: 10.

2532. "Censuur opgeheven." *Zuid-Afrika* Nov./Dec.: 164.

2533. "Experts Accuse Censors of Bias, Prejudice, Literary Incompetence." *Cape Times* 4 Dec.: 7.

2534. Faller, F. P. "Let Us Decide Who Is Right." Letter. *Rand Daily Mail* 14 Sept.: 10.

2535. "Gordimer Banning Lifted." *The Argus* 12 Oct.: 7.

2536. "Gordimer May Fight Banning." *The Star* 9 July: 3. Adapt. as "Gordimer May Challenge Censors." *Pretoria News* 9 July.

2537. "Gordimer Novel under Embargo." *The Argus* 22 June: 2.

2538. "Gordimer Sad, Angry at Banning." *The Argus* 6 July: 6.

1979.   2539. "Gordimer Seeks Reason for Ban." *Eastern Province Herald* 10 July: 4. Exp. as "Writer: We're Brothers in Arms." *Daily Dispatch* 11 July: 5.

2540. "Gordimer-boek nie verbied." *Die Volksblad* 4 Oct.: 2. Repr. as "Roman nie meer verbied." *Die Burger* 4 Oct.: 9. Adapt. as "Gordimer-boek nou nie meer taboe." *Beeld* 4 Oct.: 9.

2541. "Gordimer's Black Day." *The Natal Mercury* 6 July: 3.

2542. "Gordimer's Latest Book Joins the Banned List." *Rand Daily Mail* 6 July: 5. Also pub. as "Latest Book by Nadine Gordimer Is Banned." *The Citizen* 6 July: 12. Extr. as "Nadine's Latest Is Banned." *Pretoria News* 6 July: 7. Trans. as "Gordimer se boek verbied." *Oggendblad* 6 July: 10. Extr. as "Gordimer-boek verbied." *Die Transvaler* 6 July: 4. "Gordimer se boek verbied." *Die Burger* 6 July: 9. "Roman verbied." *Suid-Afrikaanse Oorsig* 20 July: 9.

2543. "Gordimer's New Novel Is Declared Undesirable." *The Friend* 6 July: 5.

2544. "It Was Still an Insult." Editorial. *Rand Daily Mail* 3 Dec.: 12.

2545. *Mitgang, Herbert. "The Authoress." *New York Times Book Review* 19 Aug.: 35.

2546. "Nadine Gordimer Had Own Plan to Have Book Ban Lifted." *The Daily News* 12 Oct.: 17. Exp. as "Censors Beat Me to It - SA Writer." *Weekend Argus* 13 Oct.: 11.

2547. "Nadine Talks Shop." *Rand Daily Mail* 22 Mar.: 3.

2548. "Row over Unbanned Book." *The Star* 4 Oct.: 3.

2549. "Skrywers wil nou optree ná verbod." *Die Transvaler* 9 July: 6.

2550. Swift, Penny. "Latest Gordimer Novel Banned." *Rand Daily Mail* 6 July: 1. Slightly different version pub. as "Nadine's Latest Novel Banned." *Eastern Province Herald* 6 July: 1.

2551. Venables, Hilary. "Nadine Gordimer's 'Brilliant' Book Could End in Shredder." *Evening Post* 6 July: 3.

2552. ",Vorm 'n front téén sensors!'" *Rapport* 8 July: 18.

1979. 2553. "Why the Censors Banned Nadine's Novel on Racialism and Radical Politics." *Rand Daily Mail* 6 Sept.: 11.

2554. ",Woede en frustrasie' oor die verbod." *Beeld* 6 July: 5.

2555. "Writers Slam Bannings of 'Leading' Literary Works." *The Citizen* 21 Aug.: 10.

2556. "Writers' Group Hits at Rash of Bannings." *Rand Daily Mail* 30 Aug.: 4.

1980. 2557. "Bewustheid van Afrika nodig in letterkunde: Skrywers moet weg van Europa." *Beeld* 29 July: 11. Also pub. as "G'n egte SA literatuur: Gordimer." *Die Burger* 29 July: 7. Adapt. as "Afrika-bewustheid nodig in ons letterkunde." *Die Volksblad* 27 Aug.: 11.

2558. Boekkooi, Jaap. "Baring the Flaws of Our Literary Guardians." *The Star* 3 Apr.: 25.

2559. Botha, Amanda. "Ironie rondom CNA-wenners." *Die Transvaler* 22 Mar.: 2.

2560. "CNA-prys." Editorial. *Die Transvaler* 22 Mar.: 6.

2561. "CNA-prys ook vir Opperman." *Beeld* 22 Mar.: 7.

2562. "Censorship 'a Weapon of Apartheid.'" *The Star* 18 Apr.: 1.

2563. "Censorship Is Tool of Apartheid - Gordimer." *Evening Post* 18 Apr.: 3.

2564. Charney, Craig. "Plenty to Fear, Says Gordimer." *The Star* 29 Apr.: 3.

2565. Coetzee, Ken. "Probleme van sensuur toegelig." Rev. of *What Happened to Burger's Daughter or How South African Censorship Works. Hoofstad* 24 Apr.: 25.

2566. Geyer, Arnold. "Novelist: New-Look Censors Use Same Old Gags." *Rand Daily Mail* 31 July: 3.

2567. "Gordimer Hits at Censors." *The Argus* 18 Apr.: 3.

2568. "Gordimer, Nadine." *Current Biography* [New York] (41.6): 12-15.

2569. "Gordimer Triumph: Ban Is Off - Now Book Is Honoured." *The Citizen* 22 Mar.: 7.

2570. "Gordimer versuur spogdinee." *Oggendblad* 19 Apr.: 7.

1980. 2571. Grobler, Hilda. "Sensuur uitmekaar getrek." Rev. of *What Happened to Burger's Daughter* or *How South African Censorship Works*. *Hoofstad* 24 May: 4.

2572. J. R. L. M. "The Censor's Task Is Far from Easy." Rev. of *What Happened to Burger's Daughter* or *How South African Censorship Works*. *The Natal Witness* 13 Oct.: 8.

2573. Johl, Ronl. "Wat het met *Burger's Daughter* gebeur." *Die Volksblad* 9 July: 3.

2574. "Kulturele boikot moet selektief wees - Gordimer." *Die Volksblad* 14 Jan.: 3.

2575. "Literary Award for Gordimer Novel." *The Argus* 21 Mar.: 1. Repr. as "CNA Award to Nadine Gordimer." *The Friend* 22 Mar.: 9.

2576. *Loercher, D. "South African Political Novelist Nadine Gordimer: 'I Know I Have Not Been Brave Enough.'" *Christian Science Monitor* 21 Jan.: 21.

2577. M. v. B. "Kurt Jobst - as Nadine Gordimer Saw Him." *Sunday Times* 4 May: 4.

2578. "Nadine - a Collector of Literary Laurels." *The Star* 24 Mar.: 19.

2579. "Nadine Goes in for the KO." *The Citizen* 22 Apr.: 13.

2580. "Nadine nog Nobelprys-kandidaat." *Die Vaderland* 9 Oct.: 3

2581. "Nobelprys dalk vir Nadine." *Die Volksblad* 9 Oct.: 4.

2582. "Opperman en Gordimer CNA-wenners." *Die Volksblad* 21 Mar.: 8.

2583. "Opperman wenner van CNA-prys." *Hoofstad* 21 Mar.: 3.

2584. "SA Author May Get Prize." *Evening Post* 9 Oct.: 1. Also as "Nadine May Get Nobel Prize." *The Daily News* 9 Oct.: 1. Abbr. as "Gordimer on Nobel Prize Short List." *Pretoria News* 9 Oct.: 3. Also as "Gordimer Lined Up for Nobel." *The Star* 9 Oct.: 1.

2585. Sboros, Marika. "Writing Is Now Used in Political Struggle." *Rand Daily Mail* 29 July: 3. Slightly different version as "'African Consciousness' Is Needed." *Evening Post* 29

July: 2. Abbr. as "Literature Used as Weapon - Author." *Daily Dispatch* 29 July: 4. Trans. as ",Letterkunde swartes se steun.'" *Die Volksblad* 29 July: 12.

1980. 2586. "Second Wins for Gordimer, Opperman." *Evening Post* 21 Mar.: 3. Also pub. as "Authors Are Second Time Winners." *The Daily News* 21 Mar.: 3. Adapt. as "Gordimer and Opperman Repeat Triumph." *The Natal Witness* 22 Mar.

2587. "Skryfster onthul ,vreemde proses': Verbod op *Daughter*." *Die Burger* 24 Mar.: 2.

2588. "So wek 'n mens nie simpatie." Editorial. *Oggendblad* 19 Apr.: 6.

2589. "Sonneskyn en so aan." *Rapport* 23 Mar.: 21.

2590. Sutton, Keith. "Round About: Old Hands." *Eastern Province Herald* 25 Mar.: 11.

2591. "Tributes from Her Friends." Editorial. *Sunday Express* 6 Apr.: 6.

2592. "Two SA Authors in Nobel 'Finals.'" *Rand Daily Mail* 9 Oct.: 3.

2593. Van der Byver, J. D. "Só werk SA se sensuur . . . ." Rev. of *What Happened to Burger's Daughter* or *How South African Censorship Works*. *Die Vaderland* 29 May: 18.

1981. 2594. "Another Award for Gordimer." *Rand Daily Mail* 17 Sept.: 8. Slightly different version as "SA Authoress Gets Big Literary Prize." *The Citizen* 17 Sept.: 11.

2595. "Coveted Literature Award Made to Nadine Gordimer." *The Daily News* 2 Dec.: 4. Slightly different version as "Gordimer Receives Top US Literary Prize." *The Argus* 2 Dec.: 6.

2596. "The 'Cultural Liberation Struggle' Must Be Won . . . : It's a Fight That Belongs to All of Us — Gordimer." *Sunday Tribune* 1 Mar.: 17.

2597. "Gordimer Gets US Writing Award." *Pretoria News* 2 Dec.: 5.

1981. 2598. "Gordimer Tells of the Dilemma Facing SA's White Liberals." *The Natal Mercury* 19 Feb.: 4. Exp. as "Gordimer Tells UK of Whites' Dilemma." *Eastern Province Herald* 20 Feb.: 4.

2599. "Gordimer Wins Literature Award." *The Natal Witness* 2 Dec.: 1.

2600. "Gordimer Wins Scottish Award." *The Star Tonight* (supp. to *The Star*) 8 Jan.: 1. Also pub. as "Nadine Wins Scottish Prize." *Pretoria News* 8 Jan.: 1. Trans. as "Skotte vereer Gordimer." *Die Volksblad* 10 Jan.: 2. "Skotte vereer Nadine." *Die Vaderland* 10 Jan.: 9.

2601. "Gordimer-reeks dalk nie op SATV." *Die Volksblad* 9 Nov.: 3.

2602. "Gordimer-romans vir oorsese TV verfilm: Kaapse rolprentmaker 'n regisseur." *Die Burger* 19 Nov.: 8.

2603. "Gordimer's Latest Book May Be Banned: I Don't Know What to Expect . . . ." *Sunday Tribune* 19 July.

2604. "Helping Women in the Book World." *Rand Daily Mail* 8 May: 11.

2605. Hough, Barrie. "Gordimer wen prys." *Beeld* 10 Jan.: 8. Repr. as "Gordimer wen Skotse prys." *Die Oosterlig* 13 Jan.: 10.

2606. Jansen, Ena. "'n Deurbraak vir Gordimer, Brink: Nederlanders 'ontdek' twee SA-skrywers." *Die Burger* 17 Nov.: 12. Repr. as "Gordimer-boek in Nederlands." *Die Volksblad* 19 Nov.: 24.

2607. Levin, Doreen. "Miss Gordimer Books a New Award." *Sunday Times* 29 Nov.: 50.

2608. Levin, Doreen. "Nadine Gordimer Looks into the Future." *Sunday Times* 12 July: 9.

2609. "Major US Prize for Gordimer." *Rand Daily Mail* 24 Nov.: 3. Slightly different version as "Award for Gordimer." *Daily Dispatch* 24 Nov.: 6. "US Award for Gordimer." *Eastern Province Herald* 24 Nov.: 4.

2610. *Michiko, Kakutani. "'Nadine Gordimer, South African Witness.'" *New York Times* 28 Dec.

1981. 2611. "Nadine Probes SA's 'Terrible Chemistry.'" *Pretoria News* 20 Feb.: 1.

2612. "A New Literary Prize for Nadine Gordimer." *The Star* 29 May: 3.

2613. Pienaar, Hansie. "Boekdeurbraak vir hul." *Beeld* 12 June: 6.

2614. "SA under Gordimer's TV Microscope." *The Star* 19 Feb.: 21.

2615. Smith, Margaret. "Gordimer on British TV." *Cape Times* 23 Feb.: 6.

2616. Van Rooyen, Johan. "Letterkundeprys vir Gordimer." *Hoofstad* 7 Jan.: 12.

2617. Vinassa, Andrea. "Amerika bekroon Nadine Gordimer." *Beeld* 18 Sept.: 15.

2618. "Wêreldeer aan Gordimer." *Die Volksblad* 17 Sept.: 8. Trans. as "New Books." *Pretoria News* 23 Oct.: 10.

1982. 2619. "After Apartheid by Nadine Gordimer." *The Star Tonight* (supp. to *The Star*) 10 July: 1.

2620. Albrecht, Sybelle. "Kunstenares weier skildery op boek: ‚Gordimer té onsimpatiek.'" *Die Vaderland* 22 Nov.: 4.

2621. "Censorship Essential to Apartheid Says Author." *Eastern Province Herald* 29 Apr.: 10.

2622. Collins, Anne. "South African Journal." *City Woman* (Winter): 13-16, 18, 20, 22-24, 26-27 [Gordimer: 22-23].

2623. Davis, Marlene. "Nadine on Writing and Resistance." *Cape Times* 15 July: 5.

2624. Dempster, Carolyn. "Aim of Act Is the Control of Our Minds, Says Gordimer." *The Star* 23 Apr.: 3.

2625. Dempster, Carolyn. "Is the Censor's House on Fire? Asks Gordimer." *The Star* 28 Apr.: 5.

2626. "'Don't Call Up Our Girls to Be Prostitutes' Says Kappie Kommando." *Sunday Tribune* 21 Mar.: 3.

2627. "Dust-Up over Gordimer Dust-Jacket Is Settled." *The Daily News* 17 Nov.: 10.

1982.   2628.   Feinstein, Martin. "SA 'Is Being Cut Off from Information.'" *Rand Daily Mail* 23 Apr.

2629.   "Gordimer Attacks 'Apartheid Censors.'" *Rand Daily Mail* 28 Apr.

2630.   "Gordimer geskok oor bande met SA." *Beeld* 26 May: 15.

2631.   "Gordimer, kunstenares haaks oor skildery." *Die Burger* 20 Nov.: 10.

2632.   "Gordimer on Role as Script-Writer." *Cape Times* 14 Sept.: 6.

2633.   "Gordimer Wins Her Third CNA Prize." *The Argus* 17 Mar.: 1. *Repr. as "Gordimer Wins CNA Award." *Cape Times* 18 Mar.: 3.

2634.   "'Liberation for All.'" *Rand Daily Mail* 9 Nov.: 4.

2635.   Mcapukisi, S. "Crazy Talk?" Letter. *Daily Dispatch* 11 Nov.: 16.

2636.   "Nadine Gordimer Backs Change in SA." *Cape Times* 8 Nov.: 13.

2637.   "Nadine voorsien niks goeds vir SA." *Beeld* 5 June: 7.

2638.   "Nadine's View." *Daily Dispatch* 30 Mar.: 4.

2639.   "Novelist Angry over Artist's Allegations." *The Daily News* 18 Nov.: 12. Extr. as "Gordimer Slams Artist." *Pretoria News* 19 Nov.: 16.

2640.   Richards, Jo-Anne. "Gordimer an 'Enemy of SA.'" *Cape Times* 19 Nov.: 10.

2641.   Robbins, David. "Writing Towards a Common Future." *Reality* (14.5): 10-11. [Report on Gordimer's and Rive's papers presented at a conference on "Culture and Resistance", Gaborone, July.]

2642.   Roberts, Sheila. Rev. of *What Happened to Burger's Daughter* or *How South African Censorship Works. Research in African Literatures* (13.2): 259-262.

2643.   S. M. "Gordimer Trumpets Her Own Virtues." Letter. *The Star* 23 Nov.: 16.

1982. 2644. "South African Writers: Nadine Gordimer and Es'kia Mphahlele." *Upbeat* (2.6): 8-9.

2645. Sowden, Dora. "Nadine Gordimer Feted in Jerusalem." *Rand Daily Mail* 18 May: 11.

2646. Stephenson, Bruce. "Artist's No to 'SA Enemy' Gordimer." *Rand Daily Mail* 18 Nov. Extr. as "Artist Says 'No' to Nadine Gordimer Cover." *Eastern Province Herald* 18 Nov.: 1.

2647. Thompson, Kathryn. "Time for a Common SA Culture, Says Gordimer." *The Argus Tonight* (supp. to *The Argus*) 9 July: 1.

2648. "Top Authors Hit Out at Censorship." *Pretoria News* 29 Apr.: 14.

2649. Vendeiro, Zenaide. "Artist Hits at Gordimer." *The Star* 18 Nov.: 3.

2650. "Winners Step Up for Book Awards." *Pretoria News* 29 Apr.: 14. Repr. as "CNA Prizes Awarded." *The Friend* 3 May: 5.

1983. 2651. Brownfeld, Allan C. "Gordimer praat oor die skrywer in SA: 'Gerinkel smoor die doodsroggel.'" *Beeld* 11 Apr.: 1, 3.

2652. "Eight of Nadine Gordimer's Novels Are Currently in Paperback Print." *Rand Daily Mail* 18 July: 6.

2653. "Gordimer at Wits." *The Citizen* 20 May: 19.

2654. "Gordimer Calls for New SA Society." *Daily Dispatch* 2 Sept.: 19.

2655. "Gordimer Discusses Her Work." *The Star Tonight* (supp. to *The Star*) 23 May: 1.

2656. "Gordimer Letter in Libel Suit." *Rand Daily Mail* 26 Nov.: 6.

2657. "Gordimer, Nadine 1923- ." *The Cambridge Guide to English Literature*. Ed. Michael Stapleton. Cambridge: CUP; Feltham: Newnes: 355.

2658. "Gordimer wen dalk Nobelprys." *Beeld* 6 Oct.: 2.

2659. Haresnape, Geoffrey. "Notes." *Contrast* 56 (14.4): 3, 94.

2660. "His Peers Pay Tribute." *The Daily News* 4 Jan.: 14.

2661. Lelyveld, Joseph. "South Africa on Film, as Seen by Nadine Gordimer." *New York Times* 15 May: H1, H13.

1983. 2662. Mashabela, Harry. "PFP Father 'a Great Mind.'" *Rand Daily Mail* 30 May: 3.

   2663. Mayers, Rhona. "Nadine Gordimer." *The Star* 4 Feb.: 14.

   2664. "South Africa under Siege, Says Gordimer." *Grocott's Mail* 9 Sept.

1984. 2665. Beeton, Ridley. Laudation in Presenting Nadine Gordimer at the Graduation Ceremony at U of Witwatersrand, 20 Mar. Graduation Ceremony Booklet: 9-11. Repr. *English Academy Review* 2: 149-153.

   2666. Brink, André P. "Gordimer bevestig haar meesterskap." *Rapport* 12 Aug.: 19.

   2667. "Gordimer bly hier." *Die Burger* 10 Aug.: 11.

   2668. Lipman, Beata. "A Writer." *We Make Freedom: Women in South Africa*. Lipman. London: Pandora Press: 104-106.

   2669. "New Honour for Gordimer." *The Natal Witness* 2 Mar.: 2. Different versions as "Gordimer to Be Honoured." *Daily Dispatch* 2 Mar.: 8. "Wits to Honour Writer." *Rand Daily Mail* 2 Mar.: 2. "Wits Honours Author and Senior Counsel." *The Citizen* 2 Mar.: 14. "Wits Honour for Gordimer." *Cape Times* 5 Mar.: 6.

   2670. "Out of South Africa." *Newsweek* 16 July: 42.

   2671. "Rich Body of South African Literature Shaped by Apartheid." *Sowetan* 23 Mar.: 8.

   2672. Ronge, Barry. "A Guide to South African Writers or How to Hold Your Own When People Are Talking about Books." *Fair Lady* 8 Aug.: 90-92.

   2673. Saldanha, Eugene. "Students Must Reject Sick Values - Gordimer." *The Star* 2 Mar.: 2.

   2674. Watkins, Mel. "Fiction and the State." *New York Times Book Review* 29 July: 7.

1985. 2675. "Appèlraad kyk na verbod op Boesak-video." *Beeld* 26 Feb.: 13.

   2676. ",,Bedeutende Literatin": Dortmunder Nelly-Sachs-Preis für südafrikanische Autorin Nadine Gordimer." *Westfälische Rundschau* 11 Oct.

1985. 2677. Bondy, François. "Mit Nadine Gordimer." *Die Weltwoche* [Zürich] 28 Nov.

2678. C. S. "Hieroor praat die Gilde." *Rapport* 14 July: 11.

2679. "Die Dichterin Nadine Gordimer erhält den Nelly-Sachs-Preis." *Dortmund* 11 Oct.

2680. E. B. "Nelly-Sachs-Preis an Nadine Gordimer." *Ruhr-Nachrichten* 25 Nov.

2681. E. B. "Nelly-Sachs-Preis Dortmunds für bekannte Autorin aus Südafrika." *Ruhr-Nachrichten* 11 Oct.

2682. Editorial. *The Aida Parker Newsletter* 4 June: 2.

2683. "Engagierte Kämpferin gegen Rassentrennung in Südafrika erhielt Nelly-Sachs-Preis 1985." *Dortmunder Bekanntmachungen* 29 Nov.: 1.

2684. "Gordimer, Nadine." *The International Who's Who 1985-86.* 49th ed. London: Europa: 540.

2685. "Gordimer, Nadine (1923-)." *The Oxford Companion to English Literature.* 5th ed. Ed. Margaret Drabble. Oxford: OUP: 404.

2686. "Gordimer on Short List for Nobel Prize." *The Citizen* 16 Oct.: 14. Adapt. and trans. as "Gordimer genoem vir Nobelprys." *Beeld* 16 Oct.: 14.

2687. "Gordimer Turns Down Degree." *The Star* 28 May: 3. Abbr. as "Gordimer Declines US Doctorate." *The Star* 28 May.

2688. "Gordimer Up for 1985 Nobel Prize." *Cape Times* 16 Oct.: 3.

2689. "Gordimer Wins Literary Award." *The Citizen* 23 Sept.: 20. Slightly different version in *The Windhoek Advertiser* 27 Sept.: 9. Adapt. and trans. as "Gordimer vereer." *Die Burger* 23 Sept.: 3. "Italiaanse prys vir Gordimer." *Beeld* 24 Sept.: 4. Extr. as "Gordimer Wins Award." *SA Digest* 27 Sept.: 878. Trans. as "Gordimer wen prys." *Suid-Afrikaanse Oorsig* 27 Sept.: 878.

2690. Greyling, Aletta. "Beraad eindig met gewigtige sake." *Die Vaderland* 19 July: 3.

1985. **2691.** Heyn, Ursala. "Mutige Poetin in einem leidenden Land: Misstöne bei der Verleihung des Nelly-Sachs-Preises an Nadine Gordimer in Dortmund." *Westfalenpost* 26 Nov.

2692. Imhoff, Maria. "Sachs-Preis der Stadt Dortmund an Nadine Gordimer." *Westdeutsche Allgemeine Zeitung* 11 Oct.

2693. "Kämpferin mit feiner Feder." *Ruhr-Nachrichten* 23 Nov.

2694. "Kulturpreis für Nadine Gordimer: Literatin und mutige Kämpferin." *Ruhr-Nachrichten* 11 Oct.

2695. Louw, Chris. "Waarom moet Gordimer en kie my taal so verkrag?" *Die Vaderland* 17 Apr.: 12.

2696. "Nadine Gordimer Urges US Demos to Continue." *The Citizen* 31 May: 3.

2697. "Nadine Gordimer Wins Prize." *The Daily News* 18 Oct.: 5.

2698. "Nadine Gordimer Wins Prize, Tipped for Nobel." *The Star* 17 Oct.: 2.

2699. "Nelly-Sachs-Preis 1985 geht an Nadine Gordimer." *Dortmunder Bekanntmachungen* 18 Oct.: 7.

2700. "Nelly-Sachs-Preis für Nadine Gordimer." *Düsseldorfer Nachrichten* 25 Nov. Also pub. in *Remscheider General - Anzeiger* 25 Nov. Slightly different version as "Nelly-Sachs-Preis für südafrikanische Autorin." *Die Glocke* 25 Nov. "Nadine Gordimer geehrt: Die Verantwortung der Schriftsteller in Südafrika." *Pforzheimer Zeitung* 25 Nov. "Der Befreiung dienen: Nelly-Sachs-Preis ging an Nadine Gordimer." *Münstersche Zeitung* 25 Nov. "Aufrichtigkeit: Nadine Gordimer erhielt Nelly-Sachs-Preis." *Frankfurter Rundschau* 26 Nov. Extr. as "'Militantes Engagement': Nadine Gordimer geehrt." *Lahrer Zeitung* 26 Nov.

2701. S. K. "Dissonanzen im Opernhaus bei der Kulturpreisverleihung." *Ruhr-Nachrichten* 25 Nov.

2702. Sichel, Adrienne. "Talks from Gordimer, Coetzee." *The Star Tonight* (supp. to *The Star*) 8 July.

2703. Steinert, Hajo. "Verdiente Ehrung." *Kölner Stadtanzeiger* 22 Nov.

2704. Stromberg, Kyra. "Wie lange noch? Nadine Gordimer erhält den Nelly-Sachs-Preis." *Badische Zeitung* 23 Nov.

1985. 2705. "Südafrika-Stück nicht erlaubt." *Ruhr-Nachrichten* 25 Nov.

2706. Tomlins, James. "SA Soldiers Fired from Helicopters - Gordimer." *The Sunday Star* 1 Dec.: 13.

2707. "Top German Award for Nadine Gordimer." *The Star* 26 Nov.: 2.

2708. ",,Unser Stück sollte Nadine Gordimer gewidmet sein"." *Westdeutsche Allgemeine Zeitung* 26 Nov.

2709. Walker, Richard. "Gordimer 'No' to Degree for Mrs Mandela's Sake." *Eastern Province Herald* 28 May: 5. Repr. as "Gordimer Declines Degree Honour." *Daily Dispatch* 29 May: 11.

2710. Wan. "Zum 13. Mal Nelly-Sachs-Preis: Schriftstellerin Gordimer trifft heute abend in Dortmund ein." *Westfälische Rundschau* 23 Nov.

2711. Wanzelius, Rainer. "Nadine Gordimer aus Südafrika ist Nelly-Sachs-Preisträgerin '85." *Westfälische Rundschau* 11 Oct.

2712. Wanzelius, Rainer. "Nadine Gordimer — Gegnerin des Apartheidregimes fordert Freiheit für alle Südafrikaner." *Westfälische Rundschau* 25 Nov.

2713. Wanzelius, Rainer. "Zwischenreden bei der Preisverleihung." *Westfälische Rundschau* 25 Nov.

2714. Witthaus, Michele. "Literary Gem for SA Readers." *The Star* 29 July: 18.

1986. 2715. "25 Years of Censorship." *Business Day* 24 July: 4.

2716. Asvat, Farouk, Achmat Dangor, Nadine Gordimer, Don Mattera, Mtutuzeli Matshoba, Essop Patel and Colin Smuts. "Unban This Book!" Letter. *City Press* 16 Mar.: 7.

2717. "Award for Nadine Gordimer." *The Star* 27 Nov.: 3. Exp. as "Gordimer Wins Bennett Award." *The Argus Tonight* (supp. to *The Argus*) 28 Nov.: 11.

2718. "The Bennett Award, 1986." Citation. *The Hudson Review* (39.3): 355.

2719. Boekkooi, Jaap. "The Honours Never End for Nadine." *The Star* 3 Dec.: 8M.

1986. 2720. Campbell, John. "The Varied Thoughts of Famous Writers." Rev. of *Writers at Work - The Paris Review Interviews*, ed. George Plimpton. *Business Day* 14 Apr.: 12.

2721. De Kock, Leon. "Gordimer, Nadine." *Contemporary Novelists*. 4th ed. Ed. D. L. Kirkpatrick. New York: St Martin's: 355-356.

2722. "Gordimer, Nadine (1923-)." *Companion to South African English Literature*. Comp. David Adey, Ridley Beeton, Michael and Ernest Pereira. Johannesburg: Donker: 91-92.

2723. "Gordimer, Nadine." *The Writers Directory 1986-88*. Chicago: St James: 363-364.

2724. "Gordimer word ere-doktor." *Die Vaderland* 9 Dec.: 17.

2725. Haysom, Cheetah. "Top Writers to Read at Anti-Apartheid Function." *The Argus Tonight* (supp. to *The Argus*) 17 Jan.: 1. Also as "Gordimer Spearheads Writers' Protest." *The Star Tonight* (supp. to *The Star*) 17 Jan.: 1. "Writers Read for Arts Fund." *The Daily News Tonight* (supp. to *The Daily News*) 17 Jan.: 1.

2726. "Honorary Degrees from UCT for Suzman and Gordimer." *Jewish Times* 1 Mar.: 6.

2727. "Nadine Gordimer (1923 —   )." *Lantern* (35.4): 83.

2728. "Nadine Gordimer Backs 'People's Education.'" *Cape Times* 13 Dec.: 2.

2729. "Nadine Gordimer Elected to New Anti-Censorship Body." *The Natal Witness* 12 Sept.: 7.

2730. "Nadine Gordimer to Get Honorary Degree." *The Citizen* 8 Dec.: 15.

2731. "Nadine ook vies oor Shultz en vryheid." *Beeld* 15 Jan.: 9.

2732. Obermeyer, G. A. "Gordimer's Comments on Education Are Shocking." Letter. *Cape Times* 17 Dec.: 14.

2733. Ross, Heather. "Gordimer: The Prickly Conscience of a Country." *Business Day* 24 July: 4.

2734. "SA Author on Honours List in US." *The Citizen* 6 June: 12. Adapt. and trans. as "Ere-graad vir SA skryfster." *Die Burger* 6 June: 2.

1986. 2735. Schulman, André. "Gordimer's 'Bloody' Rhetoric and Imagery Is Unjust." Letter. *Cape Times* 19 Dec.: 12.

2736. Schwartz, Pat. "Cloaked in Her Principles." *The Weekly Mail* 11 July: 16.

2737. Shelton, Glenn. "Ringside View of Strife and Fear." *The Weekly Mail* 25-31 July: 18.

2738. "South African Writers Acclaimed." *The Daily News* 21 Jan.: 9. Also as "SA Writers Attend Anti-Apartheid Function." *Pretoria News* 21 Jan.: 5. Repr. as "Applause for SA Writers, Poets." *Sowetan* 22 Jan.: 7. "Gordimer Acclaimed and Mailer Booed." *The Star Tonight* (supp. to *The Star*) 23 Jan.: 1.

2739. "Stand Fast." Editorial. *The Natal Witness* 15 Dec.: 10.

2740. "UCT to Honour Gordimer." *The Star* 7 Feb.: 11.

2741. "Universities Support Racism in SA - Gordimer." *The Citizen* 13 Dec.: 5.

2742. *Vivan, Itala. "Il Mio Sudafrica." *Quotidiano* (22) Nov.

2743. *Vivan, Itala. "L'Africa divisa di Nadine." *Corriere del Ticino* (22) Nov.

2744. Whitfield, Chris. "Gordimer Slams Varsity Education." *Sunday Tribune* 14 Dec.: 6.

2745. "A Writer's View of the Future . . . ." *Business Day* 24 July: 4.

1987. 2746. "Anti-Apartheid Writers Form National Group." *The Star* 6 July: 4.

2747. Devan, Yogin. "Go All the Way, Says Gordimer." *Sunday Tribune* 24 Apr.: 4.

2748. "Join the Struggle, Writers Told." *Cape Times* 4 July: 21.

2749. Makgabutlane, S. M. "Gordimer Hammers Election." *Pretoria News* 2 Apr.: 5.

2750. "Subsidy Ruling Greatest Threat Yet - Nadine." *The Argus* 4 Sept.: 4.

2751. Uhlig, Mark A. "Shocked by Her Own Heroine." *New York Times Book Review* 3 May: 22.

1987. 2752. Wellwarth, George. "'Criticism of My View Is Mystifying.'" Letter. *The Star Tonight* (supp. to *The Star*) 3 Apr.: 11.

1988. 2753. "The Fight to Write." *The Daily News* 24 Feb.: 17.

2754. "Gordimer Finalist for Top Literature Prize." *The Argus* 25 Feb.

2755. "Gordimer, Nadine 1923- ." *The Cambridge Guide to Literature in English.* Ed. Ian Ousby. New York: CUP; London: Hamlyn: 403.

2756. "Gordimer of Kundera? Byna R1m. wink vir SA Nadine!" *Beeld* 13 Oct.: 8.

2757. "Gordimer: I Back ANC." *Cape Times* 6 Dec.: 1.

2758. Gqubule, Thandeka. "So Few Women Writers . . . but Each Has a Story." *The Weekly Mail Review/Books* (supp. to *The Weekly Mail*) 2-8 Dec.: 27.

2759. "Het chauvinisme Nadine beroof? Skerp vrae om die Nobelprys." *Beeld* 15 Oct.: 14.

2760. "I Back ANC, Gordimer Tells Court." *The Argus* 6 Dec.: 5.

2761. "I Support Umkhonto we Sizwe, Says Gordimer." *The Star* 6 Dec.: 2. Extr. as "ANC Is Not Violent - Author." *Sowetan* 6 Dec.: 1.

2762. Joubert, Maureen. "Verhale uit Suid-Afrika in Amerika voorgelees." *Beeld* 30 May: 1. Repr. as "Broadway-gehoor hoor SA-verhale: Gordimer spreek Yanks toe." *Die Burger* 1 June: 10. Adapt. as "SA Swartes skryf anders." *Die Volksblad* 26 May: 15.

2763. *Louw, C. "Spektakel van ironie." *Die Suid-Afrikaan* Dec.: 38-40.

2764. "Mandela en Tambo hul leiers, sê twee bekendes: Hoogverraad-verhoor." *Die Volksblad* 6 Dec.: 4. Adapt. as "UWK-rektor sê hy sou ANC steun." *Die Burger* 6 Dec.: 1.

2765. McGibbon, Carolyn. "Gordimer in Bitter Clash over Censor Jibe: Top Writers Clash." *Sunday Tribune* 6 Nov.: 1, 4.

2766. "Mev. Cassirer en die ANC." *Die Transvaler* 7 Dec.: 8.

2767. Milne, Ramsay. "'Most SA Writers Support Change.'" *The Star Tonight* (supp. to *The Star*) 27 May: 4.

1988. 2768. Morris, Michael. "Gordimer Tells of Her Commitment." *The Star* 1 Mar.: 12.

2769. "Nadine Gordimer steun die ANC: Vermaarde skryfster getuig in Delmas-verhoor." *Beeld* 6 Dec.: 2.

2770. Russell, Susan. "Gordimer Backs Mandela." *Business Day* 6 Dec.: 4. Repr. as "Top ANC Pair Her Leaders - Gordimer." *Eastern Province Herald* 6 Dec.: 1. "Gasps over Gordimer's Statement on Mandela." *The Natal Mercury* 6 Dec.: 1.

2771. "White Artists Want Change - Gordimer." *Sowetan* 26 May: 10.

2772. "Women in Running for Literature Nobel Prize." *The Citizen* 13 Oct.: 14. Extr. as "Gordimer on Nobel Shortlist." *Business Day* 13 Oct.: 7. "Gordimer in Line for Nobel Literature Prize?" *Cape Times* 13 Oct.: 3.

1989. 2773. Cloete, Adrian. "Humour Lacking in SA Writing, Says Gordimer." *Eastern Province Herald* 11 Dec.: 7.

2774. "Column 89: Parliament to Be Neutralised?" *Die Patriot* 3 Nov.: 11.

2775. Dahl, Magnus. "I mina romaner måste jag få visa upp folk med vårtor och allt!" *Femina* [Stockholm] May: 104-106.

2776. "Digter van vandag skryf oor stakings." *Die Transvaler* 1 Dec.: 4.

2777. "Gordimer 'Incorrect.'" *Pretoria News* 1 Mar.: 2.

2778. *"Gordimer, Nadine (b 1923)." *Bloomsbury Guide to English Literature*. Ed. Marion Wynne-Davies. London: Bloomsbury: 566.

2779. Höög, Lars. "Nadine Gordimer på bokmässan: Sydafrika har plats för vita i Framtiden." *Västmanlandslänstidning* [Gothenburg, Sweden] 11 Sept.

2780. Joubert, Kevin. "I Saw Reds. It Was You Who Saw the 'rooi gevaar.'" Letter. *The Weekly Mail* 17-23 Nov.: 14. [Reply to Gordimer's letter in *The Weekly Mail* 10-16 Nov.]

2781. Kanfer, Stefan. "Restless White Conscience." *Time* 26 June: 48-50.

1989. 2782. "Leading Authors Challenged on Salman Rushdie." *Pretoria News* 29 Mar.: 4.

2783. Le Grange, Carina. "SA Writers Back Author of *The Satanic Verses*." *The Star* 2 Mar.: 5M.

2784. Louw, Chris. "Satan and Censorship." *Southern African Review of Books* Feb./Mar.: 13. Extr. and trans. from *Die Suid-Afrikaan* Dec./Jan. 1988/89.

2785. Mattera, Don. "Timely Bouquets for the 'Outie van Kofifi.'" Rev. of *Trevor Huddleston: Essays on His Life and Work*, ed. Deborah Duncan Honor. *The Weekly Mail Review/ Books* (supp. to *The Weekly Mail*) 28 July-3 Aug.: 29.

2786. "Nadine Gordimer May Win Nobel Prize." *The Citizen* 2 Oct.: 15.

2787. "Nobelprys dalk na SA skryfster." *Beeld* 2 Oct.: 6. Also in *Die Volksblad* 2 Oct.: 10.

2788. Tomlins, James. "Right Wing Ready for Anything - Gordimer." *The Star* 23 Oct.: 3. Exp. as "Rightists Will Halt Power Sharing - Author." *Pretoria News* 24 Oct.: 10.

2789. Van Niekerk, Philip. "I Saw Reds. It Was You Who Saw the 'rooi gevaar.'" Letter. *The Weekly Mail* 17-23 Nov.: 14. [Reply to Gordimer's letter in *The Weekly Mail* 10-16 Nov.]

2790. Vogel, Viveka. "Gordimer på mässan: Jag är ingen revolutionär." *Göteborgs-Posten* [Gothenburg, Sweden] 10 Sept.: 4-5.

1990. 2791. Britz, Etienne. "Van alles en nog wat: Nobel nie vir vroue?" *Die Burger* 15 Jan.: 6.

2792. "Censorship's Aftermath." *The Star* 6 June: 1.

2793. De Waal, Shaun. "I Couldn't Handle SA - Arthur Miller." *The Weekly Mail* 7-13 Dec.: 17.

2794. Dugdale, John. "Frontiers: Gold and the Gun." *The Listener* 31 May: 29. [Report of BBC-TV series to be screened on BBC 1 from 6 June. Nadine Gordimer to present episode on the South African-Moçambique border and South African involvement in Moçambique's civil war.]

2795. "Gordimer Speaks about Gulf between Writer and Reader." *The Natal Witness* 29 Mar.: 3.

1990. 2796. "Gordimer to Help Mandela Write Autobiography." *The Star* 20 June: 2. Slightly different version as "Gordimer to 'Ghost Write' Mandela's Autobiography." *Diamond Fields Advertiser* 21 June: 6. Extr. as "Gordimer to Help Write Mandela's Life Story." *The Daily News* 20 June: 2.

2797. Kraft, Scott. "South African Queen." *Fame* [USA] Sept.: 28, 30, 32, 34, 36.

2798. "'Kuns en politiek is onskeibaar.'" *Beeld* 22 June: 11.

2799. "Laughter, Contempt from Council's Spying Targets." *The Star* 30 Mar.: 13.

2800. Lembede, Mdu. "Gordimer, Naudé Heed Students and Snub Varsity." *Sunday Tribune* 13 May: 5.

2801. Mattera, Don. "Gordimer Acclaimed More Abroad than at Home." *Weekend Mail* (supp. to *The Weekly Mail*) 23-29 Nov.: 23.

2802. Molefe, Z. B. "Gordimer Feted at Her 70th Birthday." *City Press* 25 Nov.: 25.

2803. "Nadine Hailed at 70." *The New Nation* 30 Nov.-6 Dec.: 8.

2804. "Students Ask Naudé and Gordimer to Stay Away." *The Star* 15 May: 5.

2805. "Who Didn't Make the Booker?" *Weekend Mail* (supp. to *Weekly Mail*) 28 Sept.-4 Oct.: 7.

2806. X. P. "Patron of District Six Museum." *The Herald Times* 26 Jan.: 8.

1991. 2807. "ANC-vroue wag Nadine in op lughawe." *Beeld* 15 Oct.: 3.

2808. Abrahams, Lionel. "Gordimer dapper en toegewy aan kuns." *Die Burger* 5 Oct.: 9. Repr. as "'n Onwrikbare toewyding aan kuns." *Beeld* 10 Oct.: 4.

2809. Abrahams, Lionel. "Mannerliness Required." [Letter in response to Stephen Gray's article in *The Sunday Star* 13 Oct.] *The Sunday Star* 27 Oct.: 14.

2810. "Acclaim." Editorial. *The Natal Mercury* 4 Oct.: 6.

2811. Albert, Don. "Gordimer on SABC TV at Last." *The Star* 9 Apr.: 6.

1991. 2812. "Apartheid Remains: Gordimer." *The Citizen* 7 Oct.: 9.

2813. Arnborg, Beata. "ANC-blommor till Gordimer: Politiska frågor dominerade när litteraturpristagaren mötte svenska pressen." *Svenska Dagbladet* 5 Dec., sec. 2: 1.

2814. "Authors Join Forces to Help Students." *The Cape Librarian* (35.8): 41.

2815. "Award for Gordimer." *Pretoria News* 28 Aug.: 3.

2816. Bäckste Eva. "Nobelfest i lysande färger." *Svenska Dagbladet* 11 Dec., sec. 2: 10.

2817. Basckin, David. "Viva! Viva! Gone with the Wind." *Reality* Oct.: 20.

2818. Bentley, Kin. "Gordimer Steers Clear of Mandela Biography." *Eastern Province Herald* 18 Oct.: 3.

2819. Blatchford, M. F. "No, This Is Not the Demise of the Right." Letter. *The Weekly Mail* 8-14 Mar.: 17.

2820. Blatchford, Mathew. "After Gordimer's Prize Nothing Can Go Rong." Letter. *Southside* 10-16 Oct.: 10.

2821. "Boost for Gordimer Series." *The Star Tonight* (supp. to *The Star*) 25 Oct.: 1.

2822. Boyd-Smith, Allan. "Well Done on Nobel Nadine - However . . . ." Letter. *The Daily News* 11 Oct.: 14.

2823. Carlin, John. "Gordimer Unites Old Foes with the Write Stuff." *The Independent* [London] 4 Oct.: 11.

2824. Clingman, Stephen. "An Explorer of Buried Territory: 'Nothing I Say Is as True as My Fiction' - Gordimer." *South* 9-16 Oct.: 12-13. Different version as "'Nothing I Say Is as True as My Fiction.'" *Review/Books* (supp. to *The Weekly Mail*) 29 Nov.-5 Dec.: 4. [Extracts from his address introducing Nadine Gordimer to audience at U of Massachussetts.]

2825. "Congrats from FW." *The Citizen* 4 Oct.: 1.

2826. Crawford, B. "Two Cheers for Nadine's Nobel for Literature." Letter. *The Star* 9 Oct.: 14.

2827. Cronin, Jeremy. "Two Writers Give Praise for 'Artist of Insight and Detail.'" *South* 9-16 Oct.: 13.

1991. 2828. "'Die eensaamste beroep.'" *Beeld* 13 Dec.: 4.

2829. "Die Prys: Die skrywer Nadine Gordimer het pas die eerste Suid-Afrikaner en die sewende vrou geword wat al die Nobelprys vir Letterkunde gewen het. So praat die wêreld en Suid-Afrika daaroor." *Vrye Weekblad* 11-17 Oct.: 31.

2830. Ester, H. "Nadine Gordimer en vijftig jaar Zuidafrikaanse geschiedenis." *Zuid-Afrika* Nov./Dec.: 197.

2831. Executive Committee of the Anti-Censorship Action Group. "Nobel Recognises Courage." Letter. *The Star* 11 Oct.: 9. Repr. as "Well Done, Gordimer." *The Natal Witness* 21 Oct.: 22. "Congratulations!" *The Natal Mercury* 29 Oct.: 13. Extr. as "Gordimer's Prize Encourages." *Pretoria News* 14 Oct.: 6. Repr. as "Accord Was Imposed." *The Star* 11 Oct.: 9.

2832. "FW Can't Count on Whole Cabinet, Says Gordimer." *The Argus* 3 Jan.: 11.

2833. "Focus on Writers." *The New Nation* 12-18 Apr.: 22.

2834. "Fourth CNA Award for Nadine Gordimer." *Weekend Mail* (supp. to *The Weekly Mail*) 30 Aug.-5 Sept.: 30.

2835. "Franse eerbetoon vir Nadine Gordimer." *Die Burger* 23 Nov.: 6.

2836. "Gala Nobel Awards Ceremony Awaits Nadine Gordimer." *The New Nation* 1-7 Nov.: 5.

2837. Goldblatt, David. "Gaze at Gordimer Was Too Cold." *The Sunday Star* 13 Oct.: 8. [Letter criticising Stephen Gray's article "Basking in Gordimer's Reflected Nobel Glory." *The Sunday Star* 6 Oct.: 12]

2838. "Good for Gordimer!" Editorial. *The Argus* 4 Oct.: 14.

2839. "Gordimer Becomes First SA Writer to Scoop R2,8-m Nobel Prize." *The Star* 4 Oct.: 1.

2840. "Gordimer Calls on UN to Fight for Rushdie." *The Citizen* 9 Dec.: 13.

2841. "Gordimer 'Demoted' as Mandela's Ghost-Writer." *Pretoria News* 5 Oct.: 2.

1991. **2842.** "Gordimer Gets Nobel Prize for Her 'Magnificent Epic Writing.'" *The Weekly Mail* 4-10 Oct.: 9.

2843. "Gordimer 'Happy to Be Back Home.'" *The Natal Witness* 17 Oct.: 1. Slightly different version as "Nobel Winner Nadine Lands to an Emotional Reception." *The Natal Mercury* 17 Oct.: 7.

2844. "Gordimer i Sverige fick prata politik: 'Fel' frågor irriterade Akademiens sekreterare." *Svenska Dagbladet* 5 Dec.: 1.

2845. "Gordimer, Nadine." Programme for *New Nation* Writers Conference, D. J. du Plessis Centre, U of the Witwatersrand, Dec.: n.p.

2846. "Gordimer, Nadine 1923- ." *Major 20th-Century Writers: Vol 2: E-K.* Ed. Bryan Ryan. Detroit: Gale: 1218-1223.

2847. "Gordimer 'Not Ghost for Nelson.'" *Cape Times* 18 Oct.: 2.

2848. "Gordimer op M-Net gehuldig." *Beeld* 11 Dec.: 1.

2849. "Gordimer Plea for Writers." *The Star* 8 Nov.: 10.

2850. "Gordimer praat by kunsstigting." *Die Transvaler* 26 Feb.: 6.

2851. "Gordimer Says SA's Leaders Give Her Hope." *The Citizen* 18 Oct.: 8.

2852. "Gordimer Speaks Out in Favour of Rushdie." *The Natal Witness* 9 Dec.: 11.

2853. "Gordimer to Use Nobel Money to Boost Black Writing." *The Daily News* 4 Oct.: 1.

2854. "Gordimer wil swart werke met Nobelprys bevorder." *Die Volksblad* 4 Oct.: 1, 2.

2855. "Gordimer Will Use Prize to Aid Black Writers." *Business Day* 4 Oct.: 1.

2856. "Gordimer wyd geloof oor prys." *Die Volksblad* 5 Oct.: 5.

2857. "Gordimer: I Am Surprised: Wants to Help Black Writers." *The Citizen* 4 Oct.: 1, 2.

2858. "Gordimer's Book Voted the Best." *City Press* 1 Sept.: 15.

2859. "Gordimer's 'Masterpieces' Highlight SA Racial Woes." *Eastern Province Herald* 4 Oct.: 11.

1991. 2860. "Gordimer's Nobel Hailed." *The Natal Witness* 4 Oct.: 1.

2861. "Gordimer's Role." Editorial. *Business Day* 7 Oct.: 14.

2862. "Gordimer's Work 'Part of the Struggle.'" *Business Day* 4 Oct.: 9.

2863. Gordon, Douglas. "At Last, the SABC Yields to Nadine." *Sunday Times* 21 Apr.: 16.

2864. Grace, John and John Laffin. *Fontana Dictionary of Africa since 1960.* London: Fontana: 132.

2865. Gräslund, Thu. "Här får Gerd träffa sin stora idol." *Expressen* 10 Dec.: 18.

2866. Gray, Stephen. "Gaze at Gordimer Was Too Cold: Stephen Gray Replies." *The Sunday Star* 13 Oct.: 8. [Response to letter by David Goldblatt in *The Sunday Star* 13 Oct.: 8.]

2867. Gray, Stephen. "Nadine Gets World Recognition and Her Place in Posterity." *Sunday Tribune* 6 Oct.: 16. Also pub. as "Basking in Gordimer's Reflected Nobel Glory." *The Sunday Star* 6 Oct.: 12.

2868. Grill, Bartholomäus. "Ein Name, den keiner nennt: Süd-afrikanische Reaktionem auf die Nobelpreisverleihung." *Die Zeit* 11 Oct.: 71.

2869. Grütter, Wilhelm. "Gordimer se ondenkbare TV-debuut." *Die Volksblad* 27 Apr.: 4.

2870. Hagen, Cecilia. "Sydafrikas vita hopp." *Expressen* 5 Dec.: 19.

2871. Hall, Thomas. "Gordimer fördömer Rushdie-dom." *Dagens Nyheter* 8 Dec.: B1.

2872. Hambidge, Joan. "Gordimer as Heilige Koei." *Beeld* 24 Oct.: 3.

2873. Harpprecht, Klaus. "Das Recht auf Heimat." *Die Zeit* 11 Oct.: 71.

2874. Haysom, Cheetah. "The Pen Is Powerful - but Is It Worth Half a Million?" *The Sunday Star* 9 June: 3.

2875. "Hearty Praise for Novelist." *Daily Dispatch* 4 Oct.: 11.

1991. 2876. "Helde-ontvangs vir Nadine Gordimer." *Die Volksblad* 17 Oct.: 7.

2877. Hernbäck, Eva. "Sober Gordimer glänste utan glitter." *Dagens Nyheter* 11 Dec.: 1, A10.

2878. "High Praise for Nadine Gordimer's Nobel Win." *The Argus* 4 Oct.: 3.

2879. Holm, Birgitta. "Låt blicken avgöra: De kvinnliga Nobelpristagarna är den goda sakens tjänare." *Dagens Nyheter* 10 Dec.: B2.

2880. Hotz, Paul. "A Deserved Reward: Nadine Gordimer's Nobel Prize Widely Applauded." *The Daily News* 4 Oct.: 3.

2881. Hough, Barrie. "'n Driekuns vir Gordimer." *Rapport* 24 Nov.: 10.

2882. "Increased Demand for Nobel-Winner Gordimer's Works." *Weekend Post* 12 Oct.: 5.

2883. Johansson, Anders. ["An In-Depth Study of Gordimer's World."] *Dagens Nyheter* 7 Dec.: 1, B1.

2884. Johnson, Stephen. "CNA Literary Award 1990: The Shortlist." *Exclusive Communiqué* (17) (supp. to *The Weekly Mail*) 5-11 July: 4.

2885. Kenny, Andrew. "Did Any of the Judges Sample Wilbur Smith? The Nobel Prize for Literature Went to the Wrong South African, Argues Andrew Kenny." *The Star* 15 Oct.: 14. Repr. as "Literati in SA Should Ask: 'Why Aren't Our Books Read.'" *The Natal Witness* 26 Oct.: 7.

2886. Kent, Gilbert. "The Nobel Farce: Nadine Gordimer's Nobel Prize Raises Some Interesting Questions about the Real Meaning of This 'Prestigious' Award . . . ." *Personality* 4 Nov.: 20-21.

2887. Kierkegaard, Niklas. "Praktfull hyllning till snillen." *Svenska Dagbladet* 11 Dec., sec. 2: 9.

2888. Leeman, Patrick. "She Is No Stranger to Literary Acclaim." *The Natal Mercury* 31 Aug.: 11.

2889. Lekander, Nina. "Vit man, mörk skugga." *Expressen* 10 Dec.: 5.

1991. 2890. Levine, Duncan. "Smith and Gordimer." Letter. *The Natal Witness* 31 Oct.: 8. [Response to Andrew Kenny's article in *The Natal Witness* 26 Oct.]

2891. Lewis, Dave. "'Brave Step Forward for Cosaw.'" *South* 4-10 July: 12.

2892. Lickindorf, Elisabeth. "Gordimer Delights Academics." Letter. *The Sunday Star* 3 Nov.: 14.

2893. Lidman, Sara. "Min vän Nadine." *Aftonbladet* 8 Dec.: 4-5.

2894. Lilli, Laura. "Noi dimenticati reduci dall'apartheid: A Johannesburg 65 scrittori africani discutono sull'impegno intellettuale dopo i cambiamenti politici Sudafrica." *Cultura* (supp. to *La Repubblica*) 10 Dec.: 1.

2895. Löfvendahl, Bo. "'Författaren föds med ordet': Nadine Gordimer förklarade engagerat författarskap i nobelföreläsningen." *Svenska Dagbladet* 8 Dec., sec. 2: 4.

2896. Marincowitz, Annica. "Helde-ontvangs vir SA se Nobelpryswenner." *Beeld* 17 Oct.: 3.

2897. Marincowitz, Annica. "Nadine verheug, maar verras oor haar Nobelprys." *Beeld* 4 Oct.: 1.

2898. Marincowitz, Annica. "'Verstommende' R2,8 m. is te min vir Gordimer!" *Beeld* 18 Oct.: 4.

2899. Memela, Sandile. "Gordimer's Nobel 'a Boost.'" *City Press* 6 Oct.: 6.

2900. Ménager, S. D. "Proust among the Cannibals: Should Marcel Be Consumed?" Trans. V. M. Everson. *Theoria* (77): 143-151. [Briefly mentions Gordimer and dedicated to her.]

2901. "Menings verskil oor Gordimer se prys." *Oosterlig* 8 Oct.: 10.

2902. Milne, Ramsay. "Nobel Laureate: No One Will Know for 50 Years Why the Shortlisted SA Writer Didn't Get It Before." *Sunday Tribune* 6 Oct.: 16. Also pub. as "The Gordimer Mystery: Why Did the Nobel Prize Academy Wait So Long?" *The Sunday Star* 6 Oct.: 2.

2903. Mitchell, Dominic. "Triumph for Nadine: Nobel Literature Prize Comes to South Africa." *The Natal Mercury* 4 Oct.: 1.

1991. 2904. Mitchell, James. "Disabled Get Access to Library." *The Star Tonight* (supp. to *The Star*) 28 Nov.: 18.

2905. Mitchell, James. "Nobel Thrill for Nadine Gordimer." *The Star* 4 Oct.: 1.

2906. Mitchell, James. "Once-Banned Gordimer Books Place with Greats." *The Star* 5 Oct.: 4.

2907. Mitchell, James. "The Day the Guest of Honour Turned Up at the Finest Ball of All." *The Star* 4 Oct.: 13.

2908. Modebe, Sarah. "Gordimer's Prize." *New African* Nov.: 45-46.

2909. Moody, Chris. "Authors Mindlessly Denigrated." *The Star* 23 Oct.: 13. [Letter in response to Andrew Kenny's article "Did Any of the Judges Sample Wilbur Smith? The Nobel Prize for Literature Went to the Wrong South African, Argues Andrew Kenny." *The Star* 15 Oct.: 14.]

2910. Motsapi, Ike. "Nobel Prize for Nadine Gordimer." *Sowetan* 4 Oct.: 4.

2911. "Nadine." Editorial. *Beeld* 5 Oct.: 8.

2912. "Nadine flous die pers." *Die Transvaler* 4 Oct.: 2.

2913. "Nadine Gordimer." Editorial. *Die Volksblad* 5 Oct.: 8.

2914. "Nadine Gordimer." Editorial. *The Daily News* 5 Oct.: 6.

2915. "Nadine Gordimer." *South African Portfolio*. Text by Andrew Steele. Photographs by Ulli Michel. Cape Town: Struik: 12-13.

2916. "Nadine Gordimer Nobel Prize Winner." *Writers' World* [Somerset West, SA] (1.4): 4.

2917. "Nadine Gordimer Rewarded at Last." *The New Nation* 11-17 Oct.: 25.

2918. "Nadine Gordimer to Give Away Prize." *The Argus* 28 Aug.: 2. Exp. as "Nadine Gordimer Uses Prize to Help Writers." *Daily Dispatch* 29 Aug.: 18.

2919. "Nadine Gordimer wen Nobelprys - eerste SA skrywer." *Oosterlig* 4 Oct.: 1. Also as "Gordimer wen Nobelprys - eerste SA skrywer." *Die Burger* 4 Oct.: 1.

1991. 2920. "Nadine Gordimer Wins Nobel Prize." *Daily Dispatch* 4 Oct.: 17. Slightly different version in *Cape Times* 4 Oct.: 1, 3.

2921. "Nadine is R3 m werd." *Die Transvaler* 4 Oct.: 3.

2922. "Nadine wen dalk Nobelprys." *Die Transvaler* 3 Oct.: 4.

2923. Ndebele, Njabulo. "Two Writers Give Praise for 'Artist of Insight and Detail.'" *South* 9-16 Oct.: 12.

2924. "Nederlandse pers prys Gordimer." *Beeld* 5 Oct.: 9.

2925. "News: Authors Join Forces to Help Students." *The Cape Librarian* (35.8): 41.

2926. "News: Bekroonde boeke: Goosen en Gordimer wen." *The Cape Librarian* (35.9): 41-42.

2927. Nicol, Mike. "A Crowning Achievement for Gordimer." *Sunday Times* 6 Oct.: 6.

2928. "The Nobel Awards and South Africa." *Die Patriot* 11 Oct.: 4.

2929. "Nobel Gordimer Praised." *Eastern Province Herald* 4 Oct.: 1.

2930. "Nobel Laurate [sic]." Editorial. *The Leader* 11 Oct.: 6.

2931. "Nobel Prize." Editorial. *The Citizen* 4 Oct.: 6.

2932. "Nobel Prize." Editorial. *The Natal Witness* 5 Oct.: 6.

2933. "Nobel Prize for Gordimer." *ACAG Update* Aug./Sept.: 4.

2934. "Nobel Prize to S African Writer." *The Herald Times* 11 Oct.: 2.

2935. "Nobelprys." Editorial. *Die Transvaler* 7 Oct.: 6.

2936. "Nobelprys: Gordimer kry lof én kritiek." *Die Burger* 5 Oct.: 13.

2937. Nyatsumba, Kaizer. "Gordimer Gets Hero's Welcome." *The Star* 17 Oct.: 3.

2938. Nyatsumba, Kaizer. "Gordimer to Use Fame to Help Build New SA Culture." *The Star* 18 Oct.: 2. Also pub. in different ed. as "Nobel Award Won't Change My Work, Says Gordimer." *The Star* 18 Oct.: 2.

1991. 2939. Oliphant, Andries Walter and Barbara Schreiner, Paul Weinberg, Matthew Krouse. "Comment." *Staffrider* (9.4): 3.

2940. "Opinie: Nobelprijs voor Nadine Gordimer." *Zuid-Afrika* Oct.: 163.

2941. Pearson, Bryan. "Searching for a New Culture to Build On: Nadine Gordimer, the Girl from Springs with the Moral Tone." *The Natal Witness* 4 Oct.: 13.

2942. "Pen Is More Lonely Than Sword." *Eastern Province Herald* 12 Dec.: 5. Different version as "Writer's Lot Is a Lonely One - Gordimer." *The Citizen* 12 Dec.: 20.

2943. Petterssen, Rose. "Enson leting etter sannhet." *Klassekampen* [Oslo, Norway] 16 Oct.: 3.

2944. Prescott, Peter S., Marc Peyser and Arlene Getz. "Two Sides of Nadine Gordimer: South Africa's Great Fiction Writer Wins the Nobel." *Newsweek* 14 Oct.: 48.

2945. "Prize Day for Nobel Nadine Gordimer." *The Daily News* 11 Dec.: 2.

2946. "Programme oor Nadine Gordimer." *Die Transvaler* 10 Dec.: 13.

2947. Rautenbach, Elmari. "Gordimer *laat kykers* hul ware kleure wys." *Vrye Weekblad* 26 Apr.-2 May: 19.

2948. "Recipient Wants to Boost SA Writers." *Daily Dispatch* 4 Oct.: 17.

2949. Riordan, Rory. "Top Award and a Writer Recognised." *Eastern Province Herald* 4 Nov.: 8.

2950. Ritchie, Harry. "Read 'Noble', Not Nobel." *Sunday Times* [London] 13 Oct.

2951. Robinson, Marguerite. "Afrikaners se invloed op Gordimer." *Rapport* 21 Apr.: 16.

2952. "Sanctions Must Stay - Gordimer." *The Star* 5 Dec.: 2.

2953. Shafto, Michael. "Nobel Nadine Is Her Inspiration." *The Star* 12 Dec.: 23.

2954. Shafto, Michael. "The Guest of Gordimer." *The Star* 8 Oct.: 13.

1991. 2955. "Shortlisted Titles for Top S African Literary Award." *Eastern Province Herald* 4 July: 12.

2956. Sibiya, Khulu. "Nobel Honour Well Deserved." *City Press* 6 Oct.: 14.

2957. "Sickly Child to Grande Dame of Literature." *Cape Times* 4 Oct.: 4.

2958. "Skryf is soos waterpokke, sê Gordimer." *Die Burger* 12 Dec.: 27. Slightly different version in *Oosterlig* 17 Dec.: 14.

2959. "Snillerik jubileumsfest." *Svenska Dagbladet* 11 Dec.: 1.

2960. Swart, Freek. "'Politiek wen toe Nobelprys': 'Gordimer het nie self gely, maar in enklave gewoon.'" *Beeld* 5 Oct.: 9.

2961. Thomson, Garner. "Nobel Winner Gordimer Loses Out - Her Skin Is White." *Weekend Argus* 5 Oct.: 3.

2962. "Traditionell ceremoni i ny kostym." *Dagens Nyheter* 11 Dec.: 1.

2963. "Tutu Welcomes Gordimer Home." *The Citizen* 17 Oct.: 20.

2964. Van Gend, Cecily. "Nadine Gordimer." *The Cape Librarian* (35.10): 12-14.

2965. Visser, Nicholas. "An Explorer of Buried Territory: 'Only a Handful Can Match Her.'" *South* 9-16 Oct.: 13.

2966. Wade, Michael. Introduction to *White on Black in South Africa* to be published by Macmillan, London. *Southern African Review of Books* (4.1): 21.

2967. Wästberg, Per. "Vänskap över hudfärgsgräns: Apartheid-lager försvinner men samhällsordningen består." *Dagens Nyheter* 20 Mar.: 22.

2968. "Way Out of Line!" Editorial. *The Argus* 5 Dec.: 18.

2969. Werkelid, Carl Otto. "Litterär kvartett hyllades som hjältar: Nobelpristagare läste högt på Dramatens Lilla scen." *Svenska Dagbladet* 10 Dec., sec. 2: 1.

2970. Winder, Robert. "Nobel Prize Goes to a Muscular South African Liberal." *The Independent* [London] 4 Oct.

2971. "World Recognises a Great SA Talent." Editorial. *Weekend Post* 5 Oct.: 10.

1991. 2972. "Writing and the Struggle: Nadine Gordimer." *Financial Mail* 11 Oct.: 54.

1991/2. 2973. "Gordimer Wins Nobel Prize." *Ditaba * Izindaba* (3): 4.

2974. Ndebele, Njabulo. "To Nadine Gordimer from the Cosaw President." Letter. *Ditaba * Izindaba* (3): 4.

1992. 2975. "Arts Academy in PE." *Eastern Province Herald* 9 Dec.: 2. Exp. in *Eastern Province Herald* 11 Dec.: 16.

2976. "The Arts in Perspective." *The New Nation* 10-16 July: 14.

2977. Bauer, Charlotte. "As Many Faces as Michael Jackson." *The Weekly Mail* 10-16 July: 38.

2978. "Books of the Year: Celebrities Choose Their Favourite Reading of 1992." *Sunday Times* 13 Dec.: 18.

2979. "COSAW Meets with the Mozambican Writers Association (AEMO)." *Ditaba * Izindaba* (4): 5.

2980. "COSAW Members Out & About." *Ditaba * Izindaba* (4): 16.

2981. "Cambridge to Honour Nadine Gordimer." *The Sunday Star* 10 May: 8.

2982. D. S. "NB." *Times Literary Supplement* 19 June: 14.

2983. Dodd, Alex. "Nobel Prize Won't Help You Write." *The Weekly Mail* 4-10 Sept.: 34.

2984. *Driver, Dorothy. "Gordimer, Nadine." *Bloomsbury Guide to Women's Literature*. Ed. Claire Buck. London: Bloomsbury: 380, 438, 686, 589-590.

2985. Edelstein, Jillian. "The Tug of History." *The Independent Magazine* (supp. to *The Independent*) 13 June: 52-58.

2986. Goldstuck, Arthur. "The Great Literary Divide." *PC Review* (supp. to *The Weekly Mail*) 6-12 Mar.: 1, 2, 12.

2987. "Goodwill in the Arts Closes Racial Divide." *Daily Dispatch* 11 Nov.: 14.

2988. "Gordimer at Writers' Reading." *The Star Tonight* (supp. to *The Star*) 4 Sept.: 2.

2989. "Gordimer en Brink by fees." *Beeld* 14 May: 2.

2990. "Gordimer Honoured." *Sunday Star* 10 May: 2.

1992. 2991. "Gordimer, Nadine." *Who's Who 1992: An Annual Biographical Dictionary*. London: Black: 722.

2992. "Gordimer Praises Students." *The Natal Mercury* 27 Apr.: 2.

2993. "Gordimer to Receive Doctorate." *The Natal Mercury* 21 Apr.: 7.

2994. "Gordimer: For the Record." *The Star* 20 Apr.: 8.

2995. Gordon, Nancy. "Salute to Nadine Gordimer." *Sash* Jan.: 42.

2996. Gray, Stephen. "Literary Scene." *ADA 10* [Special edition on Johannesburg]: 81.

2997. Green, Molly. "Amongst the Best." Rev. of *Best Short Stories*, ed. Giles Gordon and David Hughes. *South African Literary Review* (2.1): 1920.

2998. Greene, Gerschom. "Much More than Literary Tiff." Letter. *The Star* 25 Feb.: 14.

2999. Irvine, Mark. "1991 Nobel Prize for Literature: Nadine Gordimer." *ADA 10*: 62.

3000. Jazbhay, Saber Ahmed and Ebi Lockhat. "Gordimer Taken to Task." Letter. *The Natal Mercury* 16 Jan.: 7.

3001. Kamp, Michael. "Nadine Gordimer." *Cue* 6 July: 5.

3002. Katzew, Henry. "South African Author's Barb against Gordimer." *The Daily News* 19 Feb.: 13. Slightly different version pub. as "Former Friend Attacks Gordimer." *The Star* 19 Feb.: 12.

3003. Kneen, Dale. "'Give Them Bread' — Gordimer." *Argus Tonight* (supp. to *The Argus*) 9 July: 7.

3004. "Literary Giants for Festival." *The Star Tonight* (supp. to *The Star*) 12 May: 1.

3005. "The Long, Hard Road to Writing Success." *Writers' World* (7): 25.

3006. "Marginalisation in Culture Criticised." *Daily Dispatch* 6 July: 7.

1992. 3007. "Nadine Gordimer: A Recorder of Our Times." *Light Years* [Old Mutual: For Anchor Club] (3.3): 12-13.

3008. Ndebele, Mfundo. "Aiming for Racial Harmony." *The Star Tonight* (supp. to *The Star*) 9 Sept.: 2.

3009. "News: Book Awards: Franse eerbetoon vir Gordimer." *The Cape Librarian* (36.2): 43.

3010. "Nobelpryse vir kommuniste." *Die Afrikaner* 3 June: 7.

3011. "Profile: Nadine Gordimer: South Africa's Controversial Daughter." *Bulletin: News for the Human Sciences* [Pretoria] (4.3): 6, 23.

3012. Robertson, Claire. "Why I Hate Nadine's Vile Politics." *Sunday Times* 24 May: 6.

3013. "Role of the Arts." *Evening Post* 15 Dec.: 8.

3014. "SA's Literary Who's Who for Festival Reading." *Grocott's Mail* 10 July: 9.

3015. Sampson, Anthony. "Writer's Enemies." Letter. *The Guardian* 22 June.

3016. "The Sixth Annual *Weekly Mail* Book Week: Johannesburg." *Review/Books* (supp. to *The Weekly Mail* 28 Aug.-3 Sept.: 6.

3017. Strydom, Marius. "Parktown se oud en nuut in harmonie." Rev. of *Parktown Centenary Souvenir. Beeld* 29 Feb.: 10.

3018. Tomlins, James. "Book of Apartheid Has Not Been Closed, Says Gordimer." *The Argus* 1 July: 9.

3019. "UD-W Graduation Day." *The Leader* 1 May: 5.

3020. "We All Need to Learn About Democracy, Says Gordimer." *Sunday Tribune* 26 Apr.: 5.

3021. Wessels, Charles. "Internationally Acclaimed SA Authors Read Their Work." *Rhodos* (4.12): 2.

3022. "White Hopes Pinned on De Klerk, Says Gordimer." *The Argus* 10 Aug.: 2.

1992. 3023. "Winter School Dominated by Literary Giants." *Coastal News* (supp. to *Grocott's Mail*) 30 June: 7. Adapt. as "Gordimer, Brink Will Be Exploring Literature." *Grocott's Festival Supplement* (supp. to *Grocott's Mail*) July: 6.

1993. 3024. "Author's Opposition to Apartheid Praised." *Evening Post* 28 Jan.: 14.

3025. Mills, Heather. "Hate-Mail Disgusting — Gordimer." *The Star* 21 Jan.: 14.

3026. Naidoo, Jayarman. "Each of Padayachee's Stories Is a Treat." *Review/Books* (supp. to *The Weekly Mail*) 26 Mar.-1 Apr.: 7.

Q. BIBLIOGRAPHIES

1964. 3027. Nell, Racilia Jilian. *Nadine Gordimer: Novelist and Short Story Writer: A Bibliography of Her Works and Selected Criticism.* Johannesburg: Department of Bibliography, Librarianship and Typography, U of Witwatersrand.

1979. 3028. Cooke, John. "Nadine Gordimer: A Bibliography." *Bulletin of Bibliography* [Westport, CT] (36): 81-84.

1985. 3029. Green, Robert J. "Nadine Gordimer: A Bibliography of Works and Criticism." *Bulletin of Bibliography* (42.1): 5-11.

1990. 3030. Dubbeld, Catherine Elizabeth. *Reflecting Apartheid: South African Short Stories in English with Socio-Political Themes 1960-1987: A Select and Annotated Bibliography.* Bibliographical Series No. 21. Johannesburg: South African Institute of International Affairs.

Nadine Gordimer and Guy Butler at NELM, 1992.

INDICES

Note: numerical reference is to the item number in this bibliography.

A. REVIEWERS

B. CRITICS, ANTHOLOGISTS AND TRANSLATORS

C. INTERVIEWERS

D. REVIEWS BY GORDIMER

E. BOOKS AND ANTHOLOGIES CONTAINING WORKS BY AND INTERVIEWS WITH GORDIMER

F. BOOKS AND ANTHOLOGIES CONTAINING CRITICAL ARTICLES ON GORDIMER

G. JOURNALS AND NEWSPAPERS CONTAINING WORKS BY AND INTERVIEWS WITH GORDIMER

H. JOURNALS AND NEWSPAPERS CONTAINING CRITICAL ARTICLES ON GORDIMER

World Literature Written in English [Arlington, Texas; later Ontario]   765, 774,
   793, 827, 899, 903, 904, 908, 919, 930, 951, 1000, 1013
Yale Journal of Criticism: Interpretation in the Humanities [New Haven, CT]
   1005

I. BOOKS, JOURNALS AND NEWSPAPERS CONTAINING REVIEWS OF GORDIMER'S WORK

Aberdeen Evening Examiner Record   1867
Advertiser [Adelaide]   1775, 2160
Afram Newsletter [Paris]   1909
Africa Digest   1395
Africa Today [Denver, CO]   1796, 2126
African Communist [London]   1522, 1724
Aftenposten [Oslo]   1385, 1510, 1577
Age [Melbourne]   1653, 1761, 1845, 1892, 1957, 2063, 2128
Amateur Photographer [Surrey]   2012
America [New York]   1594, 1737
Arabia: The Islamic World Review   1908
Argus [Cape Town]   1154, 1205, 1308, 1429, 1473, 1501, 1617, 1817, 1822,
   1943, 2074, 2134, 2179, 2275
Ariel [Calgary, AB]   1506, 2302
Artful Reporter [Manchester]   1981
Atlantic [Boston]   1220, 1223, 1250, 1258, 1348
Auckland Star [NZ]   1523
Australian [Sydney]   1292, 1374, 1670, 2144
Australian Jewish News [Abbotsford]   2139
Ba Shiru [Madison, WI]   1798
Bath & West Evening Chronicle   1660, 1876, 1960
Bedfordshire on Sunday   1682
Beeld [Johannesburg]   1264, 1433, 1463, 1573, 1609, 1652, 1719, 1831, 1840,
   1844, 1942, 1946, 1971, 2158, 2195
Berlingske Tidende [Copenhagen]   1696
Bestsellers [Detroit, MI]   1504, 1644
Birmingham Evening Mail   1302
Birmingham Post   1319, 1384, 1489, 1580, 1643, 1837, 2040, 2136
Bolton Evening News   1298
Bonniers Litterara Magasin [Stockholm]   2103
Book Review Digest [New York]   1131, 1151, 1169, 1194, 1222, 1237, 1327,
   1414, 1548, 1602, 1723, 1792, 1911, 2006, 2029, 2120, 2167, 2229, 2253, 2254,
   2265

J. TITLES OF CRITICAL ARTICLES, THESES AND WORKS ON GORDIMER

K. TITLES OF WORKS, SHORT STORIES AND ARTICLES BY GORDIMER